D1272983

Charles Mauert

Ramus and Reform

Habent sua fata libelli

SIXTEENTH CENTURY ESSAYS & STUDIES SERIES

GENERAL EDITOR
RAYMOND A. MENTZER
University of Iowa

EDITORIAL BOARD OF SIXTEENTH CENTURY ESSAYS & STUDIES

ELAINE BEILIN
Framingham State College

ROGER MANNING
Cleveland State University, Emeritus

MIRIAM U. CHRISMAN
University of Massachusetts, Emerita

MARY B. McKINLEY
University of Virginia

BARBARA B. DIEFENDORF
Boston University

HELEN NADER
University of Arizona

PAULA FINDLEN
Stanford University

CHARLES G. NAUERT
University of Missouri, Emeritus

SCOTT H. HENDRIX
Princeton Theological Seminary

THEODORE K. RABB
Princeton University

JANE CAMPBELL HUTCHISON
University of Wisconsin–Madison

MAX REINHART
University of Georgia

CHRISTIANE JOOST-GAUGIER
University of New Mexico, Emerita

JOHN D. ROTH
Goshen College

RALPH KEEN
University of Iowa

ROBERT V. SCHNUCKER
Truman State University, Emeritus

ROBERT M. KINGDON
University of Wisconsin, Emeritus

NICHOLAS TERPSTRA
University of Toronto

MERRY WIESNER-HANKS
University of Wisconsin–Milwaukee

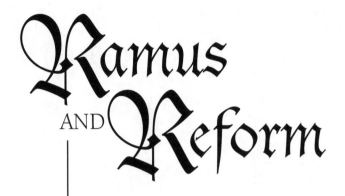

Ramus AND Reform

UNIVERSITY
AND CHURCH AT
THE END OF THE
RENAISSANCE

JAMES
VEAZIE SKALNIK

SIXTEENTH CENTURY ESSAYS & STUDIES
VOLUME LX

Copyright © 2002 Truman State University Press
Kirksville, Missouri 63501-4221 USA
http://tsup.truman.edu
All rights reserved

Library of Congress Cataloging-in-Publication Data (Applied for)
Skalnik, James Veazie
Ramus and reform: University and church at the end of the Renaissance / James Veazie Skalnik.
p.   cm. — (Sixteenth century essays & studies ; vol. 60)
Includes bibliographical references and index.
ISBN 0-943549-93-0 (alk. paper)

Text is set in Adobe Garamond 10/12. Display type is Adobe Garamond
Cover and title page by Teresa Wheeler, Truman State University designer
Printed in U.S.A. by Thomson-Shore, Inc., Dexter, Michigan

No part of this work may be reproduced or transmitted in any format by any means, electronic or mechanical, including photocopying and recording, or by any information storage or retrieval system, without permission in writing from the publisher.

The paper in this publication meets or exceeds the minimum requirements of the American National Standard for Permanence of Paper for Printed Library materials Z39.48 (1984).

For Alice Veazie Skalnik
and
Yaro James Skalnik

Contents

Acknowledgments

ONE OF THE GREATEST PLEASURES involved in researching and writing is the discovery that there are so many talented and generous people in the academic community, without whose patience and assistance (and sometimes insistence) this work could never have been completed. The following paragraphs mention only those to whom my debt is the greatest.

Several institutions granted me the facilities and support needed to carry out this project. At the University of Virginia, I owe special thanks to the staff of Alderman Library and to the Society of Fellows, which arranged for me to receive a Forstmann Foundation fellowship for research in Paris. The United States Naval Academy also provided essential support, especially through grants from the Naval Academy Research Council. I also owe a debt to the National Endowment for the Humanities and to the Folger Shakespeare Library in Washington, D.C., for their support of my research. In Paris, I found a most gracious welcome at the Bibliothèque Nationale and the Archives Nationales as well as at the Bibliothèque de l'Histoire du Protestantisme Français.

Some individuals made particularly important contributions to this work and to my understanding of history in general. The members of the Department of History at the Naval Academy were unflagging in their generous support, but my greatest debts are to the scholars of the University of Virginia who were my teachers and colleagues. Among them I owe special thanks to Lenard Berlanstein, Enno Kraehe, Duane Osheim, Thomas Robisheaux, Alexander Sedgwick, and Roberta Senechal. No one could hope for a finer group of friends and associates; certainly no one could deserve the enormous assistance they so generously provided.

For their extraordinary patience and professional courtesy, I owe special debts to Raymond Mentzer, general editor of Sixteenth Century Essays and Studies series, and to Paula Presley and her staff at Truman State University Press. I will always remember their generosity to a novice author.

My greatest gratitude goes to two exceptional scholars, for whose efforts on my behalf a simple acknowledgment is a hopelessly inadequate return. As a teacher, a scholar, and a friend, H. C. Erik Midelfort has been a constant source of inspiration, even if I can hardly hope to achieve the high standards he has established for these roles. My greatest debt of all is to my fellow graduate student and colleague Ronda

Cook, who is now my partner in work and in life. Her confidence, example, and frequent encouragement have done more than anything else to help me complete this project.

Ramus and Reform

Introduction

PETER RAMUS (1515–1572) WAS A DIFFICULT MAN.[1] His colleagues in the University of Paris found him unbearable; one of the more mild-mannered among them called him "either rabid and demented or else perverse and criminal." Scholars abroad, in London, Heidelberg, Geneva, Tübingen, and elsewhere felt the same way. Catholics labeled him a heretic, and Protestants a rebel. Even the king of France got into the act, branding him ignorant, impudent, arrogant, and a liar.[2] Ramus's ability to annoy people was remarkable, and what is more remarkable is that it has survived him by more than four centuries. Modern scholars, reviewing "the more undesirable features of [his] personality, which were many," echo the sentiments of the sixteenth century.[3]

What annoyed Ramus's contemporaries the most were his persistent, rash assaults on the most esteemed and cherished foundations of religion and learning in France. He was "always ready to upset what is best ordered,"[4] Theodore Beza complained, and his life was in fact a series of rebellions. These began on a grand scale in 1543 with Ramus's root and branch attack on Aristotle's logic, the basic framework of theology and the arts in the sixteenth century. Condemned by the king for

---

1. Even his name presents difficulties. Born Pierre de la Ramée, he adopted a Latinized form of the name, Petrus Ramus, for his scholarly work. When that work was translated into English, the translator kept the Latin form of his surname but rendered his first name as "Peter." English-speaking scholars have generally referred to him as "Peter Ramus."

2. The gentle royal professor of Greek, Denis Lambin, described Ramus as "un séditieux, un brouillon: pour dire la vérité, il est furieux et dément ou pervers et criminel"; letter to Prévost de Thérouanne, February 1554, in Henri Potez, "Deux années de la Renaissance (d'après une correspondance inédite)," *Revue d'histoire littéraire de la France* 13 (1906): 458–98, 658–92, at 663. Ramus's condemnation by Francis I is discussed below, chapter 2.

3. Neal W. Gilbert, review of Walter Ong, *Ramus, Method, and the Decay of Dialogue* and *Ramus and Talon Inventory*, in *Renaissance News* 12 (1959): 269–71, at 269. Gilbert softens his statement a bit by adding that while "Ramus is not especially attractive…the sixteenth century in general did not breed attractive personalities."

4. Beza to (Joachim Camerarius?), in Hippolyte Aubert and Alain Dufour, *Correspondance de Théodore de Bèze*, t. XIII (1572), ed. Béatrice Nicollier (Geneva: Droz, 1988), no. 925, 145: "homo ad turbanda optima quaeque comparatus."

his temerity and prohibited from teaching philosophy in the future, Ramus turned his attention to the other great thinkers of the ancient world, proclaiming that Cicero and Quintilian knew nothing of rhetoric, Galen and Euclid were ignorant of proper method, and in general that the heroes of the Renaissance had feet of clay.[5] Eventually he even challenged the worth of the common coin of the religious and scholarly world, the Latin language itself. No wonder his detractors thought him perverse and demented.

Ramus was no less tenacious in his attacks on the institutions of religion and scholarship. In 1557, he wrote and published a report which blasted the University of Paris for its structure, its teaching, and its personnel—his fellow professors. In the early 1560s, he attacked the Catholic Church in the same areas. By the mid-1560s, he was in court to oppose the royal professors of France for their recruitment and teaching practices, despite having been one of their number since 1551. And after his conversion to the Reform in the late 1560s, he lashed out at the doctrine and governance of his new church. Given his history, this last assault does not come as a great surprise. What is perhaps surprising is that Ramus persisted in his challenges to all these institutions despite the growing penalties for his actions, which included the loss of his position in the University and even years of exile from France. Only his death in the Saint Bartholomew's Day Massacre in 1572 brought a halt to his outrageous slanders. It is no wonder that he appeared "rabid" to those around him. But what made Ramus so contentious?

For modern researchers, the most bothersome thing about him is not his contentious character, but the fact that he became something of an authority himself by virtue of his academic brainchild, Ramist method. This oversimplified, unsubtle, and mechanical system of the arts and sciences, of which he was so enormously proud, was intended to supplant the works of the ancients he so strenuously attacked. It presents a major problem in the intellectual history of his era, because despite its defects—and they were many—Ramist method took sixteenth-century Europe by storm and earned him his royal professorship. The success of Ramism created resentment among his peers and puzzles historians today.[6] What made Ramism so popular?

The two most ambitious studies to date explain both Ramus's contentiousness and the popularity of Ramism as results of a fundamental change in the way Europeans looked at and thought about the world, "a discontinuity in the *episteme* of

---

5. The summary is offered in a letter from Beza to Heinrich Bullinger, 14 January 1572: "Cui enim Aristoteles est sophista, Cicero tradendae rhetorices ignarus, Quintilianus indoctus, Galenus ipseque adeo Euclides ἀμέψοδος...." in Aubert, *Correspondance*, 31.

6. Paul Oskar Kristeller and John Herman Randall Jr., "The Study of the Philosophies of the Renaissance," *Journal of the History of Ideas* 2 (1941): 449–96, at 495: "And, to take another problem, what was the appeal, the use, and the function of the logic of Peter Ramus, which became thoroughly intertwined with Calvinism in Germany and Scotland, and extended even to Puritan New England?"

western culture" which took place in the sixteenth century.[7] In both, Ramus is the herald of the new worldview, and Ramism is its embodiment. The two works are nonetheless fundamentally opposed, because they do not describe the same shift in the Western *Weltanschauung*. One sees the march of progress with Ramus in the vanguard. The other sees decadence, and Ramism as its major symptom.

Ramus is a hero in Charles Waddington's 1855 work, *Ramus: Sa vie, ses écrits et ses opinions*, which despite its age remains the best biography of Ramus yet produced.[8] Waddington used nearly all of the relevant sources in composing his clear and dramatic narrative, and as narrative it is unsurpassed. As an explanation of the place of Ramus and Ramism in history, it has serious problems. To Waddington, Ramus lived and wrote as he did because he was the prophet of a new age. He was the standard-bearer of Renaissance light against medieval darkness, of unfettered reason against bigoted authority, and of free conscience against Catholic constraint. Ramus stood alone, cloaked in virtue and light, while the forces of evil and ignorance raged against him from every side. A champion of truth and liberty, he died a martyr for the cause of humanity.

His virtue lay not in what he created but in what he cast aside. Ramism freed the mind of Europe by breaking the bonds of superstition, ancient authority, and dogmatic intolerance. That Ramus had not found anything very interesting to put in their places was of no great moment. To him belonged the credit for reason's emancipation, and left to itself it would soon enough build an edifice far more glorious than that which Ramus had torn down.

Not many modern readers will find Waddington's explanation satisfactory. His blend of romantic hero worship and Enlightenment faith in progress and reason

---

7. The phrase is from Michel Foucault, *The Order of Things: An Archaeology of the Human Sciences* (New York: Pantheon, 1971); English translation of *Les mots et les choses* (Paris: Gallimard, 1966), xxii. Foucault believed that the European mind had undergone such a fundamental change, but he dated that change to "roughly half-way through the seventeenth century" and placed Ramus firmly on the earlier side of the divide (ibid., 35). In his *Madness and Civilization: A History of Insanity in the Age of Reason* (New York: Random House, 1965), English translation by Richard Howard of Histoire de la folie (Paris: Plon, 1971), 39, Foucault chooses the year 1656 as a landmark date for the commencement of the "Age of Reason."

8. Charles [Tzaunt] Waddington, *Ramus (Pierre de la Ramée): Sa vie, ses écrits et ses opinions* (1855; reprint, Dubuque, Iowa: Brown Reprint Library, n.d.). This is an expanded French version of Waddington's doctoral dissertation, *De Petri Rami vita, scriptis, philosophia, scripsit C. Waddington-Kastus, philosophiae professor, in Parisiensi literarum facultate ad doctoris gradum promovendus* (Paris: Joubert, 1848). Waddington also published a brief reply to a critic of his work "Charpentier et Ramus," letter to the editor in *Revue des Deux Mondes* 44 (1881): 719–20, reprinted in *Bulletin de la Société de l'Histoire du Protestantisme français* 30 (1881): 286–87, and a short article on "Les panégyristes de la Saint-Barthélemy à diverses époques: Le théologien Genébrard, archévêque d'Aix: Jacques Charpentier, doyen du Collège de France: L'annaliste de l'Illustre Orbandale (Chalon-sur-Saône)," *Bulletin de la Société de l'Histoire du Protestantisme français* 1 (1853): 374–77.

seems more quaint than convincing.[9] The reader who will make allowances for his naively Whiggish tone will nevertheless find much of value in his work.

Walter Ong is not such a reader. Ong, the author of *Ramus, Method, and the Decay of Dialogue* (1958), saw Waddington's point of view as evidence of a "persecution complex" and even of "psychopathic identification" with Ramus.[10] Ong's language is extreme, but it mirrors the difference between his interpretation and Waddington's. Waddington put Ramus on a pedestal, while Ong did not care much for Ramus or Ramism and could not imagine why anyone in his right mind would.[11]

Ong paints a portrait, not of a hero, but of a particularly philistine schoolteacher, whose career was dedicated to turning the intellectual heritage of the West

9. One modern expert summarizes the problem with Waddington's interpretation by pointing out that it was "inspired by and to a certain extent biased by a passionate attachment to the martyred hero"; Gilbert, review of Ong, *Ramus, Method and the Decay*, 269. When Waddington's book first appeared, critics noticed the same feature, but for the most part they considered it a strength rather than a weakness. Thus the anonymous reviewer in *Bulletin de la Société de l'Histoire du Protestantisme français* 4 (1855): 167-72, asked: "Quelle plume était mieux qualifiée pour écrire la vie de ce dernier de nos anciens professeurs publics protestants, que la plume doublement filiale du seul protestant qui professe aujourd'hui la philosophie dans l'université de France?" Similarly, Christian Bartholmèss, in his review in *Revue chrétienne* 3 (1856): 89–106, recommends Waddington to whoever loves "les grands causes, l'humanité, la liberté de pensée, la religion, la méditation philosophique, le progrès moral et la dignité de l'âme." Critics praised Waddington's book *because* it was a moralizing tract. Bartholmèss in particular was happy to think of Ramus as a sort of Protestant saint, and of Waddington's book as an exercise in hagiography. Even at the time, however, Waddington encountered some opposition to his view. Bartholmèss thought that he might have exaggerated the value of Ramus's work, and Emile Saisset was sure of it: "La Réforme de Ramus," *Précurseurs et disciples de Descartes*, 2d ed. (Paris: Librairie Académique/Didier, 1862), 61–79, "La Réforme de Ramus." The harshest critic by far was the mathematician Joseph Bertrand, who wrote a long letter to the *Revue des deux mondes* 44 (1881): 286–322: "Jacques Charpentier: Est-il l'assassin de Ramus?" to challenge Waddington's interpretation. He was especially interested in defending Jacques Charpentier against Waddington's accusation that he had engineered the murder of Ramus, but in the course of doing so he portrayed Ramus as a poor teacher, an opponent of academic freedom, and on the whole a thoroughly bad apple. None of Waddington's critics, however, challenged his vision of the Renaissance as a fundamental shift in the European mind.

10. Walter J. Ong, *Ramus: method and the decay of dialogue: from the art of discourse to the art of reason* (Cambridge; London: Harvard University Press, 1958), 19. This work was published simultaneously with Walter Jackson Ong, *Ramus and Talon inventory: a short-title inventory of the published works of Peter Ramus (1515–1572) and of Omer Talon (ca. 1510–1562) in their original and in their variously altered forms with related material* (Cambridge: Harvard University Press, Oxford University Press, 1958), a magnificent example of careful scholarship which displays the fruits of Ong's labors in libraries all over the United States and Europe, locating, collating, and describing hundreds of editions of Ramus's works. Ong's articles on Ramus and Ramism are too numerous to be listed here; see the bibliography at the end of this study. It may be worth mentioning that, to the layman, at least, Waddington's work shows no particular signs of mental illness.

11. The different attitudes of the two authors are signaled by the epigrams they had printed on the title pages of their works. Waddington quoted Voltaire: "La Ramée, bon philosophe dans un temps où l'on ne pouvait guère en compter que trois, homme vertueux dans un siècle de crimes, homme aimable dans la société [!] et même, si l'on veut, bel esprit." Ong instead quoted Justus Lipsius's unflattering admonition: "You will never be a great man if you think that Ramus was a great man."

into the sort of pabulum adolescent schoolboys could swallow. Ramus sacrificed accuracy, subtlety, and depth to the exigencies of teaching and writing for little boys. As a result his famous logical method, and a fortiori all the works he produced with its aid, were no more than exercises in shallowness and vulgarization.

Such an evaluation presents problems, of course. If Ramus's approach to learning was so superficial, why did it enjoy such a vogue, even among educated men? Ong argued that Ramism owed its popularity to a revolution in the European mind brought on by the rise of the printed word. The Ramist method of analysis by dichotomy and diagrams was, Ong claimed, peculiarly well suited to the printed page. Together, Ramism and the printing press appealed mightily to a world which was beginning to think of knowledge in visual and spatial terms—as a thing—rather than as an oral and almost spiritual communication between teacher and disciple—in Ong's term, as a "wisdom." Ramus and the printing press helped change learning into a standardized, mass-produced commodity, "congenial to persons who habitually deal with reality in terms of accounting rather than in terms of meditation or wisdom."[12]

Ong's scholarly and meticulous study of Ramist logic and method, based on a solid knowledge of the history of logic and an exhaustive acquaintance with Ramus's works, will remain a standard work on the subject. Only a very brave or a very foolhardy author would attempt to match his massive erudition and detailed analysis. Still, his thesis has not attracted the loyalty of many historians.[13]

---

12. Walter Ong, "Ramist Method and the Commercial Mind," *Studies in the Renaissance* 8 (1961): 155-72, at 160; also in Ong, *Rhetoric, Romance and Technology: Studies in the Interaction of Expression and Culture* (Ithaca: Cornell University Press, 1971), 165-89. Ong's thesis is stated at length in his *Ramus*, in two sections entitled "Ramism and Printing as Related Epiphenomena" and "The Spatial Model as Key to the Mental World"; Ong, *Ramus, Method and the Decay*, 307–18. Several of his articles contain summaries of his hypothesis, and a few present important corollaries to the central theory. Thus in "Ramus: Rhetoric and the Pre-Newtonian Mind," in Alan S. Downer, ed., *English Institute Essays: 1952* (New York: Columbia University Press, 1954), 138–70, Ong argues that the Ramist attachment to spatial images of knowledge was a forerunner of later Cartesian and mechanistic worldviews.

13. Ong's work was greeted with praise all around, but his thesis came under attack almost immediately. Thus, Gilbert's review questioned Ong's explanations, which Wilhelm Risse, *Deutsche Literaturzeitung* 81 (1960): cols. 7–11, thought were more a product of Ong's preconceptions than of the evidence. Even D. P. Walker, who approved of Ong's effort to place Ramism in the broadest possible perspective, acknowledged that the results were "provisional and incomplete"; *French Studies* 14 (1960): 355–57. Pierre Mesnard, *Bibliothèque d'humanisme et renaissance* 21 (1959), went further than any other critic by flatly denying that the print revolution caused a "decay of dialogue", 568–76. In her study of the impact of printing on Europe, Elizabeth L. Eisenstein gave qualified support to the main features of Ong's thesis: "This line of argument dovetails neatly with Walter Ong's earlier studies of Ramism and print culture—perhaps too neatly in the judgment of some medieval scholars who see evidence in medieval manuscripts of those diagrammatic features which Ong reserves for the printed page." Still, "even if all parts of the argument are not deemed equally acceptable, the basic point still seems valid"; Elizabeth Eisenstein, *The Printing Press as an Agent of Change: Communications and Cultural Transformations in Early-Modern Europe* (Cambridge: Cambridge University Press, 1979), 67.

Where Waddington saw Ramus as the embodiment of a new free and rational age, Ong presented him as the print revolution incarnate, and Ramism as the perfect union of medium and message.[14] Both postulated a revolution in the European mind, the former from an Age of Faith to an Age of Reason and the latter from an Age of Sound to an Age of Sight. In both cases Ramus was significant primarily as a representative of a new "spirit of the age" which arose in the sixteenth century and came to dominate modern Europe.

This sort of historical explanation presents serious difficulties. To begin with, it is difficult, if not impossible, to verify the existence of a *Zeitgeist* in any era, let alone to observe it and describe its characteristics. The "spirit of the age" is an elusive wraith, and some skeptics even deny that there is such a thing. In such circumstances, attempting to explain the influence of any particular thinker or system as a reflection of that spirit is an uncertain enterprise at best. Ramus was after all a man and not a mentality, and interpretations which make him a puppet of the "European mind" are not likely to gain widespread acceptance among critical historians. A more mundane approach is likelier to carry conviction and to teach us something of value about Ramus and about the sixteenth century.

A second problem with explanations like those offered by Waddington and Ong is that their emphasis on the mind of the age neglects its social and political character. Ramus's life was to a great extent guided by his ideas, but his ideas were just as strongly influenced by the circumstances of his life. As J. W. Allen warned historians, "Ideas are begotten of circumstances on the human mind, and rarely, if ever, is their source to be found in books."[15] While it would be a grave error to ignore the literary sources of Ramist thought, it is just as serious a mistake to ignore its broader context

---

14. Along with Waddington and Ong, several other scholars have made contributions to our understanding of specific aspects of Ramus's life and thought in book-length studies and deserve to be mentioned at this point. Charles Desmaze, *P. Ramus professeur au Collège de France: Sa vie, ses écrits, sa mort (1515–1572)* (1864; reprint, Geneva: Slatkine, 1970), should be included for the sake of completeness, but is much inferior to Waddington's work. Better is Frank Pierrepont Graves, *Peter Ramus and the Educational Reformation of the Sixteenth Century* (New York: Macmillan, 1912), which, while dependent for the most part on Waddington's research and conclusions, does contain convenient summaries of Ramus's work in the different liberal arts. Perry Miller, *The New England Mind: The Seventeenth Century* (1939; reprint, Boston: Beacon Press, 1961), devotes two chapters and a valuable appendix to Ramism in the New World while Wilbur Samuel Howell, *Logic and Rhetoric in England, 1500–1700* (New York: Russell and Russell, 1961), deals extensively with the influence of Ramism in England.

Graves, Miller, and Howell all concentrate on Ramist logic and rhetoric. Reijer Hooykaas, *Humanisme, science et réforme: Pierre de la Ramée (1515–1572)* (Leiden: Brill, 1958), 167–294, looks more to his scientific and mathematical thought, a task continued by his student J. J. Verdonk in *Petrus Ramus en de Wiskunde* (Assen: Van Gorcum, 1966), and by the Soviet scholar Galina Pavlovna Matvievskaia, *Ramus, 1515–1572* (Moscow: Izd-vo., 1981). Finally, Paul Lobstein, *Petrus Ramus als Theologe: Ein Beitrag zur Geschichte der protestantischen Theologie* (Strasbourg: C.F. Schmidt, 1878), deserves mention as the first, and so far the only, major study of Ramus's theological ideas.

15. J. W. Allen, *A History of Political Thought in the Sixteenth Century* (1928; reprint, London: Methuen, 1960), 282.

---

in the economic, political, social, and religious institutions of sixteenth-century France. Unfortunately, both Ong and Waddington did just that.[16]

Ramus was no ivory-tower intellectual, if indeed anyone was in the ideologically charged atmosphere of sixteenth-century France. In an era of religious reform, political revolt, and economic dislocation, no one could escape the influence of events or the possible consequences of his public statements. Leopold von Ranke made the point even before Waddington wrote, and his words should be remembered by every historian of sixteenth-century thought. "In those times," he wrote, "a learned or religious life, entirely devoted to its own peculiar objects, and at the same time tranquil, was not conceivable."[17]

The point applies with special force to Ramus. This is not only because of his involvement with the major political and religious leaders of his day, nor even because his reform of logic challenged the understanding of man and the world current among sixteenth-century Frenchmen. Just as important, as we shall see, was Ramus's insistence that theory and practice were intimately connected, and that theory found its only validation in its application to the world. The unity of theory and practice was a central principle of his life and thought. While Ramus was far from being a Marxist in any sense of the word, he would have endorsed the classic Marxist dictum that the task of the philosopher was not to explain the world, but to change it. In fact, what Ramus developed was not an idea but an ideology. That in

16. Ong's account of Ramus's life and times takes up only twenty pages in a work of over 300 pages; Ong, "Vectors in Ramus' Career," *Ramus, Method and the Decay*, 17–35. The rest is devoted to a strictly philosophical account of Ramism. Waddington, on the other hand, spent the bulk of his work narrating Ramus's life; Waddington, "Vie de Ramus," *Ramus: Sa vie*, 17–339, and dealt with his scholarly work in isolation from it in a separate section of only sixty pages; Waddington, "Du Ramisme," *Ramus: Sa vie*, 341–400. Neither attempted to integrate the two in an explanatory scheme.

17. Leopold von Ranke, *Civil Wars and Monarchy in France, in the Sixteenth and Seventeenth Centuries: A History of France Principally during that Period*, trans. M. A. Garvey, vol. 1 (London: Richard Bentley, 1852), 213. The point applies with especial force to religious thought. Thus when Ong described Ramus's theology as "only a rather colorless, if superficially orderly, redaction of Zwinglianism," he neglects the revolutionary character of Ramus's thought in the context of the French Reformed Church of his time; "Père Cossart, Du Monstier, and Ramus' Protestantism in the Light of a New Manuscript," *Archivum Historicum Societatis Jesu* 23 (1954): 140–64, at 156. See below, chapter 5. Ranke brings up another point of some significance in his discussion of Ramus himself. While Ong treats Ramus almost exclusively as a logician and belittles his contributions in other academic fields, Ranke claimed that "Ramus cannot properly be estimated if viewed through the medium of those works which he devoted to the reformation of logic"; Ranke, *Civil Wars*, 2:111. Even before Ranke, the philosophes had emphasized the importance of Ramus's works in history and grammar; the rest, including the logic, they found "imparfait"; *Encyclopédie, ou dictionnaire raisonné...*, t. XVII (Paris: 1751), 72, col. b. Nonetheless Ong argued that Ramus's significance derived almost completely from his textbooks, and that "if we consider his life apart from his educational activity, we find very little to consider"; "Ramist Classroom Procedure and the Nature of Reality," *Studies in English Literature 1500–1900* 1 (1961): 31–47, at 31; also in Ong, *Rhetoric, Romance and Technology*, 142–64. It is to be hoped that the present study will substantially modify this view.

any case is the guiding theme of this study, and to avoid misunderstanding, it might be well to explain more clearly exactly what I take "ideology" to mean.

Definitions of the term are numerous. They range from Karl Mannheim's all-encompassing "total conception of ideology," which is "concerned with the characteristics and composition of the mind of this epoch or of this group," to such narrow and restrictive formulations as that of Harry M. Johnson, who asserts that "ideology consists only of those parts or aspects of a system of social ideas which are distorted or unduly selective."[18] And while many writers agree with Johnson that ideology necessarily involves distortion or falsification of reality, others use the term in a broader sense to include more or less accurate perceptions of "the way things are." And many also include the proviso that an ideology not only describes social situations but also prescribes appropriate responses.[19]

The definition offered by Donald R. Kelley, in his *The Beginning of Ideology: Consciousness and Society in the French Reformation,* is close to the way the term will be used here. Kelley uses the term to describe "a distinctive and more or less coherent conglomeration of assumptions, attitudes, sentiments, values, ideals and goals, accepted and perhaps acted upon by a more or less organized group of persons."[20] Kelley's usage reserves judgment on the truth or falsehood of ideological claims while making it clear that they can be normative as well as descriptive, prescriptions for action as well as diagnoses of the current scene. To an ideologist, the point is not only to explain the world, but to change it.

In this sense, Ramus was the ideologist par excellence. His works referred to a specific social situation, that of France in the middle of the sixteenth century. They recommended programs for action, whether they were ostensibly concerned with Aristotle's logic or Caesar's wars. Furthermore, Ramus attempted to put those programs into effect despite a hostile—sometimes violently hostile—environment.

Ramus's ideology was the humanist one of meritocracy. The term is appropriate, even if the sixteenth-century understanding of merit differed in crucial ways from our own, and even if the word Ramus used for it—"timocracy"—is obscure. He sought a society in which merit would be the determining factor in social and

---

18. Karl Mannheim, *Ideology and Utopia,* trans. Louis Wirth and Edward Shils (New York: Harcourt, Brace and World, 1936), 56; Harry M. Johnson, "Ideology: Ideology and the Social System," *International Encyclopedia of the Social Sciences,* vol. 7 (New York: Macmillan, 1968), 77, col. 1.

19. Among those definitions which make ideology a distorted view of the world, see Mannheim's "particular conception of ideology" (Mannheim, *Ideology and Utopia,* 55) and Marx's use of the term "for distorted or selected ideas in defense of the *status quo* of a social system" (Johnson, "Ideology," 76, col. 1). Julius Gould says in contrast that "ideology is a pattern of beliefs and concepts (both factual and normative) which purport to explain complex social phenomena with a view to directing and simplifying sociopolitical choices facing individuals and groups"; "Ideology," in *A Dictionary of the Social Sciences,* eds. Julius Gould and William L. Kolb (New York: Free Press, 1964), 315.

20. Donald R. Kelley, *The Beginning of Ideology: Consciousness and Society in the French Reformation* (Cambridge: Cambridge University Press, 1981), 4.

economic advancement, with careers open to talent and a man's standing determined by his worth.

Ramus's ideology was molded in the France of Francis I, at a time when the social structure of France was more open and fluid than it had been for centuries and than it would be for centuries to come. In his youth and early manhood, he encountered social institutions which rewarded hard work, talent, and education with advancement and material rewards, and it was this environment which enabled him to rise from the peasantry to the peak of his profession. It was Ramus's goal to make these benefits available to an ever-widening number of Frenchmen by removing what he saw as artificial barriers to learning: the high cost of a university degree, the monopoly of Latin in the academy, and the needless complexity of the arts and sciences as they were taught by Aristotle, Euclid, and Cicero.[21] Ramus sought to make education simple, inexpensive, and quick, and the Ramist method arose as a means to this end. Through Ramism, the talents of every Frenchman could be recognized and rewarded.

In the later sixteenth century, however, France experienced a reaction against popular education, careers open to talent, and social mobility in general. Elite groups, facing the problems of overpopulation, a deteriorating economic environment, and a country ravaged by religious and political strife—a "society in crisis," as J. M. H. Salmon labeled it—feared competition from their inferiors and took steps to prevent it. Birth and wealth replaced talent as the criteria of social status, and co-optation replaced competition as the mechanism of advancement. Education was no longer a key to success. Ramus discovered that he had to go beyond the classroom and into the courtroom and the consistory to challenge these new developments and to protect the claims of merit. His attacks on the self-perpetuating oligarchies which were gaining control of the University and the Reformed Church were a continuation of his struggle to ensure that talent and achievement would be properly rewarded.

Ramus fought against the social trend towards oligarchy from the 1540s down to his death in 1572, but even though he won some battles, his efforts were clearly doomed. His was already a lost cause. He was not the champion of a new age, but the defender of and apologist for a rapidly disappearing past. By the time of his

---

21. Pierre Bourdieu provides a thought-provoking analysis of how such disciplines serve as a sort of symbolic capital which confers an easily recognized legitimacy and authority on those whose mastery of them is evident in their speech and writing. His point applies especially to the monopoly of Latin in sixteenth-century education: "The competence adequate to produce sentences that are likely to be understood may be quite inadequate to produce sentences that are likely to be listened to, likely to be recognized as acceptable....Speakers lacking the legitimate competence are *de facto* excluded from the social domains in which this competence is required, or are condemned to silence." Furthermore, the "duration of study (which provides a good measure of the economic cost of training) tends to be valued for its own sake, independently of the results it produces"; Pierre Bourdieu, "The Production and Reproduction of Legitimate Language," in his *Language and Symbolic Power* (Cambridge: Harvard University Press, 1991), 43–65, at 55.

death, the conditions which had created his beliefs had vanished. In their place arose the rigidly hierarchical social structures of France in the classical age, which was to last until the Revolution. The birth of the Old Régime was the deathblow to Ramus's hopes.

Ramus's ideology failed, but it remains important for historians because of what it teaches us about sixteenth-century France and the place which Ramus and Ramism held in it. In broader terms, Ramus's life is a case study of the importance of social, economic, and political context in intellectual history, especially in the tumultuous history of Renaissance and Reformation France.

CHAPTER 1
Labor Omnia Vincit

THE YEAR 1515, WHICH SAW RAMUS'S BIRTH, was also witness to a much more significant beginning.[1] It was the year that the young Francis I came to the throne of France, greeted by a torrent of congratulations and a flood of advice on how one went about governing the greatest kingdom in Europe. Among the letters, pamphlets, and books written to prepare the novice king for his role, the best known is probably Claude de Seyssel's *The Monarchy of France.*[2] Seyssel had more right than most to claim the role of mentor to the new king. His long career of public service—he had served both in the Parlement of Paris and on the Grand Council of Francis's predecessor Louis XII—had given him an intimate knowledge of the workings of the state. Now he proposed to share the wisdom born of his long experience in public life with the untried Francis.

One chapter in Seyssel's work is devoted to the topic of "How Men Go from the Third Estate to the Second and from the Second to the First." The "estates" to which Seyssel referred were not the three legal estates of France—clergy, nobility, and commoners—but orders of society similar in many ways to social classes. He distinguished the nobility, the middling or wealthy people, and the lesser folk ("peuple menu").[3] The boundaries between these groups were clear but not rigid. In fact, Seyssel praised the ease with which talented men could rise from the lowest to the highest estate, and he warned against the danger of maintaining too strict a division between the different ranks.

---

1. According to his student and biographer Nicolas de Nancel, Ramus adopted the phrase "Labor improbus omnia vincit," "hard work conquers all," as his special motto. In his edition of Nancel's biography, Peter Sharratt identifies Virgil's *Georgica*, 1:145–46, as the source; Nicolaus Nancelius, "*Petri Rami Vita*: Edited with an English Translation," *Humanistica Lovaniensia: Journal of Neo-Latin Studies* 24 (1975): 161–277, at 249.

2. Claude de Seyssel, *The Monarchy of France*, ed. Donald R. Kelley, trans. J. H. Hexter (New Haven: Yale University Press, 1981). Written in 1515, the work was not published until three years later.

3. Seyssel, *Monarchy*, 62. See Seyssel, introduction to *Monarchy*, 19, for a discussion of the Italian influence behind this division of the social orders.

If...there were no hope of mounting from one [estate] to the other or if it were too difficult, overbold men could induce others of the same estate to conspire against the other two. Here, however, it is so easy that daily we see men of the popular estate ascend by degrees, some to the nobility and innumerable to the middling estate. The Romans always maintained this same order, for from the common people one rose to that of the knights and from that of the knights to that of senators and patricians.

Of course to reach the pinnacle of French society, the nobility, the king's assent was required, but anyone could rise from the third to the second rank by his own efforts: "everyone in this last estate can attain to the second by virtue and by diligence without any assistance of grace or privilege."[4]

It would be naive to claim that Seyssel was simply describing the society he saw around him in these passages.[5] His aim was not merely to report on the French social order but to prescribe for it. He hoped that the new king of France would see to it that his vision of French society would become, or remain, a reality. To this end, Seyssel mustered arguments to prove that the relatively open society he described was desirable and even necessary to the health of the monarchy.

To begin with, Seyssel claimed, an open society had the advantage of stability. It guaranteed domestic peace by reducing hostility between the estates, a crucial goal for any prince and one repeatedly stressed by Italian political writers of the previous century.[6] As a matter of fact, there were Italians offering the same advice to the French king even as Seyssel wrote. In a letter to Francis I written in 1515, the humanist and patron of letters Ludovico di Canossa advanced a similar rationale for maintaining a social system in which men could easily rise from one order to another. "Innumerable are the persons," he wrote, "whom we see every day rise from the third class to the second, and from the second to the first; were this not the case, it would soon be followed by an insurrection of the lower classes."[7] Canossa's testimony does not prove that Seyssel's description of French society was accurate, but it

---

4. Seyssel, *Monarchy*, 63.

5. But see J. W. Allen, *A History of Political Thought in the Sixteenth Century* (1928; reprint, London: Methuen, 1960), 275: "It has been said that we can gather from this book how France thought of herself and her political constitution at the commencement of the sixteenth century. This observation is so far true that much of the controversy that followed can be read as a commentary on or an expansion, on one side or another, of the views of Seyssel." And compare William Farr Church, *Constitutional Thought in Sixteenth-Century France: A Study in the Evolution of Ideas* (Cambridge: Harvard University Press, 1941), 22: "it is generally agreed that his ideas were representative of the conception of the state held generally by Frenchmen early in the century."

6. See Quentin Skinner, *The Foundations of Modern Political Thought*, vol. 1, *The Renaissance* (Cambridge: Cambridge University Press, 1978), 235–36.

7. Ludovico di Canossa, "Il vescovo di Bajusa al re Francisco I, 1515," excerpted by Leopold von Ranke, *Civil Wars and Monarchy in France, in the Sixteenth and Seventeenth Centuries: A History of France Principally during that Period*, trans. M. A. Garvey, vol. 1 (London: Richard Bentley, 1852), 111–12.

does demonstrate that his appraisal was reasonable and that his hopes were shared by others. Like Seyssel, they believed that an open society was not only desirable but attainable, if it were not already taking shape.

In addition to his argument from utility, Seyssel appealed to historical precedent to bolster his recommendations to Francis. The lessons of the past supported his views, he claimed, and not just the past in general, but that particular time and place most dear to the humanists of the Renaissance: ancient Rome. Rome was to provide the pattern for Renaissance society just as it provided the models for Renaissance law and Renaissance letters.

The influence of Renaissance humanism on Seyssel's work was not limited to isolated examples. His social program, his ideology, was a reflection of the humanists' optimistic assessment of man's potential to improve himself. Pico's claim that man was "a great miracle," endowed with the freedom to choose "whatever abode, whatever form, and whatever functions" he desired, was basically a proposition about man's spiritual life, but it was interpreted in a broader sense. For the humanists, man's place in this world was no more determined than his place in the next.[8] Seyssel's social program reflected this fundamental humanist view, adapted to suit a great kingdom rather than the milieu of the Italian cities.

Seyssel's views tell us something about one humanist's social ideal, but to what extent France actually matched the ideal in the early sixteenth century is a question not to be answered on the basis of political treatises or hortatory tracts. To discover just how difficult it was to ascend in the social hierarchy we must look elsewhere, especially to the many modern studies of the economic, social, and political history of sixteenth-century France. In particular, we will be concerned to find out how difficult it was for someone at the very bottom of the social hierarchy, one of the peasants who constituted the vast majority of Frenchmen, to achieve a more prominent place in society. The question is fundamental, for as Pierre Chaunu points out, "All social ascent departs from the shifting world of the countryside."[9] The question is also particularly relevant in the present context, for as we shall see, Ramus himself was born little better than a peasant and was nonetheless able to become one of the leading intellectuals of Europe.

How representative was Ramus's experience? How difficult was it for a peasant (or his urban counterpart, the wage-earning laborer) to rise above his station in Renaissance France? How difficult—compared to what? Our answer, and in fact the question itself, can only make sense in relative terms, in a contrast with conditions

8. Giovanni Pico della Mirandola, "Oration on the Dignity of Man," trans. Elizabeth Livermore Forbes, in Ernst Cassirer, Paul Oskar Kristeller, and John Herman Randall, Jr., *The Renaissance Philosophy of Man* (Chicago: University of Chicago Press, 1948), 223–54.

9. Pierre Chaunu, "L'État," in Fernand Braudel and Ernest Labrousse, eds., *Histoire économique et sociale de la France: De 1450 à 1660*, vol. 1, "L'État et la ville" (Paris: Presses Universitaires de France, 1977), 11–228, at 209.

prevailing at some other time. Here the most apt comparison is between the first and second halves of the sixteenth century. The first half of the century provided the setting for Ramus's rapid social advancement, and it was only after midcentury that he began to feel that the prospects of advancement for the lower orders were fading and to take action to preserve them.

Ramus's experience suggests that French society was a great deal more open early in the century than it was after 1550, and the evidence overwhelmingly supports that hypothesis. Compared with the later era, the reign of Francis I was a period of abundant opportunity for even the most humble to improve their lot. Toward the end of his reign, however, the upper orders of society, and especially the more privileged commoners, were beginning to erect barriers on the path to power, wealth, and status. The haute bourgeoisie, "clothing themselves with the title of the Third Estate, rejected the great mass of workers and peasants into a miserable Fourth Order without traditions, without rights, without powers, without protectors," and without much hope of rising above their condition.[10]

Jean-Richard Bloch's pessimistic conclusions were supported by Henri Drouot's study of Burgundian society in the later sixteenth century. Drouot concluded that

> the period before 1560 was one of material prosperity, in which many industrious persons had rapidly gathered together a fortune and risen to social prominence.... By 1587, however, things were very different. Social ascensions had ceased with the economic and monetary crisis, and with the permanent replacement of foreign war and internal peace by civil war.[11]

Drouot's conclusions rest on his study of the role of venal office in Burgundy over the course of the century. Under Francis I and Henry II, the sale of offices "provided able men with an easy means of entry to the upper levels of the provincial hierarchy." But under Henry III, that is, in the 1570s and 1580s, the owners of offices managed to make them hereditary possessions, and "newcomers found the path barred to situations reserved for the sons, sons-in-law, and nephews of the holders."[12] Ramus attempted to halt a similar development in Paris in the 1560s, when the royal professors also began to consider their chairs as personal property to be bequeathed or sold as the owner desired.[13]

Drouot's analysis deals only with Burgundy, of course, and with persons of higher rank than a peasant or journeyman. His description of the lower orders of society

10. Jean-Richard Bloch, *L'Anoblissement en France au temps de François I: Essai d'une définition de la condition juridique et sociale de la noblesse au début du XVIe siècle* (Paris: Librairie Félix Alcan, 1934), 215.

11. Henri Drouot, *Mayenne et la Bourgogne: Étude sur la Ligue (1587–1596)* (Paris: Auguste Picard, 1937); excerpted in English translation in J. H. M. Salmon, *The French Wars of Religion* (Lexington, Mass.: D.C. Heath, 1967), 91–92.

12. Drouot, *Mayenne et la Bourgogne*, 95.

13. See below, chapter 3.

under Francis I is less firmly grounded and tends toward the idyllic: "There were no social barriers…between the top rank of society and those lower classes on the land, whom they dominated and from whom they were derived…."[14] Certainly social barriers did exist, in Burgundy and everywhere else in France as well. But recent studies support the claim that the barriers separating the low from the high, and just as important from the middle, did in fact multiply as the century progressed.

Some of the new barriers to social advancement were erected by existing elite groups for the express purpose of defending their privileged status. Drouot illustrated this phenomenon within the provincial elite of Burgundy, but it extended farther down the social scale and all over France as well. In the towns, master craftsmen increasingly treated the mastership as a patrimony to be kept in the family, an attitude not new to the later sixteenth century, but one that spread rapidly during its course. The masters found their efforts seconded by the crown, as Richard Gascon demonstrates.[15] The Renaissance monarchs sought to use the gilds as sources of revenue and instruments of economic control, as well as to break up the patronage networks of their wealthy clients, and therefore favored the spread of gild organization into crafts which had previously been free. Under Henry III, the crown extended its policy of organizing the crafts and extracting revenue from them by the edict of 1581, which generalized the system of *métiers jurés* and levied a high fee for entering the mastership—a fee reduced by one-half, however, for the son of a master. By 1583, even fishmongers in the towns were required to take an oath and purchase their offices, and "the vast majority of offices became both inheritable and, subject to the forty-day clause, transferable."[16]

In these circumstances, Gascon asks, what became of the journeyman? "What happened to the preoccupation with social equilibrium so clearly proclaimed in the statutes, the concern to allow, within the craft, the promotion of the best at the work? For a long time the reality had been different for the richest crafts. But the freeze extended even into the most modest crafts."[17] The increased cost of mastership, together with the desire of the established masters to keep their offices within

---

14. Drouot, *Mayenne et la Bourgogne*, 91.

15. Richard Gascon, *La France de mouvement: Les Commerces et les villes*, in Braudel and Labrousse, *Histoire économique*, 231–479, at 427.

16. David Parker, *The Making of French Absolutism* (New York: St. Martin's Press, 1983), 38. Roland Mousnier, in *La Vénalité des offices sous Henri IV et Louis XIII* (Rouen: Éditions Maugard, 1945), makes the same points in relation to a much higher social stratum, the robe nobility. He finds numerous petty offices becoming venal in the second half of the sixteenth century (26), and also discovers that, from being an avenue of advancement for the lower orders, venal office had by the end of the century become a family patrimony: "les classes sociales se ferment" (63). More recently Barbara B. Diefendorf, *Paris City Councillors in the Sixteenth Century: The Politics of Patrimony* (Princeton: Princeton University Press, 1983), 17–18, suggests that the 1550s and 1560s were the crucial decades in the transformation of councillors' offices from elected positions to family possessions, and traces several dynasties of councillors which originally gained their offices in that period (37).

17. Gascon, *La France*, 427.

the family, all but eliminated the chance of a worker to become an employer in his own right. As the century wore on, the odds grew progressively worse.

The peasants were not subject to gild control, but they faced a similar situation in the second half of the century. Their desire to improve their lot came directly into conflict with the aspirations of a more powerful group, the wealthy bourgeoisie. In peasant society, wealth and prestige were measured directly in terms of landowner-ship, and to acquire land was to gain security and respect. Unfortunately for the peasants, precisely the same was true within the wealthy urban elite. There is no need to describe the well-known movement of commercial capital into investment in land in early modern France. It is a commonplace that fortunes made in trade, or in state service, were soon invested in land. Landownership offered both greater security and higher status than did the perilous and vulgar world of trade and manu-facture.[18] When the wealthy bourgeoisie entered the land market, however, the land-less peasant or smallholder was unable to compete. In bad times, he might even have to sell what land he already had to a bourgeois engrosser. As a result, the purchase of land, the peasant's main route to social advancement, became increasingly difficult for the average countryman, especially since the land market grew tighter and tighter as the century grew older.

There was one small group of peasants which was able to profit from the inva-sion of the countryside by urban capital. These were the "*coqs du village*," the peasant elite, who were in the context of their villages major landholders. Such "kulaks" might possess fifty or more acres of arable land, but their rank in rural society depended even more on their positions as managers or farmers (*fermiers*) for absentee landlords: nobles, ecclesiastics, and of course wealthy townsmen. As managers, they controlled far more land than they owned and were also responsible for employing day laborers chosen from among the landless and those whose meager holdings did not produce enough to make ends meet.[19]

What is striking about this "aristocracy of the plow" is the way its members began, around the middle of the century, to entrench themselves in their privileged positions and to prevent their less well-to-do neighbors from reaching their level. Like the magistrates in Burgundy or the gildmasters in the towns, members of the village elite began to form "peasant lineages," passing on land and offices to sons or relatives. They increasingly behaved like a separate caste within rural society, in a pattern which spread rapidly through the French countryside in the 1550s and 1560s.[20] "The rich *laboureurs* married, supported, advanced and underwrote each

18. See for example Robin Briggs, *Early Modern France, 1560–1715* (Oxford: Oxford University Press, 1977), 56–57; and Gascon, who refers to the withdrawal of merchant capital from commerce as "la 'trahison' des marchands"; Gascon, *La France*, 322.

19. Emmanuel Le Roy Ladurie, *Les Masses profondes: La Paysannerie*, vol. 2 of Braudel and Labrousse, *Histoire économique*, 483–865, at 655–66.

20. Hubert Méthivier, *L'Ancien régime en France: XVIe–XVIIe–XVIIIe siècles* (Paris: Presses Universi-taires de France, 1981), 101–2.

other," while veritable dynasties grew up to keep wealth and power within a small, closed group of families.[21] It was from this group, amounting to about 1 percent of the peasantry, that landowners and the crown selected their inferior officers and agents.[22] For these, there was some hope of escaping the peasant milieu altogether. For the rest of the peasantry, which is essentially to say for the rest of the French people, the opportunity to achieve a higher standing in society had been effectively eliminated. Clearly advancement in society was becoming more difficult at the dawn of the Old Régime. What had happened to bring about such a change in French society?

The most important difference between France in 1500 and France in 1560 was that there were more Frenchmen. According to the best estimates, the population of the country nearly doubled between 1450 and 1560, rising from between eight and ten million to between seventeen and twenty million people.[23] The course and effects of this population explosion have been traced by Emmanuel Le Roy Ladurie, whose Malthusian model of the impact of demographic change on social and economic structures in early modern France is a compelling one. His conception links land and labor, production and consumption, and population growth and decline as parts of a ramified homeostatic system, an "ecosystem." The operation of this "ecosystem" goes a long way toward explaining the rise of oligarchy at all levels of French society after the reign of Francis I.[24]

Population is the key to understanding Le Roy Ladurie's "ecosystem." The early fourteenth century had seen the population of France reach a maximum of nearly twenty million people, which was roughly the limit set by the productive capacity of French agriculture under the existing technological dispensation. French soil could not produce enough food to support more people, so demographic growth reached a plateau with production and consumption more or less in balance. Forces from outside the production-consumption equation intervened, however, to tip the balance toward demographic decline. The ravages of the Black Death were aggravated by the dislocations caused by the Hundred Years' War, and population fell precipitously after the middle of the fourteenth century, reaching a low point by about 1440.[25]

---

21. Le Roy Ladurie, *Les Masses profondes*, 656.

22. Jean Jacquart, *La Crise rurale en Ile-de-France, 1550–1670* (Paris: Armand Colin, 1974), 117–34, provides the best available survey of this phenomenon for seven seigneuries to the south of Paris around the year 1550. In the century after 1550 this small group became a "veritable clan, whose features we have traced on the eve of the Wars of Religion" (454). Membership in the group passed from father to son, and "some of the most solid of these dynasties can thus be traced for more than a century..." (509). On recruitment of royal and seigneurial agents from these dynasties see Chaunu, *L'État*, 210.

23. Estimates by Méthivier, *L'Ancien Régime*, 90; and Le Roy Ladurie, "Les paysans français du XVIe siècle," in *Conjoncture économique, structures sociales: Hommage à Ernest Labrousse* (Paris: Mouton, 1974), 333–52, at 335.

24. Brief descriptions of this model appear in Le Roy Ladurie, "Les Paysans français," and in the conclusion to his *Les Paysans de Languedoc* (Paris: S.E.V.P.E.N., 1966), 633–54.

25. Le Roy Ladurie, *Les Masses profondes*, 483–554, "La Destruction du 'monde plein.'"

The situation created by this demographic catastrophe was an ironically favorable one—for the survivors. The end of the long era of war and the decreasing incidence of the plague allowed the French to take up their normal pursuits once again, but now only ten million people enjoyed the resources which had once supported double their number. The pie was the same size as it had been, but everyone got a bigger slice. Food was abundant; between 1440 and 1520 dearth and famine were rare. Food was plentiful because land which had been abandoned during the previous century was brought back under the plow. There was a great deal of land, and it was correspondingly cheap.

Workers in the towns benefited from the demographic situation as well. Wage labor was scarce, not only because so many had died, but also because it was so easy to buy land and set up farms independently. As a result, wages were high while the price of essential commodities, in particular bread, remained stable thanks to strong agricultural production. Prosperity and peace bred confidence in the future. Men and women married earlier, had more children, raised them on a better diet, and cherished higher hopes for their futures.[26] There was plenty of opportunity for a hard worker, even at the top.

Thus it was not only the influence of Italian humanism that prompted Seyssel to describe France as an open society. In the early part of the century, that is precisely what it was. His ideology was firmly grounded in social reality. As Jean Jacquart and Bartolomé Benassar observe, "up to 1540, more or less, we can consider that prosperity was accompanied by relative growth and by a transformation, limited but real, of *mentalités* and structures...."[27] Ideologies were also transformed, as Seyssel's example makes clear.

The transformation was not to be a lasting one, however. Better health and earlier marriage meant population growth. Up to 1520, France was filling up with people at a remarkable rate, and growth continued at a slower pace until 1560, when it halted almost completely. Contemporaries were aware that France was full to bursting with people. In 1568, Jean Bodin wrote that "an infinite number of people has multiplied in this realm."[28] Seven years earlier the Venetian ambassador had already proclaimed that "France is full of people.... Every spot is occupied to capacity."[29]

"Le beau seizième siècle," marked by economic and demographic expansion and widespread opportunity, had come to a close.[30] With population again near the

---

26. Le Roy Ladurie, "Les Paysans français," 337–40.

27. Bartolomé Bennassar and Jean Jacquart, *Le XVIe Siècle* (Paris: Armand Colin, 1972), 185.

28. Jean Bodin, *La Vie chère au XVIe siècle: La Response de Jean Bodin à M. de Malestroit: 1568*, ed. Henri Hauser (Paris: Colin, 1932), 13. Bodin dated the origins of the rise in population to 120 or 140 years before he wrote in 1568 ("depuis six ou sept vint ans"), that is, between 1428 and 1448, which is in general agreement with the estimates of modern demographers.

29. Cited in Henry Kamen, *The Iron Century: Social Change in Europe, 1550–1660* (New York: Praeger, 1971), 48.

30. There is no general agreement on the chronological limits of "le beau seizième siècle." Bennassar and Jacquart, *Le XVIe Siècle*, 56, use the term to describe the period from 1490 to 1530, but elsewhere

twenty million mark, demand for food increased and prices rose. In response, arable land became more expensive. Real wages began to decline, not only because prices were higher, but also because there were more wage laborers competing for work. The lower orders were caught in a classic wage-price scissors, and the French economy as a whole suffered.

Forces from outside the demographically determined "ecosystem" compounded the economic decline. Civil war after 1560 created insecurity and economic stagnation, especially in the countryside, while even climatic conditions began to deteriorate as a "little ice age" set in after 1555. "L'offensive du froid" gained momentum during the rest of the century, lowering crop yields and hitting the poorer members of society the hardest. Taken together, these developments conspired to reduce France to a miserable state. Surveying the scene near the end of the century, Estienne Pasquier thought he was looking at his country's corpse.[31]

Economic decline and competition for scarce resources were the main reasons why class and status boundaries hardened after midcentury at all levels of society. There was less to go around, so Frenchmen deemed it essential to protect what they had and to pass it on to their heirs intact. Seyssel's vision of French society as an open arena in which merit would find its reward was out of favor by the 1560s. Guillaume de la Perrière's *Miroir Politique* (1567) suggests the new orthodoxy of the second half of the century. He described a static society, governed by an elaborate hierarchy in which one's place was determined by one's birth and family connections. Movement up the social ladder was not to be thought of. The open society had all but disappeared, both in theory and in reality.[32] In its place arose the hierarchical and oligarchic society that characterized France until the Revolution.

The economic and demographic history of sixteenth-century France helps to explain the increasingly oligarchic cast of French life after about 1550. It also provides the essential background for understanding why Ramus devoted his career to combating the growth of Old Régime institutions. He was the heir and spokesman of an earlier era, the age of Francis I, and he fought doggedly to defend its ideas and practices throughout his professional career. In the University, in the Reformed Church, and among the royal professors he was a consistent defender of the principle of merit in the face of attempts to restrict access to position, wealth, and power

---

they suggest that the period of prosperity did not end until 1540 (185) or 1550 (303). Méthivier, *L'Ancien Régime*, 90, sees the "fortunate conjuncture" extending up to 1560. The date chosen to mark the end of this era of well-being depends on which measure of prosperity is considered most important: population growth, real wages, etc. Clearly by the end of the 1560s expansion had come to an end by nearly every measure.

31. The citation from Pasquier is in Méthivier, *L'Ancien Régime*, 131.

32. Donald R. Kelley, *The Beginning of Ideology: Consciousness and Society in the French Reformation* (Cambridge: Cambridge University Press, 1981), 189–90: "Nor did he [La Perrière] envisage the sort of mobility permitted by Seyssel; for to him it was nature, which is to say birth, that destined one to these roles."

to members of privileged groups. His works were motivated and informed by the principle of merit as well, a principle spelled out in his philosophical and historical writings. As a writer, teacher, and Christian, Ramus worked to preserve the open society he remembered from his youth and to establish the meritocratic ideal he had learned from the humanists.

It is a long step, however, from the level of social structure and conjuncture to the career of an individual poor-boy-made-good, or from the ideals of the humanists to the experiences of a single sixteenth-century Parisian teacher. There are links between these levels of interpretation, but it is not immediately apparent in statistics of population growth or in Pico's high-flown oratory. The connections between French social structure and Ramus's career can be made much more explicit.

Ramus was born on his father's farm in the Picard village of Cuts, near Noyon. Jacques de la Ramée was a first generation immigrant from the Low Countries; his father had been forced out of his native Liège into exile and poverty when the town was burned by Charles the Bold in 1468. In later life, Ramus always maintained that his family had been "illustrious" in its old home, but in Picardy, his grandfather had been obliged to accept a more modest station in life than his past and his particle promised. He took up the demeaning occupation of charcoal-burner in the woods near Cuts, a circumstance which was to please Ramus's later opponents, who delighted in taunting him with his grandfather's base trade.[33]

Base it may have been, but the trade seems to have allowed the family a certain modest prosperity. Ramus's father was able to save enough from its proceeds to buy land and set himself up as a farmer. It was only "a few acres of land in a deserted, uncultivated district," according to Ramus's biographer Nicolas de Nancel, and it was not worth a great deal, either. Jacques was able to get it for "next to nothing."[34] Nevertheless it was land, and as landowners the La Ramées enjoyed greater economic security and social standing. So it must have seemed to Jacques, at least,

---

33. Ramus described his ancestry, and his adversaries' mockery of it, in his inaugural address as a royal professor in 1551: "Carbonarius pater probri loco nobis objectus est: Avus certe in Eburonum gente, familia imprimis illustri fuit: sed patria a Carolo Burgundionum duce capta & incensa, in Vermanduo-rum agrum profugus, ob paupertatem carbonarius fuit...." Petrus Ramus, "Petri Rami eloquentiae & phi-losophiae professoris Regii, Oratio," in *Collectaneae praefationes, epistolae, orationes...* (Marburg: 1609), 323–42, at 341. Ramus's biographers Banos and Freigius copy his account verbatim in their works, *Petri Rami Vita per Joannem Thomam Freigium* in *Collectaneae*, 580–625, at 581, and Théophile de Banos [Theophilus Banosius], *Petri Rami Vita*, which appeared as an (unpaginated) introduction to Ramus's *Commentariorum de Religione Christianum Libri Quatuor* (Frankfurt: A. Wechel, 1576). Nicolas Nancel's biography provides the only independent testimony to the career of Ramus's grandfather, which agrees in all essentials with Ramus's account. Nancel adds that the exiled La Ramée brought his family with him into Picardy ("cum familia et recula domestica commigravit"); Nancel, *"Petri Rami Vita,"* 172.

34. Nancel, *"Petri Rami Vita,"* 174: "coemptis vili pretio in terra deserta incultaque aliquot soli juge-ribus." Nancel adds that Jacques then turned his hand to farming ("agriculturam prisco more patrum et patriarcharum excercere instituit"), while Freigius (581) and Banos agree that Ramus's father was a farmer. Ong nonetheless credits the claim of Ramus's detractors that his father was a charcoal-burner.

who began to imagine even greater success for his son, and to prepare him for it sent him to learn Latin from a schoolmaster in the area. A farmer's son had little enough use for Latin, and schooling cost money. Still Jacques decided to send him to school, a decision that showed not only his social pretensions, but also his confidence that society would reward in a peasant the accomplishments more suitable to the higher orders.[35]

In the long run, of course, Jacques turned out to be right. Ramus's humble origins did not ruin his chances of becoming a professional man, and a very successful one at that, crowned with wealth, position, and international fame. What did almost destroy his prospects was his father's death while he was still a boy. His mother Jehanne was herself from a poor family, and she could not hope to continue her son's education without some sort of assistance. None was forthcoming. Twice Ramus traveled to Paris to study at the University, and twice was forced to return to Cuts for lack of support. The third trip seemed more promising, since his mother's brother Honoré, a Parisian carpenter, agreed to keep him while he pursued his studies. Even this arrangement proved to be too burdensome, however, and Ramus was once again thrown upon his own resources to survive and study at Paris.[36]

His solution was humiliating to the independent peasant's son. He was obliged to enter the service of a wealthy student at the college of Navarre, the Sieur de la Brosse, and to spend his days as a domestic servant.[37] By waiting on his master by day and studying by night—"making more use of lamp-oil than of wine," according to Nancel—he was finally able to take his M.A. in 1536. Just as important, he was able to attract the attention of a fellow student at Navarre who was to become one of

35. Ramus mentions his primary education in his *Aristotelicae Animadversiones* (1543; reprint, Stuttgart-Bad Cannstatt: Friedrich Frommann Verlag, 1964), fol. 23r°. His teacher does not seem to have been a very learned man, to judge by what Ramus has to say about him; beyond the basic rules of Latin grammar, "I learned nothing from him; not a word of Cicero or Virgil; but I am grateful to him, as he openly confessed that he did not know very much, and he urged me to do better [praeterea nihil ab eo didici: Ciceronis, Virgilii nullum verbum audivi: sed illi gratiam habeo, quod simpliciter se non multa scire fateretur, & me hortaretur ad meliora]." Besides proving that Ramus was not completely unlettered when he went to Paris, this testimony indicates that even the village of Cuts was able to support a schoolmaster; Ramus calls him "vici mei magister."

36. Nancel, *"Petri Rami Vita,"* 172, reports that Ramus's father and mother were both "humili de plebe parentes." Ramus himself is the authority for his repeated efforts to establish himself in Paris, in his *Defensio pro Aristotele adversus Iac. Schecium* (1571; reprint, Frankfurt: Minerva, 1976), 121: "I came to Paris to undertake the study of the liberal arts, but was twice driven away by the violence of the times. Nonetheless I twice returned despite the contrary winds.... [Lutetiam ad capessendas artes ingenuas veni, inde bis abductus violentia temporis, bis eodem tamen quamlibet reflantibus ventis reversus...]." Honoré's assistance to his nephew is attested by Nancel (176) and by Banos. Nancel adds that Honoré intended to take the boy with him on a pilgrimage to Compostella, and later to join the army with him, but apparently neither of these projects was realized.

37. Charles Waddington, *Ramus (Pierre da la Ramée): Sa vie, ses écrits et ses opinions* (1855; reprint, Dubuque, Iowa: Brown Reprint Library, n.d.), 20; Walter J. Ong, S.J., *Ramus, Method and the Decay of Dialogue: From the Art of Discourse to the Art of Reason* (Cambridge: Harvard University Press, 1958), 19,

the most powerful men in France: Charles of Guise, later cardinal of Lorraine.[38] With his academic talent and powerful friend, Ramus soon found employment in the University and began the academic career that brought him the highest scholarly honors in France and Europe.

Nancel claimed that Ramus took pride in his humble origins, and in the determination and hard work that made possible his rise from obscure poverty to wealth and prominence.[39] The Virgilian motto Ramus adopted, "Labor improbus omnia vincit," reflects that pride and his belief that diligence and constant application were the keys to success. In fact, of course, it was not only hard work that lifted Ramus out of obscurity and into celebrity, but the conditions which prevailed in French society during his youth. Would Ramus's family have been able to make its dramatic social ascent under the conditions which prevailed in the second half of the century? It seems doubtful. Jacques de la Ramée would have found it very difficult to buy land at all, let alone "for next to nothing," in the face of the tight land market and entrenched peasant oligarchy of the later sixteenth century. And without the security offered by landownership and the confidence born of prosperity, it is unlikely that the family would or could have allowed Ramus to spend his adolescence in the expensive and unproductive pursuit of learning. Furthermore, even if he had managed to earn his M.A., his chances of establishing himself as a teacher, college principal, and royal professor would have been very poor in the second half of the sixteenth century, as academics, like other officeholders and gildmasters, began to close ranks against newcomers.[40] Altogether it would have been much more difficult for a charcoal-burner's grandson to become a royal professor after midcentury.

The transformation of French society in the sixteenth century was thus something which Ramus experienced directly and dramatically, even though he would not have understood it in the terms we have been using. To understand why he reacted as he did to the birth of the Old Régime, we must look to see how his

---

suggests that Ramus resented his subordinate position: "Pierre drank at Navarre the bitter dregs of resentment, for he had got into the college only by becoming the paid valet of a wealthy fellow student." On the same page, however, Ong ridicules the notion that entering service was, as Waddington (21) suggested, a great sacrifice: "Ramus was doubtless following the general trend into the colleges and the irresistible drive of the adolescent boy to conform as exactly as possible to the crowd." Ramus seems to have been more concerned with securing a roof over his head.

38. Nancel, *"Petri Rami Vita,"* 178; Waddington, *Ramus*, 22.

39. Nancel, *"Petri Rami Vita,"* 172.

40. In the sixteenth century, disapproval of the upstart was nearly universal; "rapid movements up and down the social ladder were regarded, even by those at the bottom, as a cause for complaint"; Briggs, *Early Modern France*, 9. The poet Guillaume des Autelz sums up the reason why: "In truth when a man born of low estate arrives at honors which are due to more noble persons, he finds himself as hindered as David was when they buckled unaccustomed armor on his back to fight Goliath. He really had no idea how to conduct himself to preserve his reputation." Quoted in J. H. M. Salmon, *Society in Crisis: France in the Sixteenth Century* (New York: St. Martin's Press, 1975), 100.

experiences helped to mold his character and make him the kind of man he was, with the kinds of concerns he expressed.

The most important influence on Ramus's mature character was undoubtedly his humble birth. He was the product of a peasant home and a peasant community, and the heritage of the French peasantry left its mark on him for the rest of his life. Relating the personality of a grown man to the circumstances of his birth and child-hood is a tricky business, and even the astrologers who were Ramus's contemporaries admitted as much. Still, the attempt can be illuminating in Ramus's case. Lucien Febvre once sketched a sort of composite portrait of the Renaissance peasant-turned-academic, and I cannot do better than to borrow a page from his work to suggest the sort of man Ramus was. "Let us look at the man of the sixteenth century squarely in the face," Febvre wrote, "the rough, rustic, nomadic man of the French Renaissance."

> What we see, what we read at once on that face—on that hard and honest face, tempered by the open air, browned by sun and rain—is an immense earnestness, backed up by robust nerves, not too refined and never overex-cited, and by the inexhaustible reserves of a peasant's body, with its broad, slightly stooped shoulders.... Now I imagine such a man who sets himself to study. What will he become? We can tell a priori: a *scholar*. He will learn everything he can. He will study with the obstinate passion and mute tenacity of the vinegrower who, for the thousandth time, in broiling sun or driving rain, carries back the soil which has tumbled from the top to the bottom of his vineyard....That man, knowing what it costs to learn...will have a sort of respect for knowledge, a kind of piety...that man will throw himself entirely into his work. He will hold nothing back.[41]

Men of this stamp were not uncommon in the early sixteenth century, and Febvre mentions several of them: Thomas Platter, Jean Standonck, Guillaume Postel—and of course Ramus himself.[42] Ramus was a paradigm of the type. Physically he was tall, dark, and powerfully built, strong enough to give a beating to an armed intruder in his college of Presles and imposing enough to intimidate a gang of angry marauders at his doors.[43] His will to learn matched his strength. We may recognize Febvre's vinegrower in the boy who persisted in his determination to study in Paris despite repeated setbacks, and who eventually "submitted to servitude for many

---

41. Lucien Febvre, *Pour une histoire à part entière* (Paris: S.E.V.P.E.N., 1962), 548.

42. Febvre, *Pour une histoire*, 558.

43. Nancel, *"Petri Rami Vita,"* 226, 228, describes him as "satis densa solidaque"; Freigius, *Petri Rami Vita*, 584, confirms his height and his powerful physique, adding that his health was excellent ("valetudo firma & robusta"), while Banos goes so far as to describe him as "heroic" ("statura fuit grandis, aequabilis, & vere heroica..."). For Ramus's confrontation with intruders in the college of Presles, see Nancel, *"Petri Rami Vita,"* 246.

years," as he later put it, in order to enter the college of Navarre.[44] Between days spent attending to the needs of a young gentleman and nights spent in study, Ramus came to know the cost of learning as well as anyone.

Throughout his life, he continued to pay the price. Scholarship was his passion, and to it he sacrificed the luxuries and even some of the basic comforts he might have enjoyed. He always slept on a bed of straw and kept a frugal, though not mean, table. The more exotic temptations of wine and women attracted him hardly at all. He was drunk only twice in his life, once as a boy and once, on doctor's orders, as therapy for eye disease. And while one of his biographers implied that he sometimes visited prostitutes, the others claim that he remained celibate all his life.[45] Ramus curbed his inclinations toward sloth, gluttony, drunkenness, and fornication not only in order to avoid sin, but also because his greatest appetite was for learning, and it dominated all the rest.

His desire for knowledge was insatiable. When he felt that he had mastered one discipline, he moved on to another, with no less an aim than the mastery of all the liberal arts. Thus we find him taking up the study of Greek in his mid-thirties and beginning on mathematics at about the age of forty.[46] Ramus indeed felt the "obstinate passion" described by Febvre, although his peasant's tenacity was hardly "mute," as we shall see.

The mentality Febvre summarized is aptly summed up in Ramus's motto: "Labor improbus omnia vincit," "hard work conquers all." The maxim is a good description of Ramus's approach to life, but it is a far cry from the Renaissance ideal. To an age that valued nonchalance in its heroes, and that insisted a gentleman disguise the hard work that lay behind his accomplishments and pretend an effortless mastery of the social, artistic, and intellectual graces, the example of diligent toil offered by Ramus was unattractive and more than a little uncouth. Castiglione counseled the gentleman to "practice in all things a certain *sprezzatura*, so as to conceal all

---

44. *Collectaneae*, 341: "Fortunae necessitate coactus, multos annos duram servitutem servivi," but Ramus hastens to add "animo tamen nunquam servus fui.…"

45. Nancel, *"Petri Rami Vita,"* 230–36. Nancel claims that Ramus used to visit one or another woman in the neighborhood ("in vicina unam aut alteram mulierculam invisebat saepicule," 244), but Banos is convinced otherwise: "He lived most honestly as a bachelor; he was immune from accusation and even from suspicion of whoring [Caelebs vixit honestissime, ab scortatione non tantum crimine, sed etiam suspicione semper immunis]." Considering that there was little else Ramus was not accused or suspected of, the lack of rumor on this score suggests that he did indeed remain celibate.

46. Nancel, *"Petri Rami Vita,"* 206, says that Ramus came to Greek late. Ramus's colleague Denis Lambin wrote in 1554 that four years earlier Ramus knew not a word of Greek; Henri Potez, "Deux années de la Renaissance (d'après une correspondance inédite)," *Revue d'histoire littéraire de la France* 13 (1906): 663. Ramus described his mathematical studies in "P. Rami de sua professione Oration," *Collectaneae*, 402–15, on the occasion of resuming his chair after leaving Paris during the first of the Wars of Religion. He had almost completed his studies, he wrote, when he was forced to interrupt them because his life was in danger ("cursus industriae imo vero pene vitae nobis abruptus esset"), ibid., 409. He first fled Paris in 1562; thus he was learning mathematics at the age of forty-seven.

art and make whatever is done or said appear to be without effort and almost without any thought...."[47] But Ramus could not follow his advice.

Learning did not come easily to him. He was slow, and his memory was not the best. Hard work often had to take the place of innate talent as he struggled to understand Euclid,[48] or to compose an epigram,[49] or to escape the tangles he sometimes got into with complicated problems in addition and subtraction (which Nancel reported "caused some malicious people to smile").[50] Still he plodded away patiently, shouldering his load again and again until he had completed the task at hand. His was not the character of the courtier but of the countryman. Born a peasant, he displayed the virtues and vices of the peasantry until the day he died. His bluntness, his awkwardness, and even his frugal attitude toward money were so many indelible signs of his origin. In short, Ramus was a yokel, and neither he nor anyone else ever forgot it.[51]

Whether or not he was proud of his lowly origins, as Nancel claimed, he refused to be ashamed of them. "I am a Christian," he announced in 1551, "and I never

47. Baldesar Castiglione, *The Book of the Courtier*, trans. Charles S. Singleton (Garden City, N.Y.: Anchor Books, 1959), 43. Ramus was the sort described by Castiglione, a man doomed to "drag [his accomplishments] forth by the hair of the head, [which] shows an extreme want of grace, and causes everything, no matter how great it may be, to be held in little account."

48. *Collectaneae*, 409, tells how Ramus almost gave up on mathematics because of the difficulty he had in understanding the tenth book of Euclid, a crisis which Nancel, *"Petri Rami Vita,"* 200, also details.

49. Nancel, *"Petri Rami Vita,"* 206–8. Ramus was no better at translating than at composing poetry. On the occasion of his (short-lived) triumph over the manner of appointing royal professors in 1566, he is said to have celebrated by adapting a verse of Juvenal: "Et spes, & ratio studiorum in Caesare tantum / Solus enim tristes hac tempestate Camoenas / respexit..." in the following manner:

Des Lettres et Lettrés, l'estime et l'espérance
Ne reposent si non au grand Roi de France;
Car en cette saison il n'y a que lui seul
Qui des Muses l'ennuy regarde de bon oeil.

The Abbé Goujet remarks with some understatement that this verse "ne prouve point son talent pour la Poesie Français." Claude-Pierre Goujet, *Mémoire historique et littéraire sur le Collège Royal de France* (1758; reprint, Geneva: Slatkine, 1971), t. 1, 157.

50. Nancel, *"Petri Rami Vita,"* 200: "subridentibus nonnullis malevolis." Nancel goes to some lengths to present Ramus as a second-rate thinker: "he was slow at learning. His memory was not good.... His reasoning was extremely exquisite, but not acute or subtle....[Perceptio tardior ad discendum. Memoria non ita tenax.... Ratiocination perquam exquisita, minus tamen acuta aut arguta....]" But Nancel's descriptions should be treated warily, as he may have had ulterior motives for denying Ramus's talents. His biography of Ramus includes attempts to claim credit for several of his master's accomplishments. In particular, he stated that Ramus merely outlined his Latin, Greek, and French grammars before Nancel wrote them himself, "denique singula mea manu descripsi... (ibid., 214). Furthermore, he claims (216) to have invented the modern forms of "j" and "v" (as distinguished from "i" and "u"), an innovation which other sources credit to Ramus himself. Peter Sharratt points out, in his introduction to Nancel's biography, Nancel's desire to promote his own name at the expense of his former master (162).

51. Nancel, *"Petri Rami Vita,"* 244. After spending a great deal of money to improve the college of Presles, Ramus took to depositing his savings with the city of Paris to gain an annual dividend ("totum in aerarium publicum urbis contulit, in proventus annuos accepturus cum foenore"). Nancel also mentions

regarded poverty as an evil."[52] He did claim, like many other "new men" of the Renaissance, that his family had originally been a noble one, and that only terrible misfortune had reduced it to poverty and obscurity.[53] Still he never disavowed his ties with the peasant milieu, as his continuing contact with his relatives makes clear.[54]

It would have been difficult for Ramus to forget his roots in any case, as there always seemed to be plenty of people eager to remind him. Even in his inaugural address as royal professor, he did not bring up the poverty of his ancestors because he was proud of it, but because his opponents were making fun of him for it. He railed against the elitists "who think that without great wealth one can hardly achieve great things" and against the "malicious rich" who "reproach me for the poverty of my noble ancestors," but his complaint was futile in the face of nearly universal prejudice.[55]

The extent and intensity of this prejudice are difficult to measure, but that it existed and played an important role in the relations between men of the sixteenth century is obvious. To a Frenchman of the late Renaissance, the uppity peasant was an insult to the providential order of the world. God's plan had it that the son of a peasant should be a peasant, just as the son of an artisan should be an artisan, and the son of the king, king after his father. The Old Régime did not approve of rebellion against the Divine Order, of attempts to burst the links in the Great Chain of Being, and even those on the bottom rungs of the social ladder complained when they saw others managing to rise above their appointed places. The parvenu was an object of scorn and a figure of fun even among the peasants. How much more that was the case among the wealthy and wellborn can easily be imagined. They had no desire to rub shoulders with some rustic upstart, as Ramus was to discover to his cost.

---

that Ramus was always ill at ease in company, despite his ability to hold large crowds spellbound: "tamen in colloquio familiari, cum hominibus exteris fuisse sui longe dissimilem; ut aegre, et pauca et communia trivialiaque vix eloqueretur, imo ne eloqueretur quidem, sed magno nisu ac molimine vix tandem pectore anhelante expromeret" (ibid., 250).

52. *Collectaneae*, 341: "Christianus sum, nec unquam paupertatem malum putavi."

53. See note 1. above. Yves de la Genière traces Ramus's family back to Evrard de la Ramée, échevin of Liège in 1260, in support of his claim to nobility; "La Famille de La Ramée du XIIIe au XXe siècle," *Bulletin de la Société de l'Histoire du Protestantisme français* 88 (1939): 163. Waddington, *Ramus*, 17, adds that he found the La Ramées enrolled among the nobility in 1648.

54. At least six young La Ramées and three Charpentiers were bursars at the college of Presles while Ramus was principal there, prompting Jean Dupèbe to distinguish it as, "plus nettement que les autres collèges parisiens," "une petite affaire de famille"; "Autour du Collège de Presles: Testaments de Ramus, Talon et Péna," *Bibliothèque d'humanisme et renaissance* 42 (1980): 123–37, at 124. See also Ernest Coyecque, *Recueil d'actes notariés relatifs à l'histoire de Paris et de ses environs au XVIe siècle* (Paris: Imprimerie Nationale, 1923), 280, doc. 4986; and Charles Desmaze, *P. Ramus professeur au Collège de France: Sa vie, ses écrits, sa mort (1515–1572)* (1864; reprint, Geneva: Slatkine, 1970), 80; as well as the references in chapter 3.

55. *Collectaneae*, 341: "ut difficile puten esse praeclaras res agere, cui magnae opes desunt" and "a malo divite nescioquo...generis ingenui paupertas in nobis accusatur."

Historians have not paid much attention to the effects of this prejudice on Ramus's career, however. A case in point is the treatment given Ramus's death in the Saint Bartholomew's Day Massacre in 1572. Charles Waddington sought to prove that Ramus was killed primarily as a result of his longtime academic feud with Jacques Charpentier, who saw the massacre as an opportunity to rid himself of his most important adversary. According to Waddington, Charpentier hired killers to do away with the Protestant Ramus and to make it appear that he was simply one more victim of the enraged Catholic mob.[56] Waddington's theory has been generally rejected by modern scholars, who prefer the more straightforward explanation that Ramus was killed for his open allegiance to the French Reform.[57] At least one sixteenth-century observer, however, suggested that along with scholarly rivalry and religious bigotry, class prejudice was a strong incentive for doing away with the upstart peasant.

Christopher Marlowe's "The Massacre at Paris," written twenty years after the event and in a foreign land as well, cannot tell us why Ramus was killed. But it does suggest just how notorious Ramus's anomalous social position had become, and how willing a sixteenth-century audience would be to accept the idea that he was despised for it.[58]

Marlowe's account of the murder opens with the arrival of the assassins in Ramus's study. His friend and colleague Omer Talon urges him to flee, and when he cannot convince him to fly, Talon escapes without him. "O let him goe, he is a catholick," one of the murderers orders. Clearly these assassins are only interested in killing Protestants.

When the dukes of Guise and of Anjou arrive on the scene, however, it appears that they have a nonreligious grievance against Ramus. They make it clear that he is to die because he had challenged the authority of Aristotle: "Was it not thou that scoftes [sic] the Organon, and said it was a heap of vanities?" Ramus begs leave to reply to this new charge, and Anjou gives him permission, but his noble captors soon lose patience with his defense. Guise cries out, "Why suffer you that peasant to declaime?" Anjou agrees that Ramus is being impudent: "never was there Colliars sonne so full of pride." With that the two stab Ramus to death, bringing the scene to a close.

Marlowe's staging of the murder scene is historically impossible for a variety of reasons. Talon had been dead for a decade when Ramus was killed, and the idea that

---

56. Waddington, "Jacques Charpentier," chap. 9, *Ramus*, 258–83. Waddington's sources for this interpretation are mostly late, and its plausibility was assailed as early as 1881 in Joseph Bertrand's long letter to the *Revue des deux mondes*. Nancel, *"Petri Rami Vita,"* 270, says that he knows who the murderers are and implies that their motives were not solely religious.

57. E.g., Ong, *Ramus*, 29: "There is little doubt that the only possible objective verdict concerning Ramus's death is murder on the occasion of the St. Bartholomew's Day Massacre by persons unknown...."

58. Christopher Marlowe, "The Massacre at Paris," in *The Complete Works of Christopher Marlowe*, ed. Fredson Bowers, vol. 1 (Cambridge: Cambridge University Press, 1973), 375–77.

Guise and Anjou themselves killed him is fantastic.[59] Still, Marlowe offers an interesting insight into attitudes toward inferiors who failed to keep their place, and suggests that Ramus's humble birth was a matter of comment, if not of scandal. In Marlowe's scene, neither Ramus's heresy nor his intellectual rebellion clinches the argument for his death. Instead, it is his impudence that prompts the fatal blow. Ramus was struck down because he tried to rise above his station, a fault as heinous to his betters as either of the other two.[60]

Ramus's lowly origins cannot be dismissed from among the reasons so many Frenchmen viewed his works and his person with suspicion and hostility. Certainly his youth in the countryside contributed to his mature character, and it is tempting to follow Febvre by attributing his persistence, his bluntness, and his awkwardness to his peasant heritage. Even his desire to simplify and vulgarize the academic subjects he taught can be seen as the countryman's reaction against the oversophisticated and oversubtle scholarship of the University of Paris.

No doubt such an explanation is in part accurate, but there is no need to assume that Ramus imbibed the peasant's view of the world along with his mother's milk. Prevailing social prejudice against the upstart might in itself have encouraged him to act the way he did. Ramus's sharp temper, and even his sometimes violent behavior, can be explained in terms of his insecure social position, which promoted an aggressive response to the men and institutions which condemned him.[61] The growing contempt for the common man and the desire for greater control of society from above that characterized the later sixteenth century were bound to find a determined opponent in Peter Ramus.

Ramus's contemporaries looked to his humble birth to interpret his behavior and his ideas, but his regional origins also helped to determine the expectations they had of him. As late as 1572, when Ramus had lived in Paris for decades, Estienne Pasquier claimed that he could still detect the influence which Ramus's native land, his *pays*, exerted over him. Pasquier wrote that "there always remains in us a certain something [*je ne sçay quoy*] of the childish prattle of our homeland [*pays*]. I see its effect on you, in whom, no matter how long you have lived in the city of Paris, I recognize from time to time several traits of your native Picardy...."[62] Pasquier was

---

59. Talon died in 1562. See Dupèbe, "Autour du Collège de Presles...," 127.

60. See the discussion in John R. Glenn, "The Martyrdom of Ramus in Marlowe's 'The Massacre at Paris'" *Papers on Language and Literature* 9 (1973): 365–79. Glenn thinks that for Marlowe, Ramus "represents an acceptable standard of humanity existing outside the two warring parties" (377) and "represents a hopeful third alternative for mankind" (379).

61. Nancel, *"Petri Rami Vita,"* 246, mentions that Ramus was bad-tempered and even "fond of flogging" his pupils ("Domi...fuit valde iracundus et plagosus"). But he goes on to state that, to his credit, Ramus never swore ("ab omni jurejurando abstinebat").

62. Estienne Pasquier, "A Monsieur Ramus, professeur du Roy, en la Philosophie et la Mathématiques," 1572, *Choix de lettres sur la littérature, la langue et la traduction*, ed. D. Thickett (Geneva: Droz, 1956), 99.

thinking of Ramus's dialect in particular, but the Picard owed his unique reputation to far more than his peculiar accent and idiom.

At the time of Ramus's birth, the unification of France was as yet far from complete. Picardy had only come under the French crown late in the fifteenth century, after the dismemberment of the Burgundian state. Provincial loyalties long remained stronger there than loyalty to France, and that loyalty was the basis of a stereotyped image of the Picard among other Frenchmen. "Les méridionaux du Nord," as Michelet later called them, were considered like their southern counterparts to be particularly prone to quarrelsomeness, aggression, and revolt. It was this stereotype of the rebellious and high-tempered Picard that Victor Hugo evoked in his *Notre-Dame de Paris*, when he had Dom Claude Frollo warn his younger brother not to get mixed up with the Picards.[63]

The stereotype of the contentious Picard is best illustrated in the work of Abel Lefranc, himself a Picard by birth. His *Jeunesse de Calvin* (1888) devotes a long digression to a sketch of the Picard character. No race, he claimed, pushed so far the preoccupation with emancipation and liberty, and no people were more inclined to revolution. The concern for emancipation may belong more to the nineteenth-century world of Lefranc than to sixteenth-century Picardy, but the revolutionary impulse was indeed marked among the Picards of the Middle Ages and the early modern period. It was a Picard hermit whose words inflamed Europe at the time of the Crusades, the Picard towns which set in motion the communal movement, and the Picard peasants who began the Jacquerie. In the sixteenth century, Picardy was the birthplace of both the French Reform and of its implacable foe, the League. Lefranc sums up the character of the Picards in the words of a medieval epithet, "vaillante et colérique," and he goes on to say:

> One would say that the Picard, eager for controversy, feels the need to batter down the very ideas which he himself promoted as soon as they are admitted. He is above all an opponent. The rage for debate carries him away despite himself. Nevertheless he is neither a skeptic nor a quibbler. It is the need for commotion that animates him....[64]

Later in his work Lefranc goes on to pick out two men who seem to him "the striking personification of the Picard character": John Calvin of Noyon and Peter Ramus of Cuts.[65] Without endorsing the stereotype in general, we can at least agree

63. Quote from Michelet in Abel Lefranc, *La Jeunesse de Calvin* (Paris: Fischbacher, 1888), 24; Victor Hugo, *Notre Dame*, vol. 2 (New York: Caldwell, n.d.), 156.

64. Lefranc, *Jeunesse de Calvin*, 23–25. See also idem, *Histoire du Collège de France: Depuis ses origines jusqu'à la fin du premier empire* (1893; reprint, Geneva: Slatkine, 1970), 206–7, where he writes of "le tempérament révolutionnaire qui semble être le propre de cette race [i.e. the Picards]...." E. Doumergue, who cites Lefranc extensively in his *Jean Calvin: Les Hommes et les choses de son temps*, vol. 1, *La Jeunesse de Calvin* (Lausanne: Georges Bridel & Co., 1899), 3–4, points out that Lefranc himself was a Picard from Noyon.

65. Lefranc, *Jeunesse de Calvin*, 25.

with Lefranc that it suits Ramus perfectly. His colleagues constantly reproached him for his urge to stir up trouble. Writing to Prevost de Therouanne, professor at the college of Boncourt, in 1554, the royal professor of Greek, Denis Lambin, asked to be excused for expressing "with complete frankness my feelings about Ramus." Lambin had strong feelings on the matter. "He is a rebel and a mischief-maker: to tell the truth, he is either rabid and demented or else perverse and criminal."[66] For the most part, modern historians agree. Even Charles Waddington admits that his hero "lacked measure…and despite the practical character and merit of a part of his opinions, he was hardly more than a revolutionary."[67] To a certain extent, this view of Ramus must be allowed to be a just one. Ramus's challenges to authority did, however, have motives more solid than the mere desire to upset the establishment for the fun of it. If he did share the "Picard character," he put it to the service of a coherent and rational ideal.

Ramus was born, and in the eyes of the sixteenth century would always remain, a Picard and a peasant. The Renaissance did recognize that character was not entirely determined by birth, however. There were ways to train men out of their bad habits and into good ones, at least to some extent, and prominent among them was formal education. A man might escape the destiny imposed on him by his ancestors and his *pays* through learning. A brief look at Ramus's studies at the University of Paris reveals that for him, at least, such was not the case. The lessons he learned in school only reinforced his aggressive and rebellious attitudes.[68]

As Ramus later recalled his schooling, it consisted of little beyond disputation, contradiction, and contention. Right and wrong, truth and falsehood, were irrelevant considerations. Basically, he claimed, his three and one half years spent studying logic taught him no more than how to shout louder than the others:

---

66. Potez, "Deux années…," 663.

67. Waddington, *Ramus*, 27.

68. The setting in which Ramus pursued his studies, the college of Navarre, was founded by the queen of Navarre in 1304 and situated on the slope of the Mont Ste.-Geneviève. College life was anything but luxurious in the early sixteenth century, even in such an "extensive and splendid foundation" as the college of Navarre, built to house twenty students and including a "separate hall, kitchen, and dormitory" for each class; Hastings Rashdall, "History of the College of Navarre," *The Universities of Europe in the Middle Ages*, ed. F. M. Powicke and A. B. Emden, vol.1, "Salerno—Bologna—Paris" (Oxford: Oxford University Press, 1958), 510. From the plan of Paris drawn by Truschet in 1551, it looks to have been an imposing edifice (Truschet's plan of Paris is available in a modern edition and also appears as the endpapers of the two volumes of Jacques Hillairet's *Dictionnaire historique des rues de Paris*, 2d ed. (Paris: Editions de Minuit, 1964). Even a servant there must have lived as well as the bursars in many other colleges. Still, fires in the lecture rooms during the winter, or in the dormitories and chambers, were an unheard-of luxury; ibid., 415. For a poor scholar, it must have been difficult to get by even in such a foundation, and for a poor servant even harder. Nancel asserts that Ramus had to make do with only three hours of sleep a night, and that as a result he came down with an eye disease; Nancel, *"Petri Rami Vita,"*178. Banos agreed that Ramus suffered an eye disease as a result of insufficient sleep (Banos, *Petri Rami Vita*: "rarissimeque gravi morbo laboravit, nisi opthalmia, quam credibile est ex vigiliis immodicis contraxisse").

I believed that I should not inquire too closely into the nature of logic, into what it is and what it is for, beyond being so much disputation and clamor. So I disputed and clamored vehemently. I believed that if I were defending a thesis in class I should not yield to my opponent no matter how truly he spoke, but instead try to confuse the issue with some deceitful distinction. If on the other hand I were attacking a thesis, I tried only to put on a performance and make myself shine, not in order to teach my opponent anything but to defeat him by some argument or another, good or bad. Thus had I been taught. Aristotle's categories were like a ball we give to children to play with, which we must recover by bawling if we lost it, but which we must not return, regardless of the clamor, once we got hold of it. Thus I was persuaded that all of logic lay in disputation by vigorous and eager shouting.[69]

Or as he more formally related to the Privy Council in the 1560s, "when I came to Paris I fell in among the subtleties of the sophists, and was taught the liberal arts by questions and disputes, without ever being shown the profit or use" to be made of them.[70]

Congenial as such an approach to learning might seem to be to a man of Ramus's contentious character, he roundly condemned it and vigorously opposed it. For in looking back over his schooling, he discovered that it had not made him "more knowledgeable about history and antiquity, nor more fluent in speech, nor more skillful in poetry; nor finally had this kind of logic made me wiser in anything."[71]

Attacks on scholastic teaching methods were common among the humanists, of course, and Ramus's complaints should not be taken as a completely accurate account of the course of study at Paris.[72] Despite his harsh words for the University's

---

69. Ramus, "Scholae Dialecticae," in *Scholae in Liberales Artes* (1569; reprint, Hildesheim: Georg Olms, 1970), col. 152–53: "Credidi si thesim de categoria in schola positam defenderem, non esse adversario, etiam verisima dicenti cedendum, sed contra distinctionis alicujus captione totum clamorem conturbandum esse: sin contra ipse oppugnarem, hoc unice & singulariter agendum & enitendum, ut adversarium non docerem, sed ratione quavis, vera an falsa, nihil interesset, vincerem: Sic institutus & informatus eram. Haec categorica scilicet pila nobis juvenibus erat proposita, qua luderemus: quam amissam clamando repeteremus: quam acceptam nullo clamore nobis eripi pateremur: Id mihi persuasum erat, Logicae summum in eo esse positam, ut de ea fortiter & animose clamando disputaretur."

70. Petrus Ramus, *La Remonstrance de Pierre de la Ramée, faite au Conseil privé, en la chambre du Roy au Louvre, le 18 de Ianvier 1567, touchant la profession royalle en mathématique* (Paris: A. Wechel, 1567), 24. Waddington, *Ramus*, 411–16, prints long excerpts from the relatively rare *Remonstrance*, of which Ong knows only six copies; Walter Ong, *Ramus and Talon Inventory* (Cambridge: Harvard University Press, 1958), 364.

71. Ramus, "Scholae Dialecticae," col. 153: "Non in historia & antiquitate rerum prudentiorem: non in discendo disertiorem: non in poesi promptiorem: non denique ulla in re, talibus logicis me sapientiorem factum deprehendi."

72. Some of his teachers, at least, seem to have done a better job of instructing their charges. Ramus singled out Jean Hennuyer for praise, "both for the qualities of his soul and for his profound knowledge

curriculum, he did manage to profit from his college education. He may also have come into contact with the new religious ideas which were circulating in Paris in the 1530s, a topic to which we will return. His greatest immediate profit, however, came not from his teachers but from his fellow students. Aside from the Sieur de la Brosse, whose servant he was, Ramus came into contact with boys who were later to become important actors in the political, religious, and cultural life of France. Charles of Bourbon was his classmate, as was the poet Ronsard.[73] More important than either of these acquaintances, however, was Ramus's friendship with Charles of Guise, the future cardinal of Lorraine.

Nancel wrote that Ramus went out of his way to make himself obliging to his rich and well-born classmates, and if Nancel was right, Ramus's efforts certainly paid off.[74] Charles seems to have become a particular friend. If we can judge by a letter of 1570, a strong mutual affection grew up between the two boys during their college years. Ramus reminded Lorraine in the letter that it was "nearly thirty-five years ago, when you were a young man, that you began to feel affection for me. I was also a young man then, and since those times I have cherished you and celebrated and published your friendship for me among all men."[75] In token of their friendship,

---

of the Holy Scriptures"; Ramus, *Aristotelicae Animadversiones,* fol. 4: "Iohannis Hannonii vobis eximia & animi probitate, & sacrarum literarum cognitione...." Thus also in *Collectaneae,* 39; and Waddington, *Ramus,* 290. Hennuyer was a submaster in arts at the college of Navarre after 1533, and later became bishop of Lisieux. We also know that Ramus studied for a time under Jean Pena of the college of Ste.-Barbe, but about this master we know little beyond the fact that he was a severe man who once sought to have Ignatius Loyola flogged; ibid., 290. The teacher who had the most influence on Ramus's intellectual development was without doubt Johannes Sturm, the educational reformer of Strasbourg. Sturm had been educated by the Brethren of the Common Life at Liège, and he adopted their emphasis on practical instruction at the expense of scholastic exercise as the model for his own academy; Charles Schmidt, *La vie et les travaux de Jean Sturm* (1855; reprint, Nieuwkoop: B. de Graaf, 1970), 2–5. In 1529, Sturm traveled to Paris to try to sell the edition of Xenophon's *Memorabilia* which he and a partner had recently published, and while there he delivered a series of lectures on Cicero and on logic which Ramus attended; ibid., 8. See also M. Guggenheim, "Beitrage zur Biographie de Petrus Ramus," *Zeitschrift für Philosophie und Philosophische Kritik* 121, no. 2 (1903): 140–53, at 141. Sturm was in Paris from 1529 to 1536; Schmidt, *La Vie,* 10, writes that he lectured "dans les cours libres faits au Collège Royal," and he may have had a temporary appointment as a royal professor (see below, chapter 3). "Johann Sturm," Ramus later recorded, "excited in the University an incredible ardor for the art [of logic] whose utility he revealed. It was at the lessons of this great master that I first learned the use of logic, and since then I have taught in an entirely different spirit from that of the sophists..."; Ramus, preface to *Scholae in Liberales Artes:* "academiam academiarum principem incredibili tam insperatae utilitatis desiderio inflammavit: tum igitur tanto doctore logicam istam ubertatem primum degustavi, didicique longe alio fine consilioque juventuti proponendam esse...").

73. Waddington, *Ramus,* 289; Ong, *Ramus, Method and the Decay,* 19.

74. Nancel, *"Petri Rami Vita,"* 178: "Interea vero temporis omni officio condiscipulos, sed longe opulentiores et nobiliores promereri, obsequioque omnino devincire studebat."

Ramus dedicated most of his books and lectures to Lorraine, while the latter for his part became Ramus's patron and protector, eventually even securing him a chair as royal professor. The cardinal of Lorraine was an exceptionally good friend to have.

For all his wealthy and well-placed acquaintances, Ramus remained poor, and the numerous expenses involved in taking his degree in 1536 were almost more than he could manage. In the end, his mother had to sell off a part of the family's land, and Ramus had to borrow from his sister and his uncle as well.[76] It is a telling point that he was careful to reimburse all of his relatives, with interest, when his financial position improved.[77] He could fairly claim that he was beholden to no one, a self-made man risen from the ranks of the poor by the sweat of his brow and by his own merit. He stressed the point in another letter to Lorraine in 1570, after the two men had fallen out over Ramus's conversion to Protestantism in the 1560s.[78] In his case, at least, hard work had conquered all obstacles.

Ramus was indeed a self-made man, and he displayed most of the traits of that breed. He was brash and full of self-assurance, at least on the surface, and he was as confident that hard work was the only legitimate road to success as he was mistrustful of inherited wealth, status, and authority. Altogether his peasant birth, Picard character, and youthful self-reliance made a volatile mixture, and their effects seem to have been cumulative. They endowed Ramus with mistrust for established authority and impatience with arbitrary rules and unjustified eminence, all qualities which were only reinforced by the educational methods prevailing at Paris at the time. Finally, it can be said that Ramus came by his blunt outspokenness honestly. The "realism" of the self-made man, the "rudeness" of the peasant, and the "contentiousness" of the Picard all encouraged him to speak his mind plainly and straightforwardly, with a sometimes remarkable disregard for the consequences.

Whether Ramus came by these traits naturally, and as it were, breathed them in with the air of his native land and community, or acquired them in response to social pressures and the expectations of those around him, it is clear that French society played a dominant role in making him the sort of man he became. His character was clearly expressed in the title of the thesis he reputedly chose to defend at his inception as master of arts in 1536: "Quaecumque ab Aristotele dicta essent, commentitia

---

75. *Collectaneae*, 210–11: "Cum tu adolescens esses, anno abhinc quinto prope ac tricesimo, amare coepisti me, tum quoque adolescentum, ex eoque tempore te colui, amoremque erga me tuum apud mortales omnes praedicavi ac celebravi."

76. Nancel, *"Petri Rami Vita,"* 176.

77. Nancel, *"Petri Rami Vita,"* 176; Dupèbe, "Autour du Collège de Presles...," 124.

78. Ramus to Lorraine, 22 October 1570, in *Collectaneae*, 211–13, at 211: "by the sweat and hard work of my body I sustained the course of my studies [sudore & labore corporis animique proposita mihi studia sustenavi]." Ramus was replying to the charge that he was being ungrateful to Lorraine by converting to the Reform, and arguing that he owed his success to his own hard work rather than merely to Lorraine's patronage.

esse," "Whatever Aristotle has said is confused and contrived."[79] Walter Ong studies the content and context of this thesis with thoroughness and care, demonstrating that there is no good evidence that Ramus ever defended it and demolishing Waddington's fond belief that in maintaining it successfully, Ramus caused the whole structure of scholastic learning to totter.[80]

Ong's arguments are sound, and his conclusions about the thesis convincing, but for the most part they need not concern us here. Whether or not Ramus actually made his famous attack on Aristotle at the beginning of his career, the thesis stands as an excellent example of his outlook, not only on Aristotle, but on authority and established norms in general. It demonstrates his willingness to put his own experience and ideas up against the wisdom of the ages, and suggests that he would be no more tolerant of the customs and prejudices that controlled French society than he was of the ancient authorities that governed scholarship and learning.

In fact, as we shall see, he was not. Ramus is best known for his attacks on Aristotle and the Aristotelians, but it is not his academic iconoclasm alone that is our concern. More important is the combative, irreverent, and outspoken challenge to authority which his attacks on Aristotle represented and which would soon inform his attitudes towards society in general. Ramus's personality and beliefs were such that the new emphasis on hierarchy, authority, and inherited status in France after the middle of the century was anathema to him. French society had made him a firm believer in the value of hard work and the importance of talent in improving one's social, economic, and political standing. When the dawn of the oligarchical Old Régime threatened to undermine his belief—when he could no longer claim that even his own motto was true—Ramus would attack the new order openly, brashly, and even rudely, first in the University and then on a broader institutional and ideological front.

79. The title of Ramus's thesis was first reported by Freigius in his life of Ramus; *Collectaneae*, 585. Freigius's biography, based largely on published sources, appeared in 1575, three years after Ramus's death, and is the basis for all later reports of the thesis's title. See Phillip W. Cummings, "A Note on the Transmission of the Title of Ramus's Master's Thesis," *Journal of the History of Ideas* 39 (1978): 481.

80. Ong, *Ramus*, 36–47. See also the discussion in Pierre Albert Duhamel, "Milton's Alleged Ramism," *Publications of the Modern Language Association* 67 (1953): 1035–53, at 1036. Whether or not Ramus ever defended such a thesis, it is not a bad summary of his early attitude toward Aristotle. See Pierre Galland's attacks on Ramus in *P. Gallandi literarum latinarum professoris Regii, contra novam academiam Petri Rami oratio...* (Paris: Vascosan, 1551), and the quotations from Galland in Ong, *Ramus, Method and the Decay*, 39–40.

CHAPTER 2
Praeceptor Galliae

RAMUS EARNED HIS M.A. IN 1536 AND IMMEDIATELY SOUGHT, and found, a teaching position in the University of Paris. It was a good time to be a teacher looking for a job.[1] From the 1530s on, the demand for arts masters was growing rapidly in France. Hundreds of colleges, supported by the public, were founded in the towns and cities of France in the next few decades to meet the increased demand for education among members of the Third Estate.[2] While the propaganda of the humanists in favor of classical learning no doubt played a part in this educational explosion, another development was probably even more important. The increasingly literate and numerate worlds of justice and administration put a new premium on educational achievement and rewarded it richly. Cultural and material motives combined to create a mass market for education by midcentury, and a rising demand for arts masters to provide it.

The growing demand for education in France led not only to an increase in the number of colleges and teachers, but also to changes in what they taught and how they taught it. The young men who were flocking into the colleges were not interested in becoming scholars, as Ramus was, but in gaining the skills necessary for success in the world outside the academy. Certain components of the traditional curriculum seemed pointless to them; other subjects which they greatly desired to learn were seldom taught. Most of all, perhaps, these pragmatic students wanted to learn what they needed and be done with it. The endless complexities and refinements of scholastic logic and Latin grammar were not for them. This was the educational environment in which Ramus undertook his famous reforms of the liberal arts.

The setting in which Ramus launched his ambitious reform program was the University of Paris, and more specifically the college of Presles, where he made his

---

1. The title is modeled on the honorific epithet "praeceptor Germaniae" applied to Philip Melanchthon. I know of no contemporary who referred to Ramus as "praeceptor Galliae," but as this chapter argues he did in fact seek to be "the teacher of France."

2. George Huppert, *Public Schools in Renaissance France* (Urbana, Illinois: University of Illinois Press, 1984), xiv–xv.

home and practiced his craft from 1544 until his death. After taking his degree, he had spent several years teaching in other colleges of the University of Paris. He taught first at the collège du Mans and soon moved to the collège de l'Ave Maria in the company of another young scholar who was to become his closest associate and best friend, Omer Talon.[3] In 1544, he was able to make an arrangement with the aging Nicolas Lesage (Sapientia), principal of the college of Presles, by which, for some unknown consideration, Lesage yielded the college to him.[4] Together with the trusty Talon, he established himself in his new home and began his lifelong task of reforming the arts and sciences according to the system known to later generations as Ramism.

The college of Presles had been founded in 1324 by Raoul de Presles to house fifteen scholars from the diocese of Soissons while they pursued their studies at the University of Paris.[5] It was a relatively small college, located in the center of the university district between the rue des Carmes and the rue Saint Jean de Beauvais, adjacent to the college of Beauvais and a block from the place Maubert.[6] Raoul's charter specified that two of the scholars were to be chaplains, for the chapels of Notre-Dame and Saint Jacques, and that the latter was to be the master and governor of the rest of the scholars. University documents and modern studies usually refer to Ramus as the principal of Presles, which in a general sense he was. Technically, however, he ran Presles as the chaplain of Saint-Jacques, and it was as chaplain that he was charged to "have the students' lessons read to them, see that they attend the

3. Omer Talon (1510–60), from Beauvais, was in Walter Ong's phrase Ramus's "literary lieutenant." His province was rhetoric, and he dedicated his writings to applying Ramus's principles to that field while Ramus himself took care of the other subjects of the trivium and quadrivium. Talon also took it upon himself to defend Ramus against his numerous enemies in academe, thereby sparing Ramus the necessity of responding on his own account. Still Talon was more than Ramus's surrogate. He had considerable talents of his own, including mastery of Greek and an elegant Latin style, and at least one of his works, the *Academica*, shows him to be a capable philosopher as well. Nonetheless, his more famous colleague, Ramus, has completely overshadowed him in the eyes of historians, who are far more likely to recall his grandnephew and namesake, the seventeenth-century jurist Omer Talon.

4. There seems to have been some disagreement between Ramus and Lesage over exactly what the terms of their contract were, and Lesage took the case to the Paris Parlement, but the former principal was eventually reconciled to Ramus and to Presles, as his will forgave the debt owed him by the college—some 2100 livres—and bequeathed it the rent on a house in the rue de Postes to pay for masses for his soul. See Charles Waddington, *Ramus (Pierre de la Ramée): Sa vie, ses écrits et ses opinions* (1855; reprint, Dubuque, Iowa: Brown Reprint Library, n.d), 62–63; A.N., MM 432, "Inventaire des titres et papiers du College de Presles," fols. 28r–28v (on the bequests made by Lesage); and on Ramus's tenure as principal in general, Victor Carrière, "Pierre de la Ramée et la principalité du collège de Presles," *Revue d'histoire de l'église de France* 26 (1940): 238–42.

5. A.N. MM 432, fols. 6v–9r, Act of Raoul de Presles, 1324. On the history of Presles in the Middle Ages, see Frank Kenneth Jensen, "A History and Cartulary of the College of Presles at the Medieval University of Paris" (Ph.D. diss., University of Notre Dame, 1969).

6. See Truschet's 1554 plan of the city and the maps in A. Berty and L. M. Tisserand, *Histoire générale de Paris: Topographie historique du vieux Paris*, vol. 6, *Région centrale de l'université* (Paris: Imprimerie

Schools, and correct them if they make mistakes," or more generally to "watch over their Studies and their Behavior."[7]

While Ramus was head of the college, he also took over the task of choosing the scholars to be given a scholarship at Presles. The charter did not spell out any particular method for selecting students, beyond the requirement that they come from the diocese of Soissons and be chosen by preference from the towns of Presles, Cys, Lit, Saint-Marc, and Boves.[8] It is clear that Ramus took control of the process, however, from the names of scholars who resided at Presles during his tenure. In brief, he turned Presles into a dormitory for the younger generations of La Ramées.

The evidence for this assertion comes from the accounts of Presles between 1546 and 1573. The chaplain of Saint-Jacques was required to present these accounts to the members of the college, and the scholars signed them to show their assent to the reckoning. For each accounting period, therefore, we have a list of the scholarship students at Presles—not necessarily a complete list, but a valuable one nonetheless. On the average, nine students signed the accounts each year, and on the average two of these bore the names La Ramée or Charpentier (Ramus's mother's maiden name). More precisely, one out of five of the scholarships available at Presles in this period went to students related to Ramus.[9] The number could well be larger, since we cannot tell whether some of the scholars who bore different names were related to Ramus as well. In any case, Ramus's selection of scholars puts him squarely in line with the prevailing ethic of the time. Not merit, but family connections, were the key to a place at Presles, as they were increasingly the key to

---

nationale, 1897). The courtyards of the colleges of Beauvais and Presles were separated only by an enclosure wall, and when Ramus's colleague Omer Talon became principal of Beauvais the two had a door cut in the wall to facilitate communication. The two colleges became essentially one, as students passed freely between them and followed courses in both, an association promoted not only by the friendship between Ramus and Talon, but also by the fact that both colleges housed students from the diocese of Soissons. In the seventeenth century they were formally united. See the brief account in A.N. MM 432, fol. 12r, "Pièces relatives à l'association entre le collège de Presles et celui de Beauvais." The colleges' buildings no longer survive.

7. A.N. MM 432, fols. 6v–9r, Charter of Presles, article 10. The charter of the college consists of 21 articles, of which the first six spell out the duties of the chaplains. Article 10 describes how new chaplains are to be chosen by the scholars themselves, preferably from among qualified scholars of Presles.

8. Charter of Presles, articles 8, 18.

9. Six young La Ramées: Claude, Hugues, Anthoine, Remy, Charles, and Jehan, and three Charpentiers: Jonnes, Gudomarus, and Pierre, appear as students at Presles, for an average of three and two-thirds years each. Hugues de la Ramée spent nine years in the college. Six of these nine students appear in the first set of surviving accounts, covering 1546 to 1 May 1550. I have counted this appearance as evidence only for the last year, but obviously any or all of the six might have lived at Presles for the entire three-year period, which would raise the average period of residence considerably. Over the course of time, the number of Ramus's relatives listed declined; by 1560, none of the students bore the names La Ramée or Charpentier, and only in 1567 does a new La Ramée appear. It seems that Ramus had to wait for a new generation of nephews to reach an appropriate age.

all the valuable positions in French society. Ramus spent much of his life opposing such a system, but he was not above exploiting it himself when it was a question of his own family.[10]

Along with his duties as teacher, chaplain, and disciplinarian, the principal of Presles was also responsible for the college's finances. Raoul de Presles had laid it down that the chaplain of Saint-Jacques was to collect rents due to the college, disburse funds for its maintenance, and present his accounts to the college twice a year. Two scholars were to be appointed as procurers to assist him, but Raoul does not seem to have anticipated any problems. The 176 livres of annual income he had bequeathed to the college would cover the various expenses with money to spare. The college's charter ordained that the surplus should be kept in a double-locked coffer, to be drawn on for extraordinary expenses such as repairs and lawsuits.

Raoul composed the charter in 1324. Two hundred years later, his rules and regulations were antiquated and could no longer be made to apply. For one thing, prices had risen dramatically. During Ramus's tenure as principal, the annual cost of running the college averaged 1,350 livres, and in one year, 1554, the budget ran to 2,830 livres. Income had risen as well, but not as quickly, and the result was that the college perennially operated in the red. In the five years from 1550 to 1554, the college's income totaled 4,658 livres while expenses mounted to 9,989 livres, leaving a deficit of more than 5,000 livres. It was up to Ramus to finance the deficit, and he managed to do so, even though by 1559 the college owed him more than 9,000 livres.[11]

In the course of his tenure at Presles, Ramus managed to reduce the deficit and put the college on a balanced budget. Accounts for the earlier years are not sufficiently detailed to reveal exactly how he did so, but by the 1560s the college usually showed a

10. In addition to taking his younger relatives into the college, Ramus may have helped other members of his family to profit from his position. One means was to give them work in the college itself; for instance, the carpenter Charpentier, paid by the college for work in 1560–61, may have been related to Ramus's mother. An even more valuable favor was to put them in charge of the college's holdings in the countryside. Thus "Jean Charpentier, laboureur à Daule," rented land from the college from the early 1550s on and eventually (1564) became bailiff for some sixty arpents of land belonging to Presles; A.N. MM 432, fols. 128r–130v. Of course we cannot be certain that these men were in fact related to Ramus.

11. The accounts of Presles for the period of Ramus's governance are in A.N. H³2874², "College de Presles 1546–73," one of only four surviving sets of accounts for the college; MM 432, fol. 354r. Ramus himself prepared the itemized lists of income and expenses, along with (usually inaccurate) yearly totals, based on the year beginning May 1. Exceptions are the combined accounts for the years 1546 through 1549, which Talon prepared, and for the years 1572 through 1573, which were presented by Ramus's successor Claude Serain. Accounts for the year 1567–68 are missing. As the manuscript is unpaginated, references to it will be made by year. All accounts are in livres tournois.

Some of the accumulated debt did not represent any real outlay of cash by Ramus. Instead, it represented money which he had earned by his services to the college but was not paid. Thus in the year 1564–65, for which the accounts are clearest and most detailed, Ramus claimed a total of 175 livres for his various offices: 50 livres as his salary as chaplain, 100 for his travels on behalf of the college, and 25 for his work as principal, including drawing up the accounts themselves. As it happens, the college managed to operate in the black in this year, so Ramus actually received the money due him.

surplus or at worst a deficit of one or two hundred livres.[12] The main reason seems to have been that as Ramus's reputation as a teacher grew, paying students sought him out, and he was able to charge fees large enough to keep the college afloat out of his own purse. Total receipts and expenditures in livres are shown below in table 1.

TABLE 1: ACCOUNTS OF COLLEGE OF PRESLES, 1546–1573

YEAR	RECEIPTS	EXPENSES	SURPLUS OR DEFICIT	OWED TO RAMUS
1546–50[a]	623	1,451	-828	
1550–52	457	2,628	-2,171	4,178
1552–54[b]	2,124	4,530	-2,406	6,584
1554–55	2,077	2,830	-753	
1555–56	1,432*	1,620	-280	
1556–57	1,569*	1,552	-86	8,660
1557–58	1,180*	1,170	-128	
1558–59	1,089*	1,072	-309	
1559–60	1,424	1,103		
1560–61	4,322	1,462		5,729
1561–62	1,598	779	+819	4,910
1562–64	2,244	2,467	-223	5,133
1564–65	1,242	1,002	+241	4,892
1565–66	929	981	-52	4,944
1566–67	1,464	939	+524	4,421
1567–68	— Missing from accounts —			
1568–71[c]	2,680	3,200	-519	4,939
1571–72[d]	732	608	+124	4,816
1572–73[e]	1,590	1,697	-106	

a. From an unspecified date in 1546 to 1 May 1550.
b. From 1 September 1552 to 1 May 1554.
c. From 1 May 1568 to Christmas 1571.
d. From Christmas 1571 to 25 June 1572.
e. From 25 August 1572 to 25 August 1573.

12. The total receipts and expenditures recorded in A.N. $H^3 2874^2$ are given in tabular form below, along with the surplus (+) or deficit (-) recorded for each period—usually a year, but sometimes longer. The cumulative debt owed to Ramus, when recorded, is also shown. All totals have been rounded to the nearest livre, but are otherwise exactly as given in the source. Because of mathematical errors and unexplained deductions (in years marked with an asterisk), the sums do not work out properly. Except where noted, accounting periods extend from May 1 through April 30 of the years in question.

Another change that had taken place since Raoul's time was the nature of the costs associated with operating the college. The charter had suggested that lawsuits and court proceedings would be uncommon, not a regular feature of college life or a constant item in the budget. Under Ramus's administration, however, the college frequently resorted to the law. Whether because of the litigiousness of the age, the years which might be spent settling a dispute, or Ramus's contentious temperament, Presles was involved in expensive lawsuits throughout his career. Accounts for the period from 1546 to 1549 indicate the expenditure of 326 livres on court-related expenses during the period, a figure which rose to over 300 livres a year in two later periods, 1550–1552 and 1560–61.[13]

The lawsuits were expensive, but the money was well spent. In the long run, they seem to have been very profitable. A case in point is that of one Jean Puy, seigneur de Chéry, who was accused in 1549 before the Châtelet of Paris for having disturbed and usurped a wood belonging to the college near Daule. A verdict was reached in February of 1555 ordering Puy to pay the college the sum of 2,500 livres for his infraction. He was not in any hurry to do so. In 1557, he was once again commanded to pay, with no immediate effect.[14] Only in 1560–61 was restitution finally made to the college in the amount of 3,000 livres, nearly all of which went to Ramus in partial payment of the college's obligations to him.[15]

Such a windfall, nearly tripling the college's income for the year, was unique during Ramus's tenure at Presles. But smaller amounts from extraordinary sources trickled in irregularly, most importantly in the form of bequests to the college from former students and teachers there. Nicolas Lesage, whom Ramus had succeeded as head of Presles, left the college an annual income of eight livres from a house in Paris as well as forgiving the debt of 2,100 livres owed him by the college.[16] Jean Péna,

13. The cost of the college's legal affairs was included in a separate section of the accounts, usually an eighth chapter entitled "Huictiesme chapitre de despens a cause des proces dudict college." Other legal costs were however noted elsewhere in the yearly reckoning. See the eighth chapter of the accounts for 1546–49, 1550–52, and 1560–61 in A.N. H^{3}2874^2. The records for the years from 1546 to 1549 specify a total of 2,82 l. 19 s. 2 d. paid to sergeants, advocates, "Robichon le procureur en chatelet de Paris," Robichon's clerks, the clerks of the Parlement of Paris, the Parlement's *greffiers*, etc. One such payment of 20 l. was to Jehan Talon "pour penses, fraiz et mises par luy faicts pour les proces dudict college," an entry which suggests that Ramus's colleague Omer Talon also found a way to turn his office to the profit of relatives.

14. See A.N. MM 432 for the course of this lawsuit up to 1557. The initial action is summarized on fols. 121r–v; the 1555 verdict on fol. 122r; and the 1557 suit on fols. 122r–v.

15. H^{3}2874^2, accounts for the year 1560–61, receipts, under the heading "Daule," states: "Receu de Jehan boullenger notaire demurant a Vailly pour et au nom de monsieur de Chery a cause de cincq executiones…pour raison de proces contre luy a raison des bois dont…R[eceu] #3000."

16. A.N. MM 432, fols. 28r–v, summarizes Lesage's legacy, and the income from his Parisian property—the Jeu de Paume des Verde Gallans, on the rue des Postes—appears in the accounts from 1560 on. Ramus also forgave the debt owed him by the college at his death, a matter of some 4,816 livres. See H^{3}2874^2, 1571–72, with the note "de laquelle somme nous consentons et accordons estre prise et paiee aud. rendant compte [Ramus] sur les plus clairs deniers du tours et chacuns des biens appartenant aud. College.…" On Ramus's testaments see below, chapter 5.

Ramus's student and later his colleague, left the substantial sum of 300 livres to the college at his death in 1560.[17]

Ramus's position as principal of Presles involved him with finances, lawsuits, and the duty of providing a home for his younger relations, and it made him a great deal of money. He had in fact been co-opted into the academic world of mid-sixteenth-century Paris, where academic scholarships and teaching positions were more and more often acquired by purchase and nepotism with small regard for merit. He had become a typical academic careerist. Nevertheless, he was to emerge as the most dedicated opponent of venal office holding in the University and of practices which restricted education to the wealthy and well connected.

It was with the reform of the liberal arts, beginning with the trivium and eventually moving on to the quadrivium and the higher subjects of law, medicine, and theology, that Ramus's popularizing approach to education first became apparent. Even before settling at the college of Presles, Ramus had begun his public criticism of the University curriculum with a polemical attack on the organization and teaching of logic. The year 1543, which saw the publication of Vesalius's *De humani corporis fabrica* and Copernicus's *De Revolutionibus*, also witnessed Ramus's first appearance in print. His *Dialecticae Institutiones* was intended to reform the teaching and use of logic, while its companion volume, the *Aristotelicae Animadversiones*, was to explain why such a reform was necessary.[18] The simple, or even simplistic, version of the art of logic presented in the *Dialecticae* was enough to turn most of the arts teachers in the University against him immediately, and for those who needed more convincing that Ramus was either a simpleton or a fraud, the attacks on Aristotle in the *Animadversiones* proved to be more than enough. So strongly did the University react against Ramus's works that a commission was established to examine him and them, a commission whose deliberations were the basis of Francis I's condemnation of both books in the following year.

Francis's sentence of 10 March 1544 "condemned, suppressed, and abolished" the two books and forbade their publication while describing the author as ignorant, a liar, arrogant and impudent. It was the *Aristotelicae Animadversiones* which seems to have been the most offensive, while the *Dialecticae* was banned simply for "also

---

17. The accounts for the year 1561–62 mention receipt of the legacy and describe Péna in the following terms: "Feu maistre Jean Pena natif d'Aix en Provence a estudié au college de Prelle longtemps soub le rendant compte [Ramus] et y est passé Maistre soub maistre Aumer Talon et y a faict ung cours es ars et finalement pour soy scavoir et par layde et moyen du rendant compte fust faict lecteur du Roy en mathematiques et a esté tousiours loge au College jusques au jour de son trespas." Péna's testament is described in A.N. MM432, fols. 28v–29r, and in Jean Dupèbe, "Autour du Collège de Presles."

18. Petrus Ramus, *Petri Rami Veromandui Dialectica Institutiones* (Paris: Bogard, 1543); and idem, *Petri Rami Veromandui Aristotelicae Animadversiones* (Paris: Bogard, 1543).

containing several false and strange things."[19] Ramus himself was forbidden to teach dialectic or philosophy without the king's express permission.

Neither the fate of his books nor the restrictions placed on Ramus himself had much of an effect on his career. He himself was freed from Francis's decree soon after the king's death in 1547, thanks to the intervention of his powerful patron Charles of Guise, cardinal of Lorraine, and not long after that, in 1551, was named royal professor of philosophy and eloquence by Francis's successor Henry II, again at Charles's suggestion.

His works enjoyed even more success. In its various editions, revisions, and rearrangements and under a wide variety of titles, Ramus's textbook of logic went through about 250 printings, mostly in the sixteenth century, while his *Aristotelicae Animadversiones* (later, in an expanded version, titled *Scholarum dialecticarum*, "Lectures on Dialectic") was printed in full nineteen times.[20] Furthermore, the "method" developed in these works became the framework for Ramus's analysis and arrangement of the other liberal arts as well. What "strange things" did they contain to win them such wide popularity after they had been so roundly condemned at their first appearance?

The technical nature of Ramus's reforms, in particular his revisions of logic and rhetoric, has been studied in detail in a variety of specialized works.[21] Here we are concerned simply to show how social context played an important role in the direction Ramus's reforms took and in their enormous popularity. Some analysis of

19. The text of Francis's edict has been published several times, notably in Waddington, *Ramus*, 49–52. The books had been condemned by a panel of four judges, two appointed by the prosecution and two by the defense. Those opposed were Pierre Danès and Francisco Vicomercato, two of the most distinguished royal professors, while Ramus's defenders were relative unknowns: Jean Quentin and Jean de Beaumont, doctors of law and medicine respectively. The fifth judge, appointed by the king, was Jean Salignac, the well-known doctor of theology. Ramus's judges both withdrew before a verdict was reached, no doubt having recognized that they were on the wrong side.

20. Ong, *Ramus and Talon Inventory*, nos. 1–31, 237–473.

21. The best study of Ramism in general, concentrating on Ramist logic and rhetoric, is Walter J. Ong, S.J., *Ramus, Method and the Decay of Dialogue: From the Art of Discourse to the Art of Reason* (Cambridge: Harvard University Press, 1958). Wilbur Samuel Howell, "Ramus and English Rhetoric, 1574–1681," *Quarterly Journal of Speech* 37 (1951): 299–310, is a good introduction to Ramist rhetoric, a topic more fully explored in idem, *Logic and Rhetoric in England, 1500–1700* (New York: Russell and Russell, 1961). Wilhelm Risse, "Die Entwicklung der Dialektik bei Petrus Ramus," *Archiv für Geschichte der Philosophie* 42 (1960): 36–72, is a more technical account of Ramist logic than that in Ong; idem, *Die Logik der Neuzeit* (Stuttgart: Friedrich Frommann, 1964), is even more detailed and offers a careful look at how Ramus altered the details of his system over time. The work of Cesare Vasoli, esp. "Retorica e dialettica in Pietro Ramo," in *Testi Umanistici su la Retorica: Testi editi e inediti su Retorica e Dialettica di Mario Nizolio, Francesco Patrizi e Pietro Ramo...*, ed. E. Garin, P. Rossi, and C. Vasoli, (Rome: Fratelli Bocca Editori, 1953), 95–134; and Vasoli, *La dialettica e la retorica dell'Umanismo: "Invenzione" e "metodo" nelle cultura del XVe e XVI secolo (Lefèvre d'Etaples, J. Sturm, P. Ramus)* (Milan: Feltrinelli, 1968), concentrates on Ramus's connections with the European humanist movement and supplement the narrower focus of the works previously cited. In addition, there are numerous studies on more specific aspects of Ramus's method for the liberal arts, which can be found in the bibliography.

the principles which controlled his restructuring of the arts is essential to understanding his motives and success, but the brief outline which follows can only suggest some of their details and ramifications. Readers are referred to the specialized studies in the notes for fuller discussions.

The heart and soul of Ramism was the concept of "method" developed in successive editions of his works, and in particular his works on logic.[22] The definitive exposition of Ramist method did not emerge until a decade after Ramus's first publications, but it had been his central concern for far longer. His main criticism in the *Aristotelicae Animadversiones* was that Aristotle's logical works lacked proper method.[23] Even Ramus's (probably apocryphal) master's thesis suggested as much. Ramus's one true method for all the arts and sciences was to resolve the confusion that plagued them, and in the process to make them more loyal to nature as well as vastly easier to master.

The seeds of Ramist method were to be found in the works of Aristotle himself. Aristotle had laid down three laws for the organization of any discipline (and had then proceeded to neglect them), but Ramus had rediscovered the rules of method and expounded them as the crowning part of the art of logic.[24] Ramus called them the "lex veritatis," the "lex justitiae," and the "lex sapientiae," or in more descriptive terms the laws "de omni," "per se," and "universaliter primum."[25]

The substance of these three laws can be quickly explained. The earliest English language edition of Ramus's logic, translated by Roland MacIlmaine of St. Andrew's University in 1574, offers concise definitions of the three "documents or rules"

22. The most complete discussion of Ramus as a methodologist is in Neal Gilbert's *Renaissance Concepts of Method* (New York: Columbia University Press, 1960), 129–63.

23. In particular, in book 9 of the later expanded editions of the *Aristotelicae Animadversiones*, e.g. *Animadversionum Aristotelicarum libri viginti...* (Paris: A. Wechel, 1556). This book was later published separately under the title *Quod sit unica doctrinae instituendae methodus...* (Paris: A. Wechel, 1557), and is available in a modern English translation by Eugene J. Barber and Leonard A. Kennedy, "That There Is But One Method of Establishing a Science," in Leonard Kennedy, ed., *Renaissance Philosophy: New Translations* (The Hague: Mouton, 1973), 109–155.

24. Aristotle's discussion of these three laws appears in the *Posterior Analytics*, book 1, chap. 4 (73a21–74a3). Aristotle is hardly clear on what he intends by this discussion, and Wilbur S. Howell calls the chapter "one of the most difficult in the entire *Organon*"; Howell, *Logic and Rhetoric*, 41. Typically, Ramus saw Aristotle's lack of clarity as an opportunity rather than a difficulty. It allowed him to read his own definitions into Aristotle's words, thereby claiming classical authority without sacrificing his own notions. For the sake of comparison, relevant portions of the *Posterior Analytics* in the English translation of G. R. G. Mure can be consulted; Richard McKeon, ed., *The Basic Works of Aristotle* (New York: Random House, 1941), 115–17. Howell, *Logic and Rhetoric*, 41–43, shows how scholastic logicians, in particular Vincent of Beauvais, understood the same three laws three centuries before Ramus's work.

25. In the French version of Ramus's logic published in 1555, these three appear as the laws "du tout," "par soy," and "universel premierement"; Michel Dassonville, ed., Dialectique de Pierre de la Ramee, a Charles de Lorraine Cardinal, son Mecene (1555; reprint, Geneva: Droz, 1964). A brief definition of the three laws composed a decade later appears in the preface to Ramus's *Scholarum Metaphysicarum* of 1566 (in Scholae in liberales artes, after col. 828). Here he writes: "In arte nihil esto (ait Aristoteles) nisi κατὰ

which control the arts.[26] The law of truth simply requires "that all the rules and pre-
ceptes of thine arte be of necessitie tru, which Aristotle requirethe in the seconde
booke of his Analitikes.…" The law of justice proclaimed "that in setting forthe of
an arte we gather only togeather that which dothe appartayne to the Arte whiche we
intreate of, leaving to all other Artes that which is proper to them.…" Finally, the
law of wisdom is defined by MacIlmaine as the requirement

> that thou intreate of thy rules which be generall generallye, and those
> which be speciall speciallie, and at one tyme, without any vaine repetitions,
> which dothe nothing but fyll up the paper. For it is not sufficient that thou
> kepe the rule of veritie and justice, without thou observe also this docu-
> mente of wisedome, to dispute of every thing according to his nature.

This final law deserves a fuller explanation, not only because MacIlmaine's ren-
dering of it leaves something to be desired but also because it was the central proposition in Ramist method.

Its importance can be seen in Ramus's first French edition of his dialectic, in the
section devoted to method. The section begins with a restatement of the law of wisdom, "universaliter primum," but here it is identified with method. "Method,"
Ramus wrote, "is disposition, by which among several things the most conspicuous
is put in the first place, the second in the second, the third in the third and so on."[27]
To clarify his definition, Ramus offers the example of the art of grammar. Suppose,
he says, that all the definitions and rules of grammar are written out on separate slips
of paper and jumbled together in a jar. How do we impose the best order on the confusion?

> The dialectician chooses, by the light of natural method, the definition of
> Grammar, because that is the most general, and puts it in first place:
> "Grammar is the art of speaking well." Then, he looks in the same jar for

---

παντός omnino necessarioque verum, nisi καθ' αὐτό homogeneum, totiusque artis naturale & essen-
tiale documentum, nisi καθ' ὅλου πρωτος proprium & reciprocum, nisi denique natura prius, loco pri-
ore collocatum."

Ramus's use of Greek in this passage was characteristic. He liked to drop isolated Greek terms and
phrases into his Latin prose to suggest a close acquaintance with his sources even though his knowledge of
Greek was limited at best. His contemporaries were aware of the game he was playing and mocked him for
it. See for example the letter from Denis Lambin, royal professor of Greek, to Prévost de Thérouanne of
February 1554, where, among other accusations against Ramus, Lambin complains that "Il a employé des
mots grecs qui suivent immédiatement des termes latins du même sens: il veut nous faire savoir qu'il a lu
Aristote en grec, alors qu'il y a quatre ans il était tout à fait ignorant et inexpérimenté en cette langue." The
translation is that of Henri Potez, "Deux années de la Renaissance (d'après une correspondance inédite),"
Revue d'histoire littéraire de la France 13 (1906): 663, from the original in B.N. fonds latin 8647, fol. 114r.

26. *The Logike of the Moste Excellent Philosopher P. Ramus Martyr, Newly Translated…per M. Roll.
Makylmenaeum Scotum* (London: Thomas Vautrollier, 1574), 8–10.

27. Dassonville, *Dialectique*, 144.

the partition of Grammar and puts it in second place: "The parts of Grammar are two, Etymology and Syntax."[28]

And so on, until particular examples are reached. They are placed in the final position, and the art of grammar is properly ordered for teaching and learning. When the laws of justice and of truth are also employed, the method is perfect. Imagine that the jar also contains slips on which are written propositions in mathematics and false statements about grammar. Ramus's method teaches us to exclude these from our arrangement of the art, with the result that every proposition contained in it is true, relevant, and in its proper place.

The laws of wisdom, justice, and truth taught the proper method to arrange knowledge for learning, but Ramus recognized that it might be employed in various ways, since the most "conspicuous" element in an art or discourse would vary according to the audience being addressed. In organizing an art according to universal principles, there was no great problem. Some parts of the art were clearly more general than others, as in the case of grammar noted above, and these more general elements ought to precede the more specific examples. But in speaking to an untutored audience, it might be better to start off with those parts of the subject which were best known to them, rather than absolutely better known, and to work towards the more arcane (even if absolutely more general) parts of the topic. This second method, which Ramus labeled the "method of prudence" to distinguish it from the more scientific "method of nature," put in first place "not things which are absolutely and universally better known, but those more convenient for those who must be taught, and more likely to induce and lead them where we wish."[29] Ramus did not scorn this "method of prudence," which earned a discussion as long as that of the "method of nature" in his works.[30] He even employed it in his own theological writings.[31]

method of prudence vs. method of nature

The discovery of true method prompted Ramus to a cosmic metaphor. "In brief," he wrote,

> this artificial method seems to me a long golden chain, such as Homer imagined, whose links are these degrees depending one from the other, and all so justly strung together that none could be removed without breaking the order and continuity of the whole.[32]

---

28. Dassonville, *Dialectique*, 122–23.

29. Dassonville, *Dialectique*, 128.

30. In Dassonville, *Dialectique*, for example, the "method of nature" is discussed on 120–27, the "method of prudence" on 128–35.

31. See below, chapter 5.

32. Dassonville, *Dialectique*, 122.

So taken was he with his discovery that the great majority of his works were dedicated to defending it against his detractors or applying it to the reorganization of the arts and sciences.

This is the sum and substance of Ramist method, "a doctrine that seems the very acme of banality to us" and that struck many of Ramus's learned contemporaries the same way.[33] Nonetheless, Ramus made it his life's work to revise all of the liberal arts on the basis of his method.

The first and most famous result of Ramus's reforming zeal was the creation of Ramist logic and rhetoric. In applying his method to Aristotle's *Organon* and to Ciceronian rhetoric, he not only rearranged the study of the trivium but also jettisoned a large part of it. Hardin Craig estimated that Ramus's logic was one-tenth the bulk of Aristotle's, and as we shall see, the art of rhetoric was also drastically curtailed.[34] Their brevity stemmed in large measure from a strict application of the law of justice.

That law, which required each art to stick to its own subject matter, was the rationale behind Ramus's decision to excise whole books from the *Organon* along with three-fifths of the traditional course in rhetoric. He had seen that both disciplines treated the invention of arguments and their arrangement in discourse. Logic taught both the creation of propositions and their disposition in rational arguments; rhetoric taught the topics, or commonplaces, which provided the speaker with something to say on any subject, as well as rules for arranging the resulting sentences in a coherent discourse. Such duplication of effort was anathema to Ramus. What was the point of treating these matters twice?

Rhetoric had long enjoyed an autonomous existence as an alternative to logic for the investigation of nature, God, and society. In some eras, it had nearly eclipsed logic entirely, as its rules dominated learned discourse.[35] But without distinct theories of "invention" and "disposition," it could hardly survive as an independent discipline. Its other traditional parts, memory, eloquence, and delivery, could not stand alone. Rhetoric required material to remember, to express in terms of the tropes and figures, and to deliver with appropriate gesture and tone of voice. The law of justice denied it the right to develop that material itself.

bibliog.

33. Neal Gilbert, *Renaissance Concepts of Method*, 129, and chap. 6, "The Reaction to the Methodologies of Ramus and the Dialecticians," 145–63. See also the bibliography in Ong, "The Ramist Controversies," *Ramus and Talon Inventory*, 492–510, for attacks by Ramus's contemporaries and Ramus's published replies.

34. Hardin Craig, *The Enchanted Glass: The Elizabethan Mind in Literature* (New York: Oxford University Press, 1936), 144.

35. On the age-old competition between logicians and rhetoricians for primacy, see esp. Samuel Ijsseling's interesting *Rhetoric and Philosophy in Conflict: An Historical Survey*, trans. Paul Dunphy (The Hague: Martinus Nijhoff, 1976). Useful discussion of the relative standing of the two arts in the ancient world can be found in George Kennedy's *The Art of Persuasion in Greece* (Princeton: Princeton University Press, 1963).

Rhetoric was henceforth to be a handmaiden of logic, which would be the source of discovery and arrangement. The art of rhetoric would simply dress that material in ornate language and teach orators when to raise their voices and extend their arms to the audience. To add insult to injury, rhetoric also lost control of the art of memory. Ramus was so taken with his new method that he believed it to be a sufficient aid to memory all by itself, and method was firmly attached to the art of logic.[36]

Ramist method worked to abbreviate the study of logic as well as that of rhetoric. The law of justice allowed Ramus to remove the subject of sophistry from the study of logic, since the arts of deception had no place in the art of truth. It allowed him to eliminate the *Topics* as well, which Aristotle had intended to teach the source of arguments on matters of opinion. Like the *Sophistical Refutations*, they had no place in the study of logic because they were not properly speaking part of the art. Furthermore, in Ramus's view, the *Categories* were the source of arguments on any matter, scientific or not, and the *Topics* were redundant.

Still, there was more to Ramus's drastic pruning of the art of logic than can be explained by the laws of justice, wisdom, and truth. At a more basic level, his very conception of how the arts came to be formulated and what end they served determined the structure and content of his logic. To the questions of how the arts originated, how they should be taught, and what end they served, Ramus offered a simple answer, the same for all three questions. The answer in every case was practical use. The precepts of an art had their foundation in man's natural abilities and practices; the art was best taught by practical application as opposed to rote memorization of

---

36. The decline of rhetoric as an academic discipline was due at least in part to Ramus's emasculation of the ancient art. Several commentators on Ramus have seen his reforms as crucial in this declension. Pierre Albert Duhamel, "The Logic and Rhetoric of Peter Ramus," *Modern Philology* 46 (1949): 170–71, writes: "rhetoric was left as an art of ornamentation. It decorated the arguments discovered by logic with tropes and figures. The content of the oration became the object of reason and method; the function of rhetoric was to gild the furnished material…. Composition performed under such principles lacked the unity of conception and execution which is necessary to the highest art." The subtitle of Walter Ong's major work on Ramus—"From the Art of Discourse to the Art of Reason"—can be taken as a summary statement of Ramus's impact on rhetoric and logic, although Ong intended it to express a great deal more than the decline of a particular academic discipline. The decline of rhetoric may nonetheless be taken at least as the symbol, and perhaps as the most useful interpretation, of Ong's contention that Ramus was the representative and prophet of a turning from the spoken to the printed word, and more generally from an auditory to a visual understanding of the world.

Ramus's attempts to substitute his idea of method for the rhetorical techniques of memory have been interpreted by some as an indication that Ramist method was essentially a modification of the art of memory. Frances Yates, *The Art of Memory* (Chicago: University of Chicago Press, 1966); and Paolo Rossi, esp. "La memoria artificiale come sezione della logica: Ramo, Bacone, Cartesio," *Revista critica di storia della filosofia* 15 (1960): 22–62, develop this theme at length, and Yates argues that in sixteenth-century England, at least, Ramism was regarded *primarily* as a memory system. Her contention receives some support from the works of the Puritan divine William Perkins; see his "The Art of Prophesying" in Ian Breward, ed., *The Works of William Perkins* (Appleford, Berks.: Courtenay Library of Reformation Classics, 1970), 335–49, and esp. 344–46, "Of Memory."

abstract principles and the goal of the art was practical use in the real world. The determined practicality of Ramus's approach to learning was quite as important as his more famous methodological ideas in shortening and simplifying Aristotelian logic and the other arts as well. Indeed, the emphasis on practice may be seen as the prime motive behind his academic reforms. His contemporaries considered it a failing in his system, and labeled him "usuarius" as a result.[37]

As explained in Ramus's *Dialecticae Institutiones* of 1543, each art and science, including logic, had three aspects or moments which together determined its form and content. These were nature, doctrine, and use: "natura, doctrina, exercitatione." Together they made for the perfection of the art, each working with the others to form a unified whole.[38] Each deserves attention in turn.

Ramus believed that every man came into the world possessed of a natural, God-given ability to reason dialectically. Reason, the very image of God, was innate, and this natural faculty was the root of logic as an art.[39] As a result of this belief, Ramus

37. It is tempting to translate "usuarius" as "utilitarian," except that the latter word would apply only to the third moment of an art, its application in the world, and neglect the importance of use in the creation and transmission of an art; Ong, *Ramus, Method and the Decay*, 6, 321–22, n. 6, mocks F. P. Graves's attempt to translate the word by "utilitarian" or "pragmatist"; Frank Pierrepont Graves, *Peter Ramus and the Educational Reform of the Sixteenth Century* (New York: Macmillan, 1912), 57. Ong prefers instead "usuary" or "usufructuary" for this "technical legal term" which he sees as a reference to Ramus's borrowings from the learned authors of the ancient world and his own time. Ong's citations, however, do not provide strong support for his case. The "clear confutation" he found in a passage from Ramus's opponent Adrien Turnèbe is not so clear to me, while his reference to Nancel, "*Petri Rami Vita,*" 36, seems rather to support Graves than Ong. The passage reads, in Peter Sharratt's translation: "For this reason he was given the honorific title 'usuarius' by his opponents, who wanted to brand him with infamy, because he showed that all the liberal arts were to be directed to the benefit of human life…" [Unde et usuarius honorifico titulo ab adversarius dictus est, quem probro notare cogitabant, et quod artium omnium liberalium fines ad humanae vitae fructum referendos esse demonstravit…]; ibid., 213. Sharratt acknowledges that he follows Ong in translating "usuarius" by "usufructuary"; ibid., 212, n. 44; but the context of Nancel's statement makes it clear that "utilitarian" or "pragmatic" would be a more appropriate English equivalent. Erland Sellberg's *Filosofin och nyttan*, vol. 1. *Petrus Ramus och ramismen*, Gothenburg Studies in the History of Science and Ideas I (Göteborg, n.p., 1979), with a brief English summary, suggests some of the philosophical difficulties encountered in such an approach to knowledge.

38. Ramus summarizes the character of these three moments of an art in his *Dialecticae Institutiones*, 5v–6r: "Hi sunt tres libri ad omnis disciplinae fructum, laudemque necessarii: quorum primum aeternis characteribus in animis nostris Deus optimus, maximus imprimit, secundum naturae diligens observator imitatis notulis as aeternarum illarum notarum exemplar effingit: tertium manus, linguaque (quantum, quamque copiosum volunt) amplectuntur. Itaque de tribus dialecticae partibus prima (cuius dignitas maxima est) tertiaque (cuius secunda laus est) sunt in nobis: altera insita, tera voluntaria. Secunda (cui perpaululum loci relinquum est) sola extrinsecus a magistris assumenda est: ut nihil homini nisi perexiguum ad hanc virtutem percipiendam desit." A similar tripartite division occurs in his later logical works, though with variations in terminology. See Duhamel, "The Logic and Rhetoric of Peter Ramus," 168.

39. *Dialecticae Institutiones*, 6r: "Naturalis autem dialectica, id est ingenium, ratio, mens, imago parentis omnium rerum Dei, lux denique beatae illius, & aeternae lucis aemula, hominis propria est, cum eoque nascitur." Such a belief caused some problems for those Calvinists who later adopted Ramist logic, in that it implied that men retained at least one of their faculties in a state of prelapsarian perfection.

claimed that the art of logic must be founded on the examples offered by natural logic. Men use natural logic in speaking and writing even without formal training, and the best results reveal and illustrate the rules on which formal logic is based. The academic logician must therefore observe the operations of natural logic as the model on which he builds his art. "Experience gives rise to an art; inexperience breeds only temerity," Ramus claimed, "and no rule should be included in an art which is not observed and induced from the use and observation of true examples."[40]

Several scholars have suggested that this statement shows Ramus to have been a sort of protoempiricist, although his method falls short of scientific empiricism because the induction he enjoins is to be made from literary works rather than from nature. His use of Virgil's *Georgics* as the basis of his art of physics is a good example of how what Reijer Hooykaas called "literary empiricism" flourished in Ramism.[41] Hooykaas suggested that Ramus was the link between the "literary empiricism" of the fifteenth and sixteenth centuries and the "scientific empiricism" of later eras, initiated by the works of Francis Bacon.[42]

The demand that the arts be derived from observation, and in the case of logic and rhetoric (and, as we shall see, grammar as well) from observation of common

---

Perry Miller explains in detail how the New England Puritans got around this problem in *The New England Mind*, esp. chap. 7. On this problem see also Keith L. Sprunger, "Technometria: A Prologue to Puritan Theology," *Journal of the History of Ideas* 29 (1968): 115–22.

40. Ramus, "Scholae Metaphysicae" in *Scholae in Liberales Artes*, col. 830: "Experientia quidem artem genuit, inexperientia autem temeritatem…[ut] nullum in artibus documentum recipiendum, quod ab usu & experientia verorum exemplorum observatum & inductum non esset."

41. Ramus's commentaries on the *Georgics* and the *Bucolics* analyze the two works for the lessons they contain in fields as diverse as meteorology and beekeeping, botany and astronomy, and Ramus formed the art of physics around these lessons. See his *P. Virgilii Maronis Bucolica, P. Rami praelectionibus exposita* (Paris: A. Wechel, 1555); and idem, *P. Virgilii Maronis Georgica, P. Rami…praelectionibus illustrata* (Paris: A. Wechel, 1556). He also published lectures on Aristotle's *Physics*, but he found Aristotle almost as useless in this art as in many others, because he fell into sterile abstraction and neglected actual observable phenomema: "If one should by means of his senses and reason investigate heaven and earth and all that therein is, as a physicist ought to do, and then compare his results with the *Physics* of Aristotle, he would find in that work no observation of anything in nature, but only sophisms, theoretical speculations, and unsupported assertions." The translation is F. P. Graves's loose rendition of Ramus, "Praefatio Physica" 1, in *Collectaneae praefationes, epistolae orationes…* (Marburg: 1609), 52. See Graves, *Peter Ramus*, 168–69. Graves adds that despite Ramus's call for the "observation of nature," what he actually practiced was the observation of what the ancients had to say about nature: "Unfortunately, the real spirit of science and induction was as yet so little understood that the student gained this exercise through an interpretation of the descriptions of various classical authors rather than by actual observation, and the study became verbal rather than scientific"; ibid., 172.

42. Reijer Hooykaas, "Pierre de la Ramée et l'empirisme scientifique au xvie siècle," in *La Science au seizième siècle: Colloque International Royaumont, 1–4 juillet 1957* (Paris: Hermann, 1960), 299–313. A fuller explanation of the thesis which places Ramus even more firmly at the transition point between literary and scientific empiricism can be found in idem, *Humanisme, science et réforme: Pierre de la Ramée*

practice, dictated the method by which the arts should be taught as well. Concrete examples drawn from the greatest writers, poets, and thinkers should be the students' sources for discovering the nature of the syllogism, the use of the tropes, and the organization of discourse according to the one true method. Such an approach would bring about the reunion of philosophy and eloquence which Ramus ardently desired and for which he vigorously campaigned, from his "Address on Combining Philosophy and Eloquence" of 1546 to his appointment as royal professor of philosophy and eloquence in 1551 and beyond.[43] Philosophy, including logic and physics, would be taught from the great authors; eloquence would be taught by analyzing discourse according to logical principles and the use of method.

The way such pedagogy worked can be seen in Ramus's own classroom technique as well as in his published works, and it is reflected in the practice of later Ramists. In the classroom, Ramus concentrated on practice. One hour of lecture in the morning and one in the afternoon were to be followed by hours devoted to study and recitation, but the emphasis was on practical application of the precepts so mastered. Conversation and imitation of the classics formed the core of the teaching process, with the intent of giving students hands-on experience.[44] Typically a great work of literature, or a piece of it, would first be analyzed by the student to discover its methodological and logical structure and its use of the tropes and figures. Following that, the student would proceed to the "genesis" of his own work based on the imitation of the classical model.[45] Practical application of logical and rhetorical principles based on concrete models was the key.

The concrete models Ramus chose depended on the occasion. For physics, as we have seen, he chose the works of Virgil, and in his Latin works on logic and rhetoric

(1515–1572) (Leiden: Brill, 1958). The development of empirical and inductive methods in the sixteenth and seventeenth centuries played a crucial role in the Scientific Revolution, and Ramus's putative empiricism has therefore attracted considerable attention from historians of science and scientific method. See esp. Lisa Jardine, *Francis Bacon, Discovery and the Art of Discourse* (Cambridge: Cambridge University Press, 1974), for her careful comments on the relationship between the methods of Ramus and Bacon.

43. See Petrus Ramus, *Petri Rami Oration de studiis philosophiae et eloquentiae coniugendis Lutetiae habita anno 1546* (Paris: Jacob Bogard, 1546).

44. See the full account in Walter Ong, "Ramist Classroom Procedure and the Nature of Reality," *Studies in English Literature 1500–1900* 1 (1961): esp. 38–40. Ong relies on the work of Ramus's student Freigius for his description of Ramist classroom procedure; see his *Petri Rami Professio regia, hoc est septem artes liberales in regia cathedra per ipsum apodictico docendi genere propositae...* (Basel: Henricpetri, 1576), an attempt to gather Ramus's treatment of the arts into a single encyclopedic volume.

45. The Ramist understanding of "analysis" and "genesis" is discussed in its historical context by Gilbert, *Renaissance Concepts of Method*, 135–43; Ong, *Ramus, Method and the Decay of Dialogue*, 263–69; Howell, *Logic and Rhetoric*, 249–50, 305–6, 320–21. On imitation as an educational practice in Ramism, see esp. Peter Sharratt, "Peter Ramus and Imitation: Image, Sign and Sacrament," *Yale French Studies* 47 (1972): 19–32. The technique of analyzing a literary text to find its logical structure caught on especially among the English Puritans. As an epitome of the genre, see William Temple, *A Logical Analysis of Twenty Select Psalmes* (London: 1605), where the author's aim is to present the marrow of the psalms,

he chose from among the great Roman writers. For his French version of the art of logic, he managed to gain the cooperation of the greatest French poets of his day, the members of the Pléiade, a circumstance which has led to much speculation about possible connections between Ramus and the school of Ronsard and Dorat. It seems however that the connection was a fleeting one, based solely on the brief convergence of goals between Ramus and the poets on the occasion of his publication of textbooks in French.[46]

Finally, the teaching of every art and science was geared to practical use. The distinction between theory and practice was anathema to Ramus. The only reason for an art or science to exist was that it be useful in the world at large. The impact of such a belief on the content of the liberal arts was immense. In the case of logic, it was particularly noticeable. Out went the predicables; Ramus claimed that no one ever talked like that, and that people would laugh if anyone did.[47] Out went noncategorical syllogisms; Ramus treated them as compounds of the simple more natural

---

"stripped as it were of all outward habit, and laid forth in the first and natural lineaments…" (6). The "outward habit" is the dress in which rhetoric had cloaked the results of purely logical "invention" and "disposition," so that analysis of a literary text became for Ramists little more than application of the "law of justice," separating the logical from the rhetorical. The result was a simple outline which, according to Ong. could appeal only to "dry-as-dust analysts, polymaths with a penchant for classification…persons who habitually deal with reality in terms of accounting"; Walter Ong, "Ramist Method and the Commercial Mind," *Studies in the Renaissance* 8 (1961): 163, 172. Such an operation on a text does not, in Ong's eyes, "respect sufficiently the mysterious nature of verbal expression"; Ong, "Ramist Classroom Procedure," 40. It is hard to disagree; the poetry of the psalms analyzed by Temple is utterly lost, treated as if it played no essential role in the psalms' message.

46. On possible connections between the Pléiade and Ramus, see Michel Dassonville, "La Collaboration de la Pléiade à la *Dialectique* de Pierre de la Ramée (1555)," *Bibliothèque d'humanisme et renaissance* 25 (1963): 337–48, and Dassonville, *Dialectique*, introduction. Peter Sharratt, in "The First French Logic," in *Mélanges à la mémoire de Franco Simone*, vol. 4, "Tradition et originalité dans la création littéraire" (Geneva: Slatkine, 1983), 205–19; as well as in idem, review of Dassonville's edition of the *Dialectique, Modern Language Review* 62 (1967): 130–33, argues that the connection between Ramus and the Pléiade was not very important. His unpublished doctoral thesis on the subject of "The Ideas of Pierre de la Ramée with Particular Reference to Poetic Theory in the Sixteenth Century in France" (Ph.D. diss., University of Newcastle) concludes that "the actual relations between Ramus and the Pléiade…do not amount to much"; cited in Peter Sharratt, "The Present State of Studies on Ramus," *Studi Francesi* 16 (1972): 201–13, at 208.

47. The example is given in Duhamel, "The Logic and Rhetoric of Peter Ramus," 167, from *Aristotelicae Animadversiones*, fols. 16r–16v: "[Ramus] asks the reader to suppose what would happen if an Aristotelian, returning to his home town after studying logic, should call the people together and address them: 'I know that people have eight ways of being beautiful, such as quality, quantity…. Who would be able to stop from laughing?' [si quis Aristoteleorum (cum duos annos in dialecticorum consumpsisset) in patriam reversus populares convocaret, ut in publico conventu Aristoteleae sapientiae specimen exhiberet, tum diceret: scio populares octo pulchros habendi modos, ut qualitate, quantitate, circa corpus, in parte…quis risum teneret?]."

forms.[48] Not only in logic, but in the other arts as well (most notably in mathematics, as we shall see), Ramus's classroom texts were practical manuals and handbooks, not theoretical treatises which we would call "scientific." Their aim was use, not academic rigor, and they were intended to produce capable men rather than scholarly ones.

The complexity and theoretical bent of the arts as they were taught in the sixteenth century was a great barrier to their widespread mastery and use. Few Frenchmen could afford the years of leisure necessary to learn them, either in the university or on their own, and even fewer could see why they should bother. Thanks to the reforms of Ramus, "the greatest master of the shortcut the world has ever known," shorter, simpler, and more immediately useful versions of the academic disciplines were made available to students and the reading public.[49] For all these advantages, there remained an enormous barrier between the arts and the public. Learned works were written and published in Latin, but only a few elites understood that ancient language. Ramus set out to break down that barrier as well by bringing the arts to the people in their native tongue.

Ramus's effort to translate the liberal arts into French is a relatively neglected part of his educational reform program, even though his writings speak eloquently of his desire to bring learning to those without Latin, in order to eliminate the long years of study required before the liberal arts themselves could be mastered. In pursuit of this goal, Ramus not only translated or arranged the translation of many of his textbooks, but also worked to make instruction in the University available in French. In addition, his published work in French grammar was largely concerned with enhancing the elegance and dignity of the French language by standardizing orthography and laying down rules of syntax.

The "defence and illustration of the French language," as Du Bellay's famous work labeled the task, was a major concern in the sixteenth century.[50] Already in 1539, Francis I had ordered that French justice be conducted in French, and in every

---

48. Ong, *Ramus, Method and the Decay of Dialogue*, 185–86. Ong finds Ramus's discussion of the syllogism "devoid of any valuable and effective insights" (186), his treatment of induction "due in great part to his own obtuseness" (187), and his logic as a whole "blind...mechanistic...warped..." (188). It is generally safe to say that Ong is not impressed by any aspect of Ramist logic, not only because of his nostalgia for the era when the spoken word, and not the printed word, reigned supreme, but more convincingly because Ramus's reforms were in fact a step backwards in the scientific study and use of logic from the days of the scholastics.

49. The phrase is Hardin Craig's, in *Enchanted Glass*, 143. Ramus's works might best be compared, not to modern college texts. but to popular "how-to" works like the numerous "instant" foreign language courses that claim to teach French, Spanish, or Swahili in minutes a day.

50. The poet Joachim Du Bellay (1522–60), member of the Pléiade and associate of Ronsard and Dorat, published his *Deffence et illustration de la langue françoyse* (1549) as a sort of manifesto of the group. He defended the use of French in poetry and called for the cultivation of the language to bring it up to the dignity of Latin. The *Deffence* became one of the great symbols of the new French literature in the sixteenth century, but it actually offered little that was new or original. It was the technicians of grammar—Meigret and to a lesser extent Ramus—who actually carried out the "illustration" of the language.

field French steadily gained ground against the language of the academy.[51] The process can be studied in the authoritative work of Ferdinand Brunot on the history of the French language.[52] Here our concern is to show what part Ramus played in the general development of French as a learned language, and to see how his contributions to that development served his own educational goals.

Ramus's part in the defense and illustration of French has been a subject of debate among modern scholars, but his contemporaries were convinced that his work was important, whether they approved or not. The dramatist Jodelle, another member of the Pléiade, approved heartily, as is indicated by the verse he contributed to Ramus's 1572 *Grammaire*:

> Les vieux Gaulois avoient tous Arts en leur langage,
> Mais Dis, l'un de leurs dieux (qui riche tient couvers
> Sous les obscures nuits mille thresors divers)
> Aux champs Elysiens retint des Art l'usage.
> Il falloit doncq' avoir, pour la bas penetrer,
> Les rappeler, les faire en l'air Gaullois rentrer,
> Ce Rameau d'or, par eus redorans tout nostre age.[53]

The pun on Ramus's name, which made him a "bough of gold" by taking Ramus, the Latin nom de plume of La Ramée, and retranslating it into French as "rameau," shows Jodelle's delight in wordplay.[54] It also indicates his high regard for Ramus, who had "regilded the age" by returning the use of the arts to his countrymen.[55] The Pléiade sometimes supported and sometimes attacked Ramus, but always recognized his importance in the advancement of the French language.

In order to use French as a learned tongue, its grammar had to be standardized, and this task Ramus proposed to accomplish by employing his universal method as he had already for the Latin and Greek languages.[56] His 1562 *Gramere* was notable for more than that, however. It also represents an early attempt to

---

51. By the edict of Villers-Cotterets, 15 August 1539, articles 110–11.

52. Ferdinand Brunot's *Histoire de la langue française des origines à nos jours,* vol. 2, "Le xvi⁰ siècle" (Paris: Armand Colin, 1967), is unsurpassed, although we will have occasion to dispute some of his contentions with regard to Ramus's work in grammar.

53. Petrus Ramus, *Grammaire de P. de La Ramee, lecteur du Roy en l'Universite de Paris, a la Royne, mere du Roy* (Paris: A. Wechel, 1572), reverse of title page.

54. A seventeenth-century scholar, Guillaume Duval, was to find the problem of switching from French to Latin and back again more difficult. He hazarded the guess that Ramus was the nom de plume of "Pierre de la Verdure"—"Sappy Peter?" Guillaume Duval, *Le College Royal de France, ou Institution, Establissement & Catalogue des Lecteurs & Professeurs Ordinaires du Roy...* (Paris: Chez Mace Bouillette, 1645), 49.

55. Ramus "returned" the arts to the French because, as Jodelle's verse suggests, it was Ramus's belief that the ancient Gauls had not only taught the arts in their own tongue, but even invented them.

56. Ramus's first Latin grammar appeared in 1559 as *P. Rami, regii eloquentiae et philosophiae professoris, Grammaticae libri quatuor, ad Carolum Lotharingum Cardinalem* (Paris: A. Wechel, 1559). It had

create an orthography for French which would be strictly phonetic. By suppressing unpronounced letters and useless signs, as well as creating new characters for each sound in the language, Ramus hoped to institute a one-to-one correspondence between print and sound. The effort was unsuccessful, of course, and it was dropped in later editions of the work. The Wechel firm, as his publishers, may well have found it burdensome to maintain the weird typeface required for such a project.[57]

Aside from the new orthography, the value of Ramus's French grammar has not been rated highly. Ong, relying on Brunot, finds Ramus's work unoriginal and "undistinguished."[58] Indeed Brunot did reach such a conclusion, at least in general. Ramist grammar was derivative even to the point of copying the errors of earlier writers, in particular those of Louis Meigret.[59] Brunot concluded that "it was the method and not the material that preoccupied him," and continued:

> His work is above all a work of application: the author hastily took from others material he had not mastered, at the same time that he borrowed from himself the doctrine [i.e. Ramist method] already established.[60]

---

twenty-one more editions before the end of the sixteenth century, including an English translation published in London in 1585, and Latin editions in Leiden, Frankfurt, Basel, etc. The abbreviated version of the work, *Rudimenta grammaticae* (Paris: A. Wechel, 1559), had a similar publication history. See Ong, *Ramus and Talon Inventory*, 310–30. The Greek grammar was not quite so popular but still had a respectable run—*P. Rami Grammatica Graeca, quantenus a Latina differt* (Paris: A. Wechel, 1560) saw seven sixteenth-century editions, and its summary, *Rudimenta grammaticae graecae* (Paris: A. Wechel, 1560), was printed four times; Ong, *Ramus and Talon Inventory*, 337–46. As Ong points out, the title of the Greek grammar reflects Ramus's observance of the law of justice; "quatenus a Latina differt," or "insofar as it differs from Latin," proclaims Ramus's intention to avoid treating the same subject in more than one of the arts.

57. Petrus Ramus, *Gramere* (Paris: A. Wechel, 1562), had five more editions in standard Latin type by the end of the century. Ramus was not the only one to experiment with a new orthography. Aside from Louis Meigret, mentioned below (n. 59.), the poets of the Pléiade each followed his own spelling. In Fouquelin's Ramist rhetorics of 1555 and 1556, which used examples from their poetry as illustrations, each poet's orthography is followed in his own poems. See Nina Catach, *L'Orthographe française à l'époque de la Renaissance: Auteurs—Imprîmeurs—Ateliers d'imprîmerie* (Geneva: Droz, 1968), 130. On the subject of attempts to reform orthography in France in the sixteenth century, see also Robert E. Bousquet, "The Sixteenth-Century Quest for a Reformed Orthography: The Alphabet of Honoré Rambaud," *Bibliothèque d'Humanisme et Renaissance* 43 (1981): 545–66.

58. Ong, *Ramus and Talon Inventory*, 348.

59. Louis Meigret, *Le Tretté de la grammere françoeze* (Paris, 1550) also attempted a revised orthography, as his title indicates, and recommended the construction "ce suis-je" rather than "c'est moi." Ramus recommends the same, and much of his orthographic reform follows Meigret's. Brunot, *Histoire de la langue française*, 150, includes texts to demonstrate Ramus's dependence on Meigret, and they are entirely convincing.

60. Brunot, *Histoire de la langue française*, discussion of Ramist grammar is on 150–55; quotations from 151, 153.

The grammar on the whole was not very valuable in his eyes, but Brunot does find some worth in Ramus's method. He credits him with being the first to separate etymology from syntax in French, and finds the second edition of the work much improved.[61]

Brunot's verdict on Ramist grammar may have been a bit harsh. Ramus certainly copied from his predecessors. Few in the sixteenth century did not. But he did not follow them slavishly. Nor did he allow his method to impose structure and order where he could find none. Newton Bement pointed out several cases where previous grammarians had attempted to impose rigid paradigms on the language, paradigms copied by Ramus only with explicit reservations. Ramus repeated Meigret's scheme for the second conjugation verbs, for example, only with the qualification that the conjugation is "in almost every verb irregular."[62] Bement in fact constructed a strong defense for Ramist grammar not only on a variety of technical points but in more general terms as well, and concluded that "Ramus must be granted full credit…for being the first to expand French grammar as a science and to attempt to give it that full treatment which Latin grammar had begun to receive."[63]

Whatever the merits of Ramus's grammar may be, it has one major feature which deserves our attention here. Ramus always reserved the last word on the structure of the French language to those who were, in his opinion, the real experts: the speakers and writers of French. In his first edition, he concluded:

> Now up to this point I have declared to you the rudiments of our French language, which (as I hope) will be little by little augmented by the study and diligence of good and learned French minds, which will more and more devote themselves to ornament and enrich their country not only by such teachings, but by *examples and true usage*, which you will suggest to yourselves much more by writing than by all the rules of grammar that one might invent. (emphasis added)[64]

Or in more concise terms, "the people are sovereign lords of their language."[65]

---

61. Brunot, *Histoire de la langue française*, 150, 153–54. One of Ramus's orthographical innovations which has survived was the use of the letters "v" and "j" to represent their respective sounds, instead of following the Latin practice of using "u" and "i". This distinction, introduced in the 1555 *Dialectique*, was carried over into his Latin grammar in 1559. See Catach, *L'Orthographe française*, 131, who says the type for these letters was cut in the summer of 1559.

62. Newton S. Bement, "Petrus Ramus and the Beginnings of Formal French Grammar," *Romanic Review* 19 (1928): 309–23, at 318.

63. Bement, "Petrus Ramus," 315. See also 311: "He may be considered the first of the philosophical grammarians of the French Renaissance." Bement also points out that Ramus's orthography represented "the only such reforms to find favor outside of France"; ibid., 317; cf. 320.

64. Cited in Bement, "Petrus Ramus," 317. Bement calls this "the most significant paragraph produced by any French grammarian in the sixteenth century."

65. Ramus, *Grammaire*, 30.

The idea that grammar should be governed, at least in part, by the people's usage was not one of Ramus's more successful proposals, at least not in France. It is an accurate reflection, however, of the principles which controlled his approach to all of the liberal arts. Practical use was the goal of every art and science; it was the key to mastering every art and science; and it was the source and origin of the art or science itself. For Ramus, grammar, like all the other arts and sciences, was to be derived from, learned through, and employed in practice.

The arts, therefore, were not rightfully the possession of an academic elite which studied them in a vacuum. It was common human experience which determined their content, and they should be tailored to the use of ordinary men. And for that to occur, they had to be made accessible to men of ordinary means and talents, in particular by making them available in French.

In the dedicatory letter to his French grammar of 1572, Ramus addressed the queen mother Catherine and claimed that

> it was because of your persuasion that the king commanded me to pursue the liberal arts not only in Latin, for the learned men of every nation, but also in French for France, where there is an infinity of good minds capable of all the sciences and disciplines, who nonetheless are deprived of them because of the difficulty of the languages. And in truth it is harder for us today to learn Greek or Latin than it ever was for Plato or Aristotle to learn all of philosophy.[66]

Ramus announced a program of vulgarization of the arts and sciences through translation, but its results were noticeably scant. French editions of Ramus's logic and rhetoric had appeared in the mid-1550s, and of course his French grammars were also published in French. In addition, two of Ramus's historical studies, on Caesar's wars and on the ancient Gauls, appeared in French soon after their Latin versions appeared.[67] Otherwise, however, Ramus's learned works in arithmetic, algebra, geometry, and theology remained accessible only to those who could read Latin. Compared with the enormous numbers of editions of his works in Latin, the number of published translations seems almost negligible. How can we reconcile Ramus's avowed interest in using the vulgar language to teach the arts with the paucity of French works he published or supervised?

---

66. Ramus, *Grammaire*, preface. This preface seems to be the appeal addressed to Charles IX and Catherine on Ramus's return from Germany in 1571, when he sought their assistance in regaining his offices and income (see below, chapter 5). His Latin summary of the appeal in a letter to Theodore Zwinger in Basel is nearly identical in wording to the published version of the preface (Ramus to Zwinger, March 1571, in Waddington, *Ramus: Sa vie*, 430–31).

67. Ong lists two French versions of the *Dialectica* made during Ramus's lifetime, one in 1556 and one in 1557, as well as two other French adaptations in the sixteenth century. Antoine Fouquelin's French version of Talon's rhetoric appeared in 1555 and was reprinted in 1557, while Ramus's histories appeared in the vernacular in 1559, 1581, and 1583.

One possible explanation is that Ramus did not adopt his aim of translation until very shortly before his murder, which dramatically ended whatever plans he might have formed. Another and perhaps stronger argument relates to the prospective market for Ramist works in French. André Wechel was a businessman, and if Ramus's 1555 *Dialectique* had sold well, or if its companion volume, the *Rhetorique françoise* of Antoine Fouquelin, had found a market, new editions would certainly have been forthcoming. Even if Wechel had not provided them, someone would have. The point is only emphasized by the prevalence of English editions of the *Dialectica* and *Rhetorica* across the channel. Ong counts five English editions of the *Dialectica* in eight separate issues during the 1500s, with another eleven editions in the seventeenth century.[68] England provided a market for vernacular learning; France did not. The reason why cannot be certainly ascertained, but I would suggest that it has a great deal to do with the relatively open character of English society after 1550, compared to the increasingly rigid French social structure, a point to which we shall return.

Ramus's program of reform can be best seen in its application to the mathematical sciences, a branch of learning to which he turned after being barred from teaching philosophy in 1544. All of the elements of reform: method, practicality, simplicity, and accessibility, were brought to bear by Ramus and his students to make the esoteric discipline of mathematics available to a wide public.

Ramus's career as a mathematician was far more notable for his efforts to publicize the art than for any particular contributions he made to mathematics as a science.[69] He did serve the mathematical scholarship of his time by gathering mathematical manuscripts in the college of Presles and having his students translate them into Latin. Ong describes the college as "a translation factory comparable to the picture factories of the Renaissance painters, assembling both workers and materials."[70] At least one extant letter to the English mathematician and mystic John Dee survives as an example of Ramus's search for mathematical manuscripts in the European world, and several of these manuscripts appeared in print through the labors of Ramus's students.[71]

---

68. Ong, *Ramus and Talon Inventory,* 184.

69. Johannes Jacobus Verdonk, *Petrus Ramus en de Wiskunde* (Assen: Van Gorcum, 1966) is by far the best available study of Ramist mathematics. Unfortunately only a Dutch edition of the work is available. Verdonk argues for Ramus's authorship of several mathematical works not listed by Ong; see the arguments, pro and con, in Sharratt's "The Present State of Studies on Ramus," 205.

70. Walter Ong, "A Ramist Translation of Euripides," *Manuscripta* 8 (1964): 18–28, at 25.

71. Ramus to Dee, January 1565, in *Collectaneae,* 174–75. Ramus had heard that Dee had a copy of Archimedes' *Isoperimetra* and was eager to get a look at it. In Sharratt's account, "his search for more manuscripts was almost as keen as that of the early Renaissance"; Sharratt, "The Present State of Studies on Ramus," 206. Jean Péna, mathematical prodigy and Ramus's pupil, is responsible for editions of Euclid's *Optica et Cataoptrica* and *Rudimenta Musices* with Latin translations, both published in 1557. Ramus could not have played a very great role in this activity, since all the evidence suggests that his Greek was rudimentary at best.

While some have claimed that Ramus's efforts in mathematics did indeed advance the art, it is difficult to credit him with much in the way of original work. His own mathematical work was oversimplified and cursory.[72] Certainly that is the impression conveyed by his textbook of geometry, first published in 1569.[73] As Ong points out,

> it specializes in practical applications—e.g., methods of calculating distances by triangulation, such as one associates with Boy Scout manuals today. Ramus is perhaps at his best in producing this sort of schoolbook.[74]

One of the reasons why Ramus's geometry so resembles a recipe book is that he could not see the practical value of the Euclidean procedure of axiomatizing geometry and proceeding by theorem and proof. Such mistrust of theory was typical of him. Man's own reason can judge the truth or falsehood of a proposition, and the elaborate apparatus of rigorous proof is merely distracting. According to Florian Cajori, in his nineteenth-century history of mathematics, Ramus

> did not favour investigations on the foundations of geometry; he believed that it was not at all desireable to carry everything back to a few axioms; whatever is evident in itself, needs no proof.[75]

Or, as Pierre Duhamel suggests, "one of the more or less explicit assumptions of the

---

72. Among those who believe that Ramus deserves more credit as a mathematician, see Joachim-Otto Fleckenstein, "Petrus Ramus et l'humanisme bâlois," in *La Science,* 119–33. Fleckenstein, 121–22, credits Ramus, among other accomplishments. with the introduction of the term "radius" for a semidiameter, the logical establishment of the rule "minus times minus equals plus," and the "pratique de chiffres-zeros." He also traces Ramus's influence on the Basel mathematician Christian Urstitius, on whom see also Walter Ong, "Christianus Ursitius [*sic* for Urstitius] and Ramus' New Mathematics," *Bibliothèque d'humanisme et renaissance* 36 (1974): 603–10.

73. Petrus Ramus, *P. Rami Arithmeticae libri duo, geometriae septem et viginti* (Basel: Episcopius, 1569). As Peter Bietenholz points out in "Peter Ramus," chap. 8 of *Basle and France in the Sixteenth Century: The Basle Humanists and Printers in Their Contacts with Francophone Culture* (Geneva: Droz, 1971),153–63, Ramus's stay in Basel in 1569 resulted in his seeing several of his mathematical works through the press.

74. Ong, *Ramus and Talon Inventory,* 370.

75. Florian Cajori, *A History of Elementary Mathematics with Hints on Methods of Teaching* (New York: Macmillan, 1897), 276. As old as Cajori's work is, I have found no other discussion of Ramus's geometrical thought that sums it up so neatly. The passage is worth quoting in full: "[Ramus] brought out an edition of Euclid, and here again displayed his bold independence. He did not favour investigations on the foundations of geometry; he believed that it was not at all desirable to carry everything back to a few axioms; whatever is evident in itself, needs no proof. His opinion on mathematical questions carried great weight. His views respecting the basis of geometry controlled French textbooks down to the nineteenth century. In no other civilized country has Euclid been so little respected as in France. A conspicuous example of French opinion on this matter is the text prepared by Alexis Claude Clairaut in 1741. He condemns the profusion of self-evident propositions, saying in his preface, "It is not surprising that Euclid should give himself the trouble…; but in our day things have changed face; all reasoning about what mere good sense decides in advance is now a pure waste of time and fitted only to obscure the truth and to disgust the reader."

Ramist dialectic was the inevitability of the mind's assent to a true proposition, once it was presented to the mind."[76]

A striking example of this typically Ramist approach to knowledge comes from Ramus's comments on astronomy, which he treated as a part of mathematics. Ramus's belief that the arts must be founded on observation and not speculation, and his disdain for useless theory, received its best-known formulation in his correspondence with the German astronomer Joachim Rheticus on the *De Revolutionibus* of Copernicus. Sympathetic to Copernicus on the whole, Ramus nonetheless objected to the fictionalist nature of his heliocentric theory and called for a purely observational astronomy, an "astronomy without hypotheses."[77] He went so far as to promise his chair as royal professor to whoever might create such an astronomy.[78] Johannes Kepler later claimed that his discoveries entitled him to the chair, stating that if what Ramus meant was an astronomy without false and unprovable hypotheses, he had provided one. If, Kepler went on, Ramus meant to reject all hypotheses, then Ramus was stupid. Consulting the honor of both men, Kepler concluded, he would prefer to call himself royal professor than to call Ramus stupid.[79]

Ramus's effort to reform the study of mathematics included an attempt to make the art available to those who had no Latin. Pierre Forcadel, the author of important arithmetic texts in French, became royal lecturer in mathematics thanks to Ramus's support and despite the fact that he knew neither Latin nor Greek. Not only did he lecture in French, causing a scandal among the other royal lecturers, but he taught arithmetic—the most elementary part of mathematics—and he taught it with a special emphasis on its use in business and trade.[80]

---

76. Duhamel, "The Logic and Rhetoric of Peter Ramus," 169.

77. Ramus did not know that the preface to Copernicus's work, describing heliocentricity as mere theory, was added later by Osiander. The text of his letter to Rheticus appears in Marie Delcourt, "Une lettre de Ramus à Joachim Rheticus (1563)," *Bulletin de l'Association Guillaume Budé* 44 (1934): 3–15. Delcourt's article should be read together with Edward Rosen's "The Ramus-Rheticus Correspondence," *Journal of the History of Ideas* 1 (1940): 363–68.

78. Petrus Ramus, *P. Rami Scholarum Mathematicarum, libri unus et triginta* (Basel: Episcopius, 1569), 50: "Ac si quis caducae utilitatis fructus tantae virtutis praemio proponi possit, regiam Lutetiae professionem praemium conformatae absque hypothesibus Astrologiae tibi spondebo; sponsionem hanc equidem lubentissime, vel nostrae professionis cessione, praestabo."

79. Johannes Kepler reprinted Ramus's promise on the reverse of the title page of his *Harmonice Mundi* of 1609, and went on to defend Copernicus against the charge of fabricating a fictional explanation of the world. It is here that Kepler identifies Osiander as the author of the preface to Copernicus's work. See *Johannes Kepler Gesammelte Werke*, ed. Max Caspar (Munich: C.H. Beck, 1937). His claim to the chair appears first in a letter of October 1597, to Michael Mästlin, where he expresses his preference for being called royal professor rather than calling Ramus stupid: "Verum ut utriusque honori consulatur malo me Professorem Regium, quam Ramum stultum appelare," ibid., 141, and again in a letter to the same in January 1598; ibid., 165.

80. On Forcadel in general, see Natalie Zemon Davis, "Sixteenth-Century French Arithmetics on the Business Life," *Journal of the History of Ideas* 21 (1960): 18–48. The scandal caused by Forcadel's teaching in the vulgar tongue is indicated by the reaction of Dorat in his "Decanatus, hoc est in P. Ramum decanatum

While we cannot survey Ramus's treatment of all the arts, enough has been said to make the general character of his reform program clear. It aimed to recast the arts simply, briefly, and accessibly, with an emphasis on their practical use. It was, in essence, an attempt to make learning available to a wide audience, to spread the benefits of education in a society which was more and more bent on restricting them to an elite. One author has even credited Ramus with a "democratic ideal" of learning for France.[81] How successful was he? Pierre-Albert Duhamel claimed that:

> by his translations and use of the vernacular, plus his reduction of the arts
> to a few principles, he made logic readily available to, and employed by, a
> large group of people and filled the world with logic choppers.[82]

For a while, at least, Ramism seemed to be doing just that. As the graph in appendix B indicates, his works were extremely popular in France in the second half of the sixteenth century. With the dawn of the seventeenth century, however, they quickly disappeared from publishers' lists. Their popularity in other parts of Europe lasted a bit longer, but even in Germany they were no longer printed after the 1620s. What had given them their immense popularity and then made them disappear altogether?

Were it not for the evidence of the German presses, it might be possible to argue that Ramism's collapse by 1600 was largely due to Ramus's conversion to Protestantism. How many French Catholics would willingly embrace a system of learning tainted with heresy? But the Protestants dropped him too, as the evidence from abroad shows. A more general explanation of what had happened is required.

One thing that had happened was that the French educational boom of the period from 1530 to 1560 had come to an end. The colleges which had been so eagerly established in the towns and cities of France faced diminishing support after about 1560 for reasons which are not too hard to fathom.[83] Education was no longer the path to wealth and security in a French society which was closing the door on members of the less privileged orders. The spread of oligarchy, nepotism, and venal office, hallmarks of the Old Régime, made the meritocratic ideal of careers open to talent an anachronism, as we saw in the first chapter. The rewards of education diminished, and its attractiveness diminished for that very reason. Ramus's accessible, practical, and simple method for mastering the arts lost the mass market for which it had been created.

Perhaps even more importantly, the new rulers of society openly declared war on education for the masses. In the Renaissance, an educated peasant might become

---

collegii professorum Regiorum sibi vindicantem," in Jean Dorat, *Ioannis Aurati Lemovicis Poetae et Interpretis Regii Poemata* (Paris: Linocier, 1586), Liber 3, 275–91, at 279–80: "Francice docere/De regis solitus (nefas) cathedra, linguarum omnia prisca iura mutans...."

81. The phrase is Dassonville's, in his introduction to the 1555 *Dialectique*, 9.

82. Duhamel, "The Logic and Rhetoric of Peter Ramus," 171.

83. Huppert, *Public Schools*, xv.

a royal professor. In the Old Régime, he was far more likely to remain a peasant, and quite probably a disgruntled one. Pamphleteers in the early seventeenth century were making the point openly. One lamented the presence of numerous colleges in the realm,

> even in the smallest towns of the kingdom, to the great detriment of the state, since by such means, merchants and even peasants find ways of getting their children to abandon trade and farming in favor of the professions.

And another,

> It is the ease of access to this bewildering number of colleges that has enabled the meanest artisans to send their children to these schools, where they are taught, free of charge—and that is what has ruined everything![84]

What such public education threatened was summed up by Cardinal Richelieu in his *Political Testament* of 1642. It was not that the sons of peasants were entering the professions; it was precisely that educated sons of peasants could not become professionals and were therefore the more likely to be subversives:

> A body with eyes all over it would be monstrous, and in like fashion so would a state if all its subjects were learned; one would find little obedience and an excess of pride and presumption....If learning were profaned by extending it to all kinds of people one would see far more men capable of raising doubts than of resolving them, and many would be better able to oppose the truth than to defend it. It is for this reason that statesmen in a well-run country would wish to have as teachers more masters of mechanic arts than of liberal arts.[85]

If, as I have suggested, Ramism was designed to make education accessible and practical, to appeal to the masses, then its success in the mid-1500s and its near disappearance later is not hard to explain. The earlier period saw a market for mass education, since education led to greater wealth and status for anyone. In the later period, it offered no such reward, and besides was actively discouraged. Ramus's effort to democratize the content of education failed because his society no longer wanted educated subjects.

This was not the case everywhere. In England and even more in England's New World colonies, Ramism held on. There Ramism's democratizing potential was recognized from the outset. As Abraham Fraunce wrote, "Coblers be men; why therefore

---

84. Both quotations are from Huppert, *Public Schools*, 116.
85. From *The Political Testament of Cardinal Richelieu*, trans. Henry Bertram Hill (Madison: University of Wisconsin Press, 1961), 14–15.

not Logicians? and Carters have reason, why therefore not Logike?"[86] Nowhere was Ramism preserved longer than in New England, where Massachusetts encompassed the most open and least oligarchic society in the Western world in the seventeenth century. There, at Harvard University, Ramism maintained its ascendancy all the way down to the Enlightenment.[87]

The anonymous Cambridge play "Pilgrimage to Parnassus," performed in 1598, summarizes our answer to the problem of Ramism's appeal. One of the characters tells the audience:

> I have spent this day to my great comfort: I have…analised a peece of an homelie according to Ramus and surelie in my mind and simple opinion Mr. Peter maketh all things verie plaine and easie.

The anonymous author of "Pilgrimage to Parnassus" did not intend to recommend Ramus to his hearers, a point made sufficiently clear by the fact that he puts Ramus's praises into the mouth of the character Stupido. To the playwright, Kepler's choice was the wrong one. But his summary of the character of Ramism is accurate and telling. Ramism was, and was intended to be, "plaine and easie," and its appeal to Europeans, stupid or not, was based mainly on its simplicity. In the words of another Cambridge play of the same vintage,

> For tidy Peter like a pretty primmer
> May well be learned ere thou go to dinner.[88]

That was precisely the source of his appeal, and Stupido was precisely the audience Ramus was looking for. That the Stupidos of France were increasingly barred from education and its rewards under the Old Régime was the result of forces beyond his control. He had attempted to make it available to them with his "plaine and easie" course of study. As we shall now see, he sought to improve access to education by altering its institutions as well as its curriculum, with no more lasting success.

---

86. Cited in Lawrence Stone, "The Educational Revolution in England, 1560–1640," *Past and Present* 28 (July 1964): 80.

87. Miller, *The New England Mind*, abundantly documents the primacy of Ramism at Harvard and among Puritan divines throughout the seventeenth century.

88. Both Cambridge plays are in J. B. Leishman, ed., *The Three Parnassus Plays, 1598–1601* (London: Nicholson & Watson, 1949), and the quotations are on 112. The second quotation is from the play "Tyros Roring Megge."

CHAPTER 3
Professor Regius

RAMUS'S REFORM OF THE STRUCTURE AND CONTENT of the liberal arts turned out to be enormously successful.[1] Ramus applied his method to more and more parts of the curriculum, and the number of Ramist works in print constantly increased. Frenchmen who had been barred from pursuing learning by the length, complexity, and impracticality of the liberal arts, as well as by the length of time required to master Latin, now found a growing number of simple, short guides to the arts available in their native tongue. As time went on, however, Ramus became aware that popularization of the arts themselves was not enough to guarantee that all talented Frenchmen could reap the benefits of an education.

Ramus discovered that the structure of France's educational institutions was frustrating his ideal of social advancement through education. The expense of a University education was one effective barrier to higher learning for most of his countrymen. Perhaps everyone could learn grammar, logic, rhetoric, and the other liberal arts from Ramus's textbooks and apply them to their own lives with profit. But only the well-to-do could attend the University of Paris for professional training, and only a formal university degree certified educational achievement. If social advancement was to be open to all talented Frenchmen, then a university education had to be open to all as well.

But even as Ramus was beginning his campaign to lower the cost of higher education, education was becoming less important as the key to social advancement. French elites were closing ranks against newcomers from the lower orders no matter how well educated they were. Venal office holding was an especially effective means of keeping positions of wealth and status in the hands of a self-perpetuating oligarchy, and as venality spread within elite groups, educational achievement lost its relevance as a qualification for positions of profit, status, and power. Family connections and wealth became far more important.

What was true of France as a whole was true of France's educational institutions as well. Venality of office appeared among the professors of the University of Paris by

1. Ramus was named "Eloquentiae et Philosophiae Professor Regius," "royal professor of eloquence and philosophy," in July of 1551.

the 1560s, and Ramus was its earliest and most outspoken opponent. Faculty appointments, in his view, should be reserved for the most learned, rather than for the sons and sons-in-law of faculty members. His program for the reform of France's institutions of higher education thus became two-pronged. It sought both to make education available to all talented Frenchmen regardless of wealth and position, and to ensure that educational merit and achievement received their proper reward. This chapter traces Ramus's efforts to institutionalize both parts of that program in the University of Paris and among the royal professors.[2]

It was not until the late 1550s that Ramus began his campaign to reform the University, and his first public statements on the subject date from May 1557. They appear almost as an afterthought in a harangue addressed to Henry II and published in French the next month.[3] Ramus had been chosen by the University as part of a delegation sent to plead with the king, who had ordered harsh repressive measures against its students after an outbreak of violence between them and the monks of Saint-Germain-des-Prés. We will return to the quarrel between the monks and the students in the next chapter. What concerns us now is that in the course of pleading with the king, Ramus gave the first indications of his interest in institutional reform.

In the middle of his speech, Ramus suggested that professors at the University be paid not by the students but from public funds. Certain buildings in the Pré-aux-Clercs west of the city had been an object of dispute between the students and the monks, and Ramus recommended that revenue from them be used to pay salaries to faculty members.[4] He did not expressly state that his concern was to lower the cost of an education by shifting the burden of supporting the faculty from the shoulders of the students, but he did show that he was aware of the poor scholars' plight. The king had ordered that students not resident in colleges be expelled from the University, so that the number of unsupervised teenagers in the city would be reduced. Ramus entered a plea on their behalf:

> There is a large number of poor students who cannot afford to pay twenty or thirty écus a year to be shut up [renfermé] in a college, who most of the time survive on the bread they are able to beg.[5]

2. There is more than a little irony in Ramus's stance as the champion of merit against venality and nepotism, since as we have seen he gained his own office as principal of Presles through a financial arrangement with his predecessor and used his office to favor his own relatives.

3. Petrus Ramus, *Harangue de Pierre de la Ramee touchant ce qu'ont faict les deputez de l'Université de Paris envers le Roy: Mise de Latin en François...* (Paris: A. Wechel, 1557).

4. Ramus, *Harangue*, 8v: "Parquoy l'Université requiert, que le revenu de chasque année de ces edifices qui sont tenuz par quelques particuliers, s'emploient aux gages des lecteurs des quatre facultés, de Theologie, de Droict, de Medecine, & des artz liberaux." Ramus repeats his request on 10r.

5. Ramus, *Harangue*, 16v: "Il y a un grand nombre de pauvres escoliers, qui n'ont la puissance de donner vingt ou trente escuz tous les ans pour estre dans un college renfermé, lesquelz la plus part du temps vivent du pain qu'ilz mandient."

Ramus's harangue implicitly suggests that faculty members should be supported not by the students but by some other means, and he soon had an opportunity to make the suggestion explicitly. In the same year, 1557, the king appointed a commission to continue the reform of the University begun under Francis I.[6] Ramus was chosen as a member of that commission, and seems to have been the only member to carry out the task. For whatever reason, the report which finally appeared was the work of Ramus alone. It reveals a great deal about his vision of the University and, by implication, of the proper structure of French society as a whole.

The fruit of Ramus's investigation, the *Advertissements sur la réformation de l'Université de Paris*, appeared in 1562 in both French and Latin editions. In it, Ramus inveighed against the pedagogical practices of the University and the colleges, as might be expected, and presented a brief for his own teaching methods. His main concern, however, was with the cost of a University education, a subject which he took up at the beginning of the work and pursued throughout its first half. His thesis was that "it is a most unworthy thing that the road leading to knowledge of philosophy be closed and forbidden to the poor, even when they are wise and learned...."[7]

Indeed education was an expensive business. Ramus allowed that the student should be responsible for his own food, lodging, clothing, and books, but he was aghast at the other outlays required to be received as a degree candidate. Dinners had to be given to the regents, along with seals, hats, gloves, and a variety of other irrelevant gifts, many of which went to faculty members who played no part in the student's education at all.

As a result, the cost of education was rapidly rising at a time when most Frenchmen saw their incomes falling (although Ramus does not mention, and was probably unaware of, the latter fact). The fees associated with a degree in philosophy, for example, had been set by statute at four écus, or six at the most, but the actual cost to the student had grown to 56 livres 13 sous, about four times the legal amount.

The situation was even worse in the higher faculties. Ramus's itemized account of the expenses incurred revealed that the total cost for two years of study leading to the M.D. approached 900 livres, while a degree in theology commanded the even more

---

6. See the accounts of the commission in César Egasse Du Boulay, *Historia Universitatis Parisiensis*, vol. 6 (1665–73; reprint, Frankfurt: Minerva, 1966), 524–25; Jean Baptiste Louis Crevier, *Histoire de l'Université de Paris depuis son origine jusqu'en l'année 1600*, vol. 6 (Paris: Desaint et Saillant, 1761), 90–96; and Charles Waddington, *Ramus (Pierre de la Ramée): Sa vie, ses écrits et ses opinions* (1855; reprint, Dubuque, Iowa: Brown Reprint Library, n.d.), 141–48. Henry's appointment of the reform commission, dated 28 January 1557, is printed in Du Boulay, *Historia Universitatis*, 6:489.

7. Petrus Ramus, *Advertissements sur la réformation de l'Université de Paris* (Paris: A. Wechel, 1562), reprinted in the nineteenth century in L. Cimber and F. Danjou, *Archives curieuses de l'histoire de France*, vol. 5 (Paris: Beauvais, 1835), 115–63, at 122–23. The work was originally published in Latin as *P. Rami Proœmium Reformandae Parisiensis academiae*; I have used the version in *P. Rami Scholae in Liberales Artes* (Basel: Episcopius, 1569), cols. 1063–102. Citations to the French version are to the edition of Cimber and Danjou.

outrageous price of 1,200 livres![8] The situation in law was not nearly so bad, as the "jurisconsultes" were obliged to follow the *arrêt* of 13 June 1534, limiting fees to a total of 28 écus, but they were as eager as the doctors and theologians to make more.[9]

Ramus spoke from experience as well as conviction, and there is a personal note in his exclamation that such excessive costs are unworthy of the University, as he urges that

> the only legitimate expense that should face the student is to have clothed and fed himself, to have purchased books, and to have passed entire nights in study, to have devoted the better part of his life to letters.[10]

The greed of the teachers was one of the reasons for the rising costs of a University education, but Ramus took his analysis beyond the purely personal level and attempted a kind of institutional analysis of the phenomenon. The problem, as he saw it, was built into the system of higher education itself. Too many students were being received as M.A.'s, and all of them (at least according to Ramus) were teaching. Or at least they claimed to be teaching. Many were "régents honoraires," professors in name only.[11] As Peter Sharratt put it, "In our terms, the staff-student ratio was unacceptable because there were far too many staff."[12] A limited number of students had to support an ever-growing number of idle professors, and thus, Ramus concluded, "this infinity of masters charges the students with infinite costs, with the result that one can hardly believe how honest studies are oppressed."[13]

What was to be done? Ramus conceived a plan which went far beyond the ineffectual royal edicts regulating fees. His idea was to end the system of private payment of professors altogether by putting the University's teachers on royal salary. The king's liberality was famous, and already the royal professors were paid from the royal treasury. Why not extend the practice to University teachers as well? Ramus returned to this theme several times in the course of his report.[14] He also suggested mechanisms for keeping the cost to the royal treasury at a minimum, suggestions which reflect in embryo his later public stands on the royal professors and the Catholic Church.

---

8. Ramus, *Advertissements*, 125–27, for Ramus's calculations of the cost of a medical degree; ibid., 129–30, for the fees levied by the theology faculty. Typically, Ramus's totals do not quite match the actual sum of expenses, but the errors are not of sufficient magnitude to affect his general point.

9. Ramus, *Advertissements*, 123–24. The suggestion that the lawyers are also hiking up their fees despite the edict appears on ibid., 127.

10. Ramus, *Advertissements*, 123.

11. Ramus, *Advertissements*, 119, 122.

12. Peter Sharratt, "Peter Ramus and the Reform of the University: The Divorce of Philosophy and Eloquence?" in Peter Sharratt, ed., *French Renaissance Studies 1540–70: Humanism and the Encyclopedia* (Edinburgh: Edinburgh University Press, 1976), 4–20, at 12.

13. Ramus, *Advertissements*, 120.

14. E.g., Ramus, *Advertissements*, 123, 128, 135, etc.

Ramus reminded the king that in ancient times, under the statutes of the University laid down by Charlemagne, the rule was that the various colleges did not support their own lecturers in each of the arts, but instead sent their students to public lectures on the rue du Fouarre. He claimed that the University should return to this practice, which would provide superior teaching at a reduced cost. The modern method, which required each college to maintain four philosophy teachers, meant that the students had to support twelve times as many professors as under the old system. Not only did this create added expense, but it also inevitably led to a less skilled teaching staff. If large public lectures were resumed, eight teachers could do the job of one hundred current ones, and those eight could be chosen from among the cream of the crop.[15]

How to choose the public professors? Ramus only hinted at the method he endorsed, but it was a hint confirmed in his later attempts to reform the selection of royal professors. Competitive examinations of applicants for teaching posts should be instituted. Conducted publicly, these would demonstrate which of the candidates was most qualified for the job and ensure that the University's staff was the very best.[16]

The king was less likely to be concerned with precisely how University professors were chosen, however, than with the problem of how they were to be paid. The royal treasury was poor enough as it was—even the royal professors frequently missed their wages—and the last thing any French king wanted was to multiply permanent charges against it. Ramus, however, anticipated this difficulty. "So many monasteries and colleges of canons in your city of Paris would count themselves lucky and greatly honored to take on this expense," he proclaimed, that the salaries of the public professors need not become a royal charge. Even now there were two unfilled prebendaries at Notre Dame that could support such a scheme.[17] The idea that the clergy of Paris would willingly forfeit a portion of their wealth for such a purpose was of course disingenuous at best, and subversive at worst. It is a mark of Ramus's changing attitudes toward the Catholic clergy and the Catholic Church in general that he should suggest such use of church property. As we shall see later, the year the *Advertissements* was published, 1562, was the crucial one in Ramus's decision to abandon the Catholic faith.

Ramus anticipated other objections to his proposed scheme of reform as well, notably the difficulty of controlling the large audience of adolescent boys which

15. Ramus, *Advertissements*, 133–35.

16. In Ramus, *Advertissements*, 123–24, Ramus notes with approval that the edict of June 1534 required the legal faculty to choose six "lecteurs ordinaires" by this method. These professors were not however to have the freedom later vouchsafed to the royal professors to design their own courses; "books, hours, lessons and disputes, all that is regulated."

17. Ramus, *Advertissements*, 123, for Ramus's suggestion that the monks and canons would vie for the honor of paying teachers' salaries; ibid., 132, for the specific suggestion to use revenues from Notre Dame.

would attend such public lectures.[18] His major concern for the remainder of the report, however, was not with the cost of education, but with the proper method of providing one in the lecture hall and classroom. Here he reiterated the points which his earlier works had already made: an end to barren disputations, abandonment of scholastic authors in favor of the ancient sources of knowledge themselves, emphasis on the practical use of lessons, and of course the institution of Ramist principles in the organization of the liberal arts.

Ramus was to press for such reforms from the publication of the *Advertissements* until his death a decade later. The institution with which he became most concerned was not, however, the University of Paris, but a more elite academic group, the royal professors. Ramus's career as a royal professor deserves detailed consideration, as it forms the setting for his most dramatic protest against changes in French society and institutions.

Ramus was named royal professor of philosophy and eloquence in July of 1551 and delivered his first lecture in that distinguished capacity a month later. More than 2,000 people came to hear his address, and the lecture hall was so packed that several of them nearly suffocated and had to be carried out. The combination of the size of the crowd and the heat of Paris in August was so overpowering that Ramus himself nearly fainted.[19]

Such at least is the way Ramus told the story. He was not the sort of man who hesitated to exaggerate his own popularity, and he may well have inflated the number of his auditors and the drama of the scene. Still, his inaugural address was probably well attended. He was after all one of the best orators of the age, and beyond that he was a great showman, shouting and waving and contorting his face to keep his audience interested. He played to the crowd shamelessly, to the extent that many of his colleagues thought him positively undignified. Adrien Turnèbe called him a mere clown. Whatever his fellow professors thought, his students loved it. Ramus knew how to harangue a crowd, especially a not very sophisticated one.

18. Discipline was a very real concern for the University and the king. The dangers involved in assembling large numbers of teenagers in one place were real and clearly perceived, and the Pré-aux-Clercs riot of 1557 was only one of numerous examples of the potential for violence. Ramus claimed that discipline could be maintained in the large public lectures he envisioned. Public lectures had been the rule for 750 years without major problems, and if the University returned to the path of virtue the students would too. In any case, Ramus added, if the practice of some virtue opens the way to vice, the solution is not to abandon the virtue but to correct the vice; Ramus, *Advertissements*, 136.

19. "Petri Rami eloquentiae & philosophiae professoris Regii, Oratio," in *Collectaneae praefationes, epistolae, orationes*...(Marburg: 1609), 323–42, at 323; Nicolaus Nancelius, "*Petri Rami Vita*: Edited with an English Translation," *Humanistica Lovaniensia: Journal of Neo-Latin Studies* 24 (1975): 190: "Dies habendae orationi publice indicitur. Fit concursus Academiae totius ad oratorem longe disertissimum audiendum; tota Curia, totus Clerus eodem effunditur; locus licet amplissimus aulae Cameracensis, capiendo non est. Multi abeunt minime audito eo, quem audire percupiebant; nonnulli prae turba prope exanimes efferuntur; denique (ut ipse scribit in prooemio orationis eodem die habitae) duo millia audientium non audivere."

If Ramus's oratorical skills attracted many people to his lecture, his reputation as a troublemaker probably drew even more listeners. Few could challenge his talent for invective, and he had plenty of scores to settle. Ramus had been at loggerheads with the University ever since the edict of 1543 had barred him from teaching or publishing his philosophical ideas, and he had earned more enemies in the interim through his writings on rhetoric. His most recent dispute had been a shrill and vituperative quarrel with the royal professor Pierre Galland over the relative merits of Cicero and Quintilian, and their "Petromachie" was notorious all over France as the subject of a poem by Joachim du Bellay and of a satirical fable by Rabelais.[20] Even abroad Ramus's enemies dreaded his venomous pen.[21] If he was a foe to be reckoned with even when his pen was shackled and his position modest, what might his adversaries have to fear now that he held one of the most prestigious academic positions in France? The wheel of fortune had turned, and the academic brawler who had been condemned by the University and the Parlement of Paris, by the king of France, and by most of the scholars of Europe could now take his revenge with impunity and with authority few of them could ever hope to match. His inaugural lecture promised to be an entertaining spectacle.

If the crowd that came to hear Ramus speak was expecting him to rant and rave and make his enemies look like fools, his address must have been a disappointment to them. There were harsh words for those who had attacked him in the past, but Ramus named no names, and for the most part the tone of his lecture was dignified rather than combative. He was less interested in revenge than in promoting his educational reforms, and most of his speech either defended the changes he had already proposed in logic and rhetoric, or outlined his ideas on reforming the other liberal arts.

20. Joachim du Bellay, "Satyre de Maistre Pierre du Cuignet sur la petromachie de l'Université de Paris," in *Oeuvres poétiques*, vol. 2, "Recueils lyriques," ed. Henri Chamard (Paris: Librairie Hachette, 1923), 236–51; and François Rabelais, "Prologue de l'Auteur," in *Le Quart Livre...*, in *Oeuvres complètes*, vol. 2 (Paris: Éditions Garnier Frères, 1962), 11–29. Rabelais was apparently inspired to mock the squabbling professors by a comment in one of Galland's diatribes against Ramus: "Melior pars eorum qui hasce tuas nugae lectitant, Rame (ne hinc tibi nimium placeas), non ad fructum aliquem ex iis capiendum, sed veluti vernaculos ridiculi Pantagruelis libros ad lusum & animi oblectationem lectitant"; Pierre Galland, *P. Gallandi literarum latinarum professoris Regii, contra novam academiam Petri Rami oratio: Ad illustrissimum Cardinalem & Principem Carolum a Lotharingia* (Paris: Vascosan, 1551), fol. 9v.

21. A letter from Roger Ascham to Johannes Sturm in 1552 suggests how little European scholars outside of France relished a quarrel with Ramus. Ascham had heard that someone was spreading the rumor that he had attacked Ramus, and he was afraid that Ramus would respond by annihilating him in print. He begged to hide from the expected onslaught behind Sturm's shield, and in a curious mixture of timorousness and bravado pleaded with Sturm to crush the insolent upstart while denying that he felt anything but the deepest respect for the French logician: "Quid ergo impedit quo minus ego tanquam Teucer clypeo tectus Sturmiano, aut arceam aut contemnam ictus istos Rami? Potes in Nidrusiano tuo sermone, apto aliquo loco, vel tribus verbis, et illius refutare insolentiam et meum purgare consilium, quum ego non eo animo quicquam scripsi, ut publice convellerem Ramo." Ascham to Sturm, 29 January 1552, in J. A. Giles, ed., *The Whole Works of Roger Ascham...* (1864; reprint, New York: AMS Press, 1965), 318–22, at 320.

To begin with, however, he neither attacked his foes nor advertised his own program, but instead expressed his gratitude to the men who had put him into the august chair from which he spoke: Henry II, king of France, and Charles of Guise, cardinal of Lorraine, Ramus's old schoolmate.

Without for a moment doubting that the honor of a royal professorship was one he richly deserved, Ramus did recognize his debt to the two men to whom he owed his just desserts. In typical humanist fashion, he thanked them effusively and praised them lavishly. The first place for gratitude went naturally to the king. He was a "Gallic Hercules" who had unchained Ramus from the restrictions placed upon him in 1543 and who now, in his magnificent kindness, honored him with a royal professorship as well. To say merely that Ramus owed his life to Henry would have been base ingratitude. He owed him his very soul, and he promised to remember the debt for as long as he lived. [22]

Henry's name did appear on the order which freed Ramus from the ban of 1544 as well as on the decision to create a royal chair for him, but few of those attending the lecture could have been naïve enough to believe that either edict had been Henry's idea. The king was the tool of his advisers, and no one had him so firmly in hand as Charles of Guise, cardinal of Lorraine. Lorraine's influence over Henry may not have been the best thing for France during this critical period in her history, but for Ramus a more fortunate situation could hardly have been imagined. For years the cardinal had been his leading supporter, and since Henry had succeeded Francis I on the throne, the support and comfort Lorraine could offer had grown immensely. He had seen to it that his protégé was released from the ban on teaching and publishing, and he had exerted his influence to save Ramus when the University hauled him into court in 1550 for violating teaching regulations and corrupting his students. Now he had not only convinced Henry to make Ramus a royal professor, but even caused a new royal chair to be created for him.

Ramus did not forget to thank Lorraine in his inaugural address; only after he had thanked the king, of course, but then at considerably greater length. Henry may have been a French Hercules, but Lorraine claimed descent from a hero more dear to the French: Charlemagne himself. Ramus reminded his audience of the connection between his patron and the greatest of French kings by portraying the cardinal as Charlemagne reborn. Just as Charlemagne had founded the University of Paris (at least as far as the sixteenth century was concerned), his descendant had as much as founded it all over again by bestowing on it an "enormous and truly infinite benefit"

---

22. "Petri Rami...Oratio," 324: "Interea misero Rex Henricus, Hercules videlicet Gallicus, adfuit, meque quarto ab hinc anno ad postulationem Caroli Lotharingi Cardinalis, & manibus & lingua solvit....Quapropter, Henrice Rex Christianissime, si tibi vitam, quae hoc corpore continetur, debere me dicam, quod liberas, quod alis, quod ornas, parum dicam. animi, qui corpore longe charior est, animi (inquam) vitam potius debeam, cujus labores ac vigiliae beneficiis tuis aluntur & vivunt...."

for which future generations would venerate his name. He had renewed the arts and letters and returned the University to its pristine practices and goals, and he had done it by a single and simple action. He had given it Ramus.[23]

As it turned out, Lorraine's reputation among future generations did not benefit a great deal from his concern for Ramus, but it was not because Ramus did less than his best for his distinguished patron. He went out of his way to advertise Lorraine's virtues both before and after his appointment as royal professor, in orations, prefaces, and dedications to his numerous published works. Between 1550 and 1560, no fewer than seventeen books by Ramus carried dedications to Lorraine, praising him as a protector of the arts and letters and thanking him repeatedly for his "singular grace" in raising Ramus to the loftier and more distinguished chair he now held. Again and again he promised Lorraine that "as many ages of men as there will be ages of learning will speak of Charles, cardinal of Lorraine, the unparalleled patron of letters."[24]

Ramus did all that he could for his patron's reputation, and his gratitude to Lorraine was probably sincere. It was beyond all doubt appropriate. Appointment to a royal chair was the highest academic honor in France, and one of the most prestigious in Europe, just as an appointment to the Collège de France is today. In some ways, the royal chairs of the sixteenth century were even more prized, since unlike the modern Collège de France they were open to qualified candidates from all over Christendom, not from France alone.

Such at least had been the intention when the chairs were established. Francis I appointed the first royal professors in 1530 to provide free public instruction in Greek and Hebrew in his capital city. The appointments were a triumph for French humanism in general and for Guillaume Budé in particular. Budé had been after the king ever since his coronation to create a humanist college in Paris, and while Francis's actions fell short of Budé's hopes, they were a substantial step in the right direction. Four lecturers—Pierre Danès and Jacques Toussaint in Greek and François Vatable and Agathias Guidacerius in Hebrew—began their courses in

23. "Petri Rami...Oratio," 329: "[The University of Paris] non solum te Cardinalibus illis antiquis, Simoni, Aegidio, Joanni, Gulielmo legislatoribus nostris comparabit, sed in Carolo Lotharingo Carolum Magnum conditorem suum divinitus sibi redditum judicabit...."

24. Ramus, "[Praefatio] Octava, Rami pro C. Rabiro (1551)," in *Collectaneae*, 101: "Jam vero ex ampliore atque altiore suggesto, tua singulari gratia nobis instituto..."; idem, "Nona, Rami in Agrarias (1552)," in *Collectaneae*, 102–7, at 106: "Loquentur, Mecoenas, aetates hominum tam multae (quam multa disciplina seculae futura sint) Carolum Lotharingium Cardinalem, literarum patronum singularem fuisse...." Ramus's most fulsome praise of the cardinal is perhaps in his 1546 preface to the "Dream of Scipio"; *Collectaneae*, 113–15, where for example he asks: "Enimvero tam popularis illa tua & facies, & oratio, tam magnificus animus, tam aperta omnibus ad gratificandum beneficentia, nonne admirabiles illas in te laudes apertissime demonstrant?" (113). This, of course, was even before Lorraine had procured him the royal chair.

March of 1530 and became overnight celebrities. Students flocked to them, and it even became a fad for members of the court to attend a few lectures.[25]

The professorships were a publicity bonanza for the king as well, as humanists all over Europe praised the new foundation and the wise, generous, and powerful monarch who had brought it into being. Francis knew a public relations coup when he saw one. He wasted little time in extending the program with chairs in mathematics (1531) and Latin eloquence (1534) as well, and more chairs followed until by midcentury there were ten royal professors altogether.

Francis could well afford to create as many royal chairs as he wished, since he gave little thought to the problem of how they were to be paid. Nor did he trouble to build them a college, despite his often-repeated assurances. It was not until 1610 that the royal professors had a home of their own.[26] The financial support of the crown was not the main thing Budé had been after, however. More important was Francis's open allegiance to the humanist program, the clear endorsement that the creation of the royal chairs implied. Henceforth in the battles between humanist scholars and the University of Paris, the University would have to step carefully. Its opponents were very often favorites of the king.

The first royal professors were the forerunners of the Royal College and the later Collège de France, but neither of these two bodies existed in the 1500s. Just as they had no building of their own, the royal professors were without a legal corporate identity or defined institutional structure. Throughout the sixteenth century, each

25. The best available guide to the history of the Royal College is Abel Lefranc, whose works on the subject provide the basis of the following discussion. See especially his *Histoire du Collège de France: Depuis ses origines jusqu'a la fin la du premier empire.* (1893; reprint, Geneva: Slatkine, 1970). On the foundations of the Royal College, idem, "La Fondation et les commencements du Collège de France (1530–1542)," in *Le Collège de France (1530–1930): Livre jubilaire composé à l'occasion de son quatrième centenaire* (Paris: Presses Universitaires de France, 1932), 27–58, should now be supplemented by the collection *Les Origines du Collège de France (1500–1560),* ed. Marc Fumaroli (Paris: Collège de France/ Klincksieck, 1998). Less reliable but with detailed accounts of individual professors is Claude-Pierre Goujet, *Mémoire historique et littéraire sur le Collège Royal de France* (1758; reprint, Geneva: Slatkine, 1971). Serious students of the Royal College should also consult Guillaume Duval, *Le College Royal de France, ou Institution, Establissement & Catalogue des Lecteurs & Professeurs Ordinaires du Roy…* (Paris: Chez Mace Bouillette, 1645), whose accuracy can be suggested by the fact that he identifies Ramus as "Pierre de la Verdure" (49). In the eighteenth century, the antiquarian Martin Billet du Fanière collected a considerable body of notes to assist him in writing his own history of the Royal College, which are preserved in the Bibliothèque Nationale, MS. français 24526, "Extraits de l'histoire du College de France de Guillaume Duval (Paris, 1644?, in 4) et notes pour l'histoire de cet établissement que Fanière se proposait d'écrire." His own notes are on 61r–216 of the manuscript. He also left "Notes pour servir à la redaction d'un dictionnaire biographique" in B.N., MS. fr. 24510, "I. Akakia–Guyon," and MS. fr. 24511, "II. Hallé–Vignal." Du Fanière's information is if anything less reliable than Duval's.

26. Ramus was one of many to urge the king to build the royal professors their own college. See Petrus Ramus, *Grammaire de P. de La Ramee, lecteur du Roy en l'Université de Paris, a la Royne, mere du Roy* (Paris: A. Wechel, 1572), where he urges Catherine to convince her son that he could not create "ung trophee plus Royal, ny plus magnifique, ny de plus longue duree, que cestuy la."

royal professor was, in legal terms, an independent officer of the crown, appointed at the king's pleasure and answerable to him alone. The independence of the professors, the lack of rules governing their selection and duties, is of enormous importance for understanding their initial success as well as their later decline.

From the very foundation of the professorships in 1530, candidates were selected by the king on the basis of recommendations by those closest to him. Guillaume Budé, whose decade of lobbying had convinced Francis to establish the offices in the first place, was directly responsible for the appointments of the Latinist Barthelemy Latomus and the Greek scholar Jacques Toussaint to royal chairs, while Marguerite de Navarre gained a royal chair as well as an abbey near Rouen for her client, the Hebraicist François Vatable, and was responsible for the appointment of the third royal professor of Hebrew, Paul Paradis, as well.

This method of staffing the new chairs produced a highly skilled and justly acclaimed group of scholars. On the face of it, the royal professorships were just the sort of sinecures which might have been employed to reward faithful service, without particular attention being paid to the character or qualifications of the candidates. Powerful figures at court needed as many such sinecures as they could get to maintain the numerous clients who were the measure of their honor and power. For various reasons the professorships did not become the preserve of marginally qualified place-seekers, however, at least in the first twenty or thirty years of their existence.

The most obvious reason for the high caliber of the royal professors in the first decades of their existence is the conscientiousness and commitment of the leading patrons of the age. Guillaume Budé and Marguerite de Navarre were themselves dedicated to the same humanist goals as the royal chairs were meant to promote, and in scholarly and literary achievement they were in the front rank of sixteenth-century French letters.

Even patrons less committed to the humanist goals of the royal chairs found themselves constrained in their choice of nominees. For one thing, while the royal professors had considerable latitude in choosing the manner and matter of their lectures, they could not entirely escape the demands of their profession. It might have been possible for a nonspecialist to bluff his way through a course in Latin eloquence, but the more specialized and esoteric chairs created in 1530 did not leave much leeway for bluff. Mathematics, Greek, and Hebrew demanded application and understanding far beyond what the standard liberal education of the day supplied. Most unqualified clients would have shied away from the demands of such a position, which could only lead to humiliation if they attempted to fill their duties or to dismissal if they neglected them.

Another and probably more important reason why patrons generally chose talented scholars for the royal chairs in the early years of their existence stems from the nature of literary patronage itself. The great patrons of Renaissance humanism did not support scholars because the scholars brought them wealth or political influence or military aid. They were more interested in the less tangible benefits to be derived from a grateful writer: reputation, honor, and a certain measure of immortality. Humanists were not so fulsome in their praise of their patrons because they were sycophants by nature, but because fulsome praise was their half of a clearly understood literary bargain. The writer used all the means at his command to spread the word of his patron's merits and achievements, and in return he expected (even if he did not always get) financial support and preferment. The patron looked after his client's fortune, while the author looked after his benefactor's fame.

Naturally, the greater the fame of the humanist, the greater the publicity for his patron. There would be little point in patronizing the incompetent or mediocre writer, whose efforts might do his patron's reputation more harm than good. The greatest men and women in society sought the greatest and most talented pens as their creatures, just as they sought the finest brush among the painters and the finest chisel among the sculptors. The best scholars found the best patrons, or vice versa, by a sort of natural selection. Among the humanists, the fittest ended up with the most prestigious and lucrative positions, even perhaps appointments as royal professors.

Over the course of the sixteenth century, both the method of choosing the royal professors and the scholarly merit of the successful candidates changed dramatically. The patron-client system, for all its flaws and disadvantages, tended to reward merit among humanists whether it was intended to or not. If its methods were dubious, its results were excellent. After the middle of the century, however, the practice of selecting new professors on the basis of their place in the clientage system increasingly gave way to a system which paid almost no attention to merit, even accidentally. From 1560 on, the royal chairs became, like positions in the Parlement of Paris, a form of property which the holder could dispose of as he wished, by gift, legacy, or sale. Not surprisingly, the quality of the royal professors declined as more and more of them came to their posts by transfer, inheritance, or purchase.[27]

The locus classicus for the deterioration of the quality of royal professors in the last third of the 1500s is a passage in Estienne Pasquier's *Recherches de la France*.... It is worth quoting at length, since it provides a neat and eloquent summary of the argument which follows. Pasquier describes Ramus's unsuccessful attempt to keep Jacques Charpentier from holding a royal chair for which he was not qualified, and went on to write:

> And since then, since we are in a kingdom of precedents, what occurred by connivance in the person of Charpentier for his merits, opened the door to others, in such a manner that we have seen a Royal Professor resign his place in favor of his son-in-law, and a very young child being given the chair of his late father, to honor his memory, as if it were a patrimony and

27. See now the important article by Jean-Eudes Girot, "La Notion de lecteur royal: Le Cas de René Guillon (1500–1570)," in *Les Origines du Collège*, 43–108, for a careful study of the transmission of the royal chairs.

hereditary. Not that I do not consider them to have been and to be capable and sufficient in the profession they exercised and exercise; but the method cannot please me, fearing that with time these chairs might fall into disrespect. I see the learned Cardinal du Perron putting everything into the effort to build the College I have been speaking of above. God grant that hereafter it not be a body without a soul, and a magnificent college of stones, in place of that which King Francis originally built of men.[28]

Pasquier's fears were justified by the event. As the sixteenth century drew to a close, the royal professors entered on what their modern historian refers to as "a period of effacement and decadence" which lasted down to the French Revolution. Abel Lefranc attributed their problems to the very cause Pasquier had identified, namely, defective recruitment of the royal professors through sale or inheritance of the royal chairs.[29]

An analysis of the royal professors appointed between 1530 and 1610 shows that the problem began well before the seventeenth century. The extraordinary methods of recruitment which Pasquier and Lefranc lamented began to appear by the 1560s, as the royal professors followed the broader trend toward oligarchy. Not surprisingly, Ramus was the first to challenge the new practices in propaganda, appeals to the king, and lawsuits. His attempts to preserve a more meritocratic selection process form a case study in resistance to the rising tide of oligarchy in France in the second half of the century, and add another piece to the puzzle of the meaning of Ramus's life and works.

From the foundation of the royal chairs to the accession of Louis XIII in 1610, eighty-two royal professors were named, a rate of about one each year.[30] Along with the chairs in Hebrew, Greek, mathematics, and Latin eloquence, chairs were established in medicine (1547), in Greek and Latin philosophy (also in 1547), and in Arabic (1586). In addition, two chairs were created especially for individual scholars and were abolished at the end of their tenure; the chair in oriental languages held by

28. Estienne Pasquier, *Les Recherches de la France...* (Paris: Laurens Sonnius, 1621), 839: "Dieu veuille que par cy apres ce ne soit un corps sans ame, & un magnifique College de pierres, au lieu de celuy qui fut premierement basty en hommes par le Roy François."

29. Abel Lefranc, *Histoire du Collège de France*, 237. Elsewhere Lefranc discusses the great disparities in wages as one reason for the decline of the royal professors' prestige, and goes on to say: "The recruitment of professors also left a great deal to be desired. Chairs were sold and ceded to individuals who were not worthy to occupy them, without the royal government doing anything about these irregular choices. Certain courses were indefinitely suspended or taught in such an inadequate manner that little by little the establishment's former prestige was seriously tainted" (243).

30. See the list of royal professors in the appendix to this work, and also Abel Lefranc, "Liste des lecteurs et professeurs du Collège de France," in *Le Collège de France*, 15–23, which supersedes the list provided in his *Histoire du Collège de France*, appendix T, 377–82. Useful bibliography on several of the royal professors is to be found in Simone Guenée, *Bibliographie de l'histoire des universités françaises des origines à la Révolution*, vol.1, "Généralités: Université de Paris" (Paris: A. & J. Picard, 1981).

Guillaume Postel from 1538 to 1543, and the chair in Latin eloquence and philosophy created for Ramus in 1551.

Biographical data on the holders of the royal chairs is often sketchy and occasionally entirely absent. A few are the subject of full-length scholarly biographies, while fifty of them appear in standard biographical dictionaries. For the rest, little information is available outside of the histories by Duval, Goujet, and most importantly Lefranc, but even Lefranc is often unable to supply more than a name and a date of appointment for the less well known incumbents. In two cases, it is not even possible to be certain that the individuals named as royal professors ever really held a royal chair.[31]

Despite the sketchy evidence, it is possible to show that Pasquier's fears were justified, and that new methods of recruitment in the later sixteenth century did indeed lead to a deterioration in the quality of appointees to royal chairs. We will first investigate how recruitment changed, and then turn to the effects of this change on the overall character of the royal professorships.

In the early part of the century, as has already been noted, royal professors were appointed by the king on the basis of recommendations from his advisors, but no formal mechanism for selecting them existed. This situation prevailed through the 1550s, a decade which is generally considered the peak of prestige and scholarly merit among the royal professors. Soon thereafter, however, sale and inheritance of offices came to be the norm. We can trace several "dynasties" of royal professors which arose in the 1550s and 1560s, within which royal chairs became family possessions, handed down through the generations from father to son or to son-in-law. Thus Leger Duchesne turned his chair in Latin eloquence over to Frederic Morel, who had married his daughter Isabel. Martin Akakia awarded his chair in medicine to Pierre Seguin, husband of his daughter Anne, and Pierre saw to it that Akakia's son Martin II held the chair after him. Simon Piètre, another medical professor, also handed his chair on to his son-in-law. Louis Duret simply passed his medical chair on to his son Jean, while also arranging the marriage of his daughter Catherine to the royal professor of Arabic, Arnoul de l'Îsle.

While the royal professors of medicine provide the most examples of nepotism in the 1500s, the most successful dynasty was established by the Greek professor Jean Dorat. The table below illustrates how his royal chair was passed on from generation to generation of his descendants, and suggests how the royal professors, like

---

31. Among the standard compilations consulted for this study, the most useful have been the new *Dictionnaire de biographie française* (Paris: Letouzey, 1933–); Didot's *Biographie universelle* (Paris: C. Desplaces, 1854–65); the *Dictionary of National Biography* (London: Oxford University Press, 1950); the *Dictionary of Scientific Biography* (New York: Scribner, 1970–80); Belgium's *Biographie Nationale* (Brussels: Émile Bruylant /Académie royale des sciences, des lettres et des beaux-arts, 1957–); and the *Dizionario biografico degli Italiani* (Rome: Istituto della Enciclopedia Italiana, 1960–).

the peasant "kulaks" described by Le Roy Ladurie, "married, supported, advanced and underwrote each other."

TABLE 2: DESCENDANTS OF JEAN DORAT

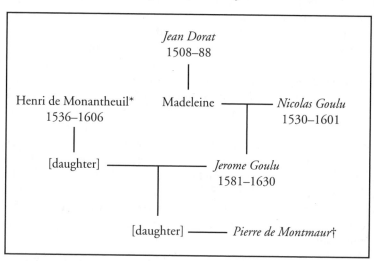

(Royal professors of Greek appear in *italics*)
* Royal professor of mathematics
† Obtained the chair by promising to marry Jerome's daughter, but reneged

Inheritance was only one of the methods by which the royal chairs were kept within a closed circle of privileged incumbents. Outright sale of the professorships also occurred in the last third of the century. The most notorious example is that of the sale of the chair in mathematics held briefly by Dampestre Cosel to Ramus's old enemy Jacques Charpentier, which we will deal with in detail later. But Jacques Hélias, royal professor of Greek from 1572 to 1590, also sought to profit from his retirement by resigning his chair to one Claude Collin, principal of the college of Ste.-Barbe. In a *placet* addressed to the duc de Mayenne in October of 1590, he sought permission to make the transfer without disclosing the considerations offered by Collin in return. Mayenne granted the request, but to no avail, as his decisions regarding the royal professorships were voided when he was forced to yield Paris to the king.[32]

32. Henri Drouot, "Documents sur Dorat et Hélias," *Revue du XVIe siècle* 17 (1930): 126–27.

What is most striking about Hélias's request is that it clearly reveals how the royal professorships had become just one more royal office, subject to the same terms of transfer as a seat in the Parlement or any other venal office. Hélias explicitly requests "dispanse de quarante jours et mesmes de pourveoir par mort," rules of succession promulgated by the crown to raise revenues from venal officeholders and now extended to the royal professorships as well.[33] The implication of Hélias's request is that if the royal chairs were subject to the same rules as other royal offices, they enjoyed the same privileges as well, especially those that permitted their holders to dispose of them as private possessions. Altogether at least sixteen out of the fifty royal professors appointed between 1560 and 1610, nearly one-third, were definitely involved in transfers of royal chairs by inheritance or by sale, and the scarcity of evidence suggests that the number could well be much higher.

The spread of venal office holding among the royal professors was part of a widespread development in sixteenth-century France, one which saw the crown increasingly willing to sacrifice its control over royal officers to the need for cash. Henry III in particular sought to enrich his treasury by selling positions of authority, prestige, and profit, and to attract buyers went so far as to prepare an edict in 1586 which would have guaranteed that all such offices would be hereditary. The edict was never published, but the trend was clear. As the most careful study of venality in the Old Régime concluded,

> It was infeudation of offices pure and simple, the creation of a feudalism of officers, the ruin of royal authority; the risk, also, of increasing the anger of those who could not achieve office and who saw more and more the upper classes of society close themselves off.[34]

That anger appeared as early as 1560, when the Third Estate opposed the First and Second in the Estates General with its demand that venal office holding be abolished along with all new offices created since the reign of Louis XII. The Third repeated its demands at Blois in 1576 and in the Estates General of 1588 as well, at which time Henry III agreed to forbid venality.[35] But for all their protests and Henry's capitulation, the sale and transfer of venal offices continued to sap the authority of the king and to play their part in making it harder and harder to break into the upper ranks of the social order.

While the royal professors were trying to keep their chairs in the family, they were also attempting to keep them in the hands of Frenchmen. Francis I had hoped

---

33. On the forty-day rule and other restrictions on the transfer of venal office established by the crown in the 1500s, see Mousnier, "Les Temps modernes: Le xvie Siècle," chap. 2, *La Vénalité*, 20–71, The forty-day clause itself is described on 28–30.

34. Mousnier, "Les Temps modernes," 36.

35. Mousnier, "Les Temps modernes," 66–68.

that all European scholars would be able to compete on an equal footing for the chairs, and only half of the appointments made in the decade of the 1530s went to native Frenchmen. By the 1540s, that number had risen to 70 percent, and by 1560, 90 percent of the newly appointed professors were Frenchmen, a situation which was to continue through the 1570s and 1580s. Contemporaries were aware of this trend and of its possibly pernicious effects, and the royal professor of mathematics Henri de Monantheuil sought to reverse it with some small success.[36]

In the latter decade another trend became apparent, as geographical preferences were narrowed even further. It was important to be a native Frenchman, but even better to be a Parisian born and bred. Between 1530 and 1580, only three native Parisians had been appointed, one each in the 1530s, 1560s, and 1570s, and none at all in the 1540s or 1550s. Their numbers rose abruptly in the 1580s, and by the 1590s nearly half of all new appointees were natives of Paris.

The result of these developments was to restrict the pool of candidates for royal professorships to a narrower and narrower group, based on ties of blood, marriage, and nationality. As might be expected, one result of these restrictions was to lower the overall quality of the royal professors compared to appointments made before 1560. While there is no way to construct a completely objective scale for comparing the merits of the successive generations of royal professors, there are strong indications of declining quality within their ranks. Among these are the lower age of appointees to royal chairs after 1560 and the absence of most appointees after 1560 from the standard reference sources.

The declining age of appointees to royal chairs concerned Pasquier, and with good reason. For the first fifty years of their existence, the royal chairs were filled by mature scholars who had proven their ability to teach and their scholarly worth. Only three appointments went to individuals less than thirty years of age, and these were young scholars of undoubted genius: Guillaume Postel, appointed to the chair of oriental languages in 1538 at the age of twenty-eight; Gilbert Génébrard, the Hebraicist and theologian, appointed in 1566 at the age of twenty-nine; and Ramus's protégé Jean Péna, the mathematical prodigy who attained his chair in 1557, also aged twenty-nine.

After 1580, however, the situation changed dramatically. In the next thirty years, seven different appointments went to men still in their twenties, two of them only twenty-two years old and barely out of college. Jean Duret, the son of Louis who took over his chair of medicine in 1586, was a mere twenty-three years old and

---

36. Henri de Monantheuil (1536–1606, royal professor of mathematics 1573–1606) was one of Ramus's pupils from the Vermandois in Picardy and may well have developed his views on recruitment of professors from his old master. On the other hand, he did not scruple to join in the professorial "caste" by marrying his daughter to Jerome Goulu. See Lefranc, *Histoire du Collège*, 231–33, and Goujet, *Mémoire historique*, 2:83–95.

had received his medical degree only two years previously.[37] The general trend appears clearly in the dynasty established by Jean Dorat and depicted graphically above. Dorat was forty-eight when he took over the royal chair of Greek; his son-in-law, Nicolas Goulu, succeeded him at the age of thirty-seven; and Nicolas's son Jerome was only twenty-two when he took over from his father. It is not impossible that some of these very youthful appointees did a creditable or even excellent job in their posts, but there is no solid evidence that they were any better than mediocre as scholars and teachers.

The accomplishments and reputations of the royal professors are not easy to measure, but however the attempt is made, the decline in scholarly ability among them after the 1560s is evident. As one rough indicator, we might simply count the royal professors considered significant enough to be included in the *Biographie universelle* of Didot. Clearly this can provide only a biased estimate of their achievements, since it applies nineteenth-century standards to the work of sixteenth-century scholars, but it does show a suggestive trend.

Splitting the period from 1530 to 1610 into two equal parts, we find that a roughly equal number of appointments to royal chairs were made from 1530 to 1570 (40) and from 1570 to 1610 (42). Twenty-four of the professors appointed in the first forty-year period appear in Didot, or three-fifths of the total number, while only thirteen of the forty-two appointed after that date are listed—less than a third. The later appointees made less of a mark in their fields and were presumably less qualified than their predecessors.

The new character of the royal professorships became a concern for contemporaries such as Pasquier towards the end of the 1500s, but long before that time Ramus had seen its damaging potential. Not only was the quality of instruction likely to decline, but scholars of merit would be denied an opportunity to compete for the prestigious positions. In order to stop this threat to the integrity of Francis I's foundation, Ramus needed an alternative plan for recruitment, a strong backer to support it, and an occasion to challenge the new system. He found all three in the controversy over the royal chair of mathematics that began in 1565.

Ramus's confrontation with the advocates of a new form of recruitment to the royal chairs began with the contested succession to the royal professorship held by

37. The evidence available does not permit a rigorous analysis of appointees by age, date of degree, or other numerical measure, since such data are lacking for many of the royal professors. The value of a statistic like that of average age at appointment would be dubious in any case. For example, of the ten appointments made in the 1590s, we know the ages of only six royal professors. Their average age on appointment to their chairs is 43.3 years. But the average includes Pierre-Victor Palma Cayet, appointed in 1596 at the age of seventy-one, the oldest of whom we have record. It also includes the royal professor of Hebrew Pierre Vignal, appointed in 1592 at the age of 54. Vignal's age was calculated on the basis of the Abbé Goujet's not-always-reliable information, however; in this case, the claim that Vignal died in 1640 at the age of one hundred and five; Goujet, *Mémoire historique*, 1:313–16. I hope to be able to refine the data at some future point so that they may be treated statistically.

Pasquier Du Hamel. Du Hamel had served for twenty-five years as royal professor of mathematics, from 1540 to his death in October of 1565, and was generally considered the dean of the royal professors.[38] In his place, a Sicilian by the name of Dampestre Cosel was appointed, a man of whom little more was known at the time than is known today. Pasquier recorded that he could speak neither French nor Latin, and Ramus that he was ignorant of mathematics as well.[39] How he came to be appointed to the chair is a mystery. Ramus wrote that Cosel, "seeing that our professor was dying, went posthaste and with great diligence to ask for his chair, thinking to have the best right to it if he was the first to ask for it"; but Ramus does not tell us whom Cosel approached with his request.[40] Pasquier simply stated that Cosel "was provided" with the chair.[41] Modern accounts are similarly imprecise.[42]

However Cosel managed to slip into Du Hamel's old chair, he did not stay there long. Ramus's interest in mathematics gave him a strong motive for interfering in the appointment, and he claimed standing to do so as well, since Du Hamel's death had left him the senior royal professor, and he claimed the title of dean. He took it upon himself to preserve the integrity of Francis's foundation, and when Cosel failed to heed Ramus's advice on the proper method of teaching mathematics, the new dean took more vigorous action to chase the incompetent newcomer away. The hostile reception given Cosel in his initial lectures seems to have been orchestrated by Ramus,[43] and when that failed to intimidate the Sicilian, Ramus took the case to Parlement and wrote to the king, the queen, and the cardinal of Châtillon to complain.

> "I cried murder, that brigands had entered the lecture hall of the king, that they were cutting the throats of the royal professorships to enrich themselves with the spoils."[44]

---

38. See *Dictionnaire de biographie française*, 12, cols. 20–21; and Goujet, *Mémoire historique*, 2:21–23.

39. Pasquier, *Recherches*, 838, "homme qui entrant en la chaire se trouva si disgracié, qu'il ne sçavoit parler Latin ni François." Ramus goes on at greater length about Cosel's complete lack of qualifications for teaching mathematics; *Remonstrance de Pierre de La Ramee faite au conseil privé, en la chambre du Roy au Louvre, le 18 de Ianvier 1567: Touchant la profession Royalle en Mathematique* (Paris: A. Wechel, 1567), 4–14. Cosel was "estonné du nom d'Euclide...," "n'entendant rien à cest a b c...."

40. Ramus, *Remonstrance*, 4.

41. Pasquier, *Recherches*, 838.

42. E.g., Lefranc, *Histoire*, 216: Du Hamel's succession "fut attribuée par faveur" to Cosel. Lefranc here follows Waddington, *Ramus*, 168: "sa succession fut donnée par faveur." On the other hand, M. L. Am. Sédillot, "Les professeurs de mathématiques et de physique générale au collège de France: Deuxième période. Les derniers Valois. 1547–89," *Bullettino di Bibliografia e di Storia delle Scienze Matematiche e Fisiche* 2 (1869): 387–448, at 400, claimed that "Dampestre était nommé par Lettres Patentes...," but provides no source for the claim, an especially curious omission in this almost obsessively well documented article. It is probably safe to say that Cosel did hold letters patent to his chair, even if we cannot put our hands on them, but the more important question is who was behind his appointment.

43. Pasquier, *Recherches*, 838: "il fut deux & trois fois chiflé et baffoué par tout l'auditoire."

44. Ramus, *Remonstrance*, 13–14.

Faced with hostile students, an antagonistic dean, and the threat of a lawsuit, Cosel caved in and decided to abandon his royal professorship. Not only that, but at Ramus's urging Charles IX issued an ordinance, dated 24 January 1566, requiring that all future candidates for royal chairs undergo a competitive examination to prove their fitness for the profession. Such a method had been used to choose royal professors before, notably in the concourse held in 1557 which selected Jean Péna over Etienne Forcadel for the other mathematical chair, but the intent of Charles's ordinance was to make the practice standard for all new appointments. As he explained in letters patent issued on 7 March 1566, Charles meant the ordinance to recall the original purpose of the royal chairs as established by Francis and to specify the procedure for examining new candidates. Charles wrote that under Francis "the most learned persons in Europe were called to teach, and so fruitfully that there went forth an infinite number of learned men, who throughout the world testified to our ancestor's grandeur." In order that in the future the professors be recruited from among the most learned and capable,

> we have ordered that in the case of a vacancy in any of our professors' places in whatever sciences and languages it may be, it be made known in all the famous universities and other places, and that those who wish to present themselves and submit to disputation and reading for the vacant chair, as the dean and other professors propose, be received there, and afterwards the most sufficient and capable of those who have read and disputed, of which we will be advised by the dean and other professors, be chosen by us....[45]

According to the letters patent, the king would simply confirm the choice made by his royal professors, who would evaluate the candidates according to their performance in a concourse of scholars drawn from all over Europe. The form of the examination was not specified, but the one surviving document certifying that such a test took place suggests that it was intended to be quite thorough. Before Nicolas Goulu was appointed to the royal chair of Greek in late 1567, he was heard and tested for six days by a jury which included the royal professors Louis Duret, Jacques Charpentier, Jean Dorat, and Leger Duchesne as well as Ronsard and J. A. de Baïf. There is no indication, however, that Goulu faced any competition from other Greek scholars.[46]

Goulu's examination suggests that by driving Cosel from his chair, Ramus had achieved a complete success. Not only had he protected the reputation of the royal

---

45. Petrus Ramus, *Lettres patentes du roy, touchant l'institution de ses lecteurs en l'université de Paris, avec la preface de Pierre de la Ramee sur le proeme de mathematique: A la royne, mere du roy* (Paris: A. Wechel, 1567), 3–6.

46. The document, dated 15 September 1567, was discovered by Abel Lefranc and published in his "La Pléiade au Collège de France," in Abel Lefranc, *Grands Ecrivains de la Renaissance* (Paris, 1914), 387–411, at 388–89. Each of the examiners signed a brief statement endorsing the general conclusion that Goulu was worthy of the royal chair on the basis of his honest life and a six-day-long audition by the signers ("a nobis in regia cathedra perorantem et Graece interpretantem per sex dies auditum et probatum").

professorships for the present; he had guaranteed that only qualified candidates would be appointed in the future. As it happened, however, his triumph carried the seeds of his failure, and Nicolas Goulu was the only candidate for a royal chair to have been tested under the terms of the letters patent. The collapse of Ramus's meritocratic scheme began with Cosel's resignation. In forcing him out, Ramus created the occasion for the first attested transfer of a royal chair as if it were personal property. His own words tell the story:

> Now Dampestre, finding himself surrounded by so many nets, both of the Parlement and of the king, proceeds simply and frankly; recognizing that he could not sell his wares retail, he seeks a market to barter or sell them wholesale, and addresses himself to Master Jacques Charpentier, M.D., and traffics, at what price I leave to your imagination.[47]

Whatever the price, Charpentier claimed Du Hamel's old chair by right of resignation. Ramus had no doubt that Charpentier bought the office from Cosel, and Charpentier never actually denied it. Whether he did or not is irrelevant. The heart of the problem was that Charpentier had acquired a royal chair through a private transaction, without public scrutiny or consideration of qualifications. As Pasquier put it, "a new monster had been introduced in their company, to proceed in this matter by resignation, and not by merit."[48]

Ramus was just as determined to get rid of Charpentier as he had been to drive out Cosel, and perhaps more so. Not only was Charpentier his oldest and most determined foe, but Cosel, bad as he was, was a veritable Archimedes compared to Charpentier, at least in Ramus's eyes.[49] The problem was that Charpentier was a far more formidable opponent than Cosel had been. As *procureur* of the Picard nation and rector of the University as a whole, Charpentier had made powerful connections during a long career.[50] In addition, he enjoyed letters patent from the king confirming him in the chair. He had no intention of allowing Ramus to bully him, or of undergoing an examination in a field—mathematics—about which he knew little

---

Ramus's is not among the signatures to the certification; apparently he did not attend the examination. His colleague Denis Lambin does not seem to have been there either, even though his signature does appear on the document. As the senior royal professor of Greek, his attendance would have been appropriate, but it is characteristic of the man that he was happy to let others make the decision: "Si collegis meis, et ceteris doctis viris dignus videatur, qui in nostrum collegium cooptetur, ego eis libenter assentiar."

47. Ramus, *Remonstrance*, 14–15.

48. Pasquier, *Recherches*, 838.

49. Ramus, "Actiones duae, habitae in senatu, pro regia mathematicae Professionis cathedra" (Paris: A. Wechel, 1566), in *Scholae in Liberales Artes*, col. 1125: "Sic enim primum statuo, Dampestram prae Dampestrae successore in mathematicis rebus Archimedem quendam esse."

50. On Charpentier's life, see Joseph Bertrand, "Jacques Charpentier: Est-il l'assassin de Ramus?" *Revue des deux mondes* 44 (1881): 286–322.

and cared less. He proposed in fact to teach philosophy from his new royal chair and leave mathematics for the less advanced teachers and students.

Ramus was not about to let him get away with it. His personal dislike of Charpentier, his professional interest in reviving mathematics, and his meritocratic beliefs all combined to make him attack once again. His immediate recourse was to return to Parlement. There he accused Charpentier of violating the king's new ordinance by refusing to undergo examination and of lacking competence to perform the duties of his office. He demanded that Charpentier demonstrate his proficiency in mathematics before being permitted to take over the royal chair.

Ramus's plea came before the Parlement of Paris on 8 March 1566, the same day as Charles issued the letters patent reaffirming his desire that royal professors be chosen by merit. The two old opponents confronted each other in the high court, and as Pasquier described it, it was

> a grand cause, and two brave champions, who without the help of counsel entered the field, in the presence of Parlement and of an infinity of people. And I can say, as one who saw the affair unraveled, that it was well attacked and well defended, and to a good thrust a good riposte. Both of them, speaking Latin, were heard from their own mouths, with an admirable facility and faculty of speech.[51]

The hearing, and the affair as a whole, is exceptionally well documented, not only in the records of the Parlement itself, but in published pleas by both Ramus and Charpentier and in the many polemical writings by their allies. The sources reveal the enormous distance between the competing interests and ideologies of the conservative, meritocratic Ramus and the more up-to-date, oligarchic Charpentier.

Ramus's complaints against Charpentier were basically three in number: that he knew no mathematics, that he knew no Greek, and that he had failed to obey the king's edict by undergoing examination. His brief formal plea to the Parlement pointed out that Charpentier himself had admitted his ignorance of Greek and geometry in print, and so was clearly not qualified for the post he claimed. Ramus requested that the Parlement confirm the king's edict requiring examination of new professors, in the clear expectation that Charpentier would fail such a test.[52]

Charpentier found a strong defense in his rather clever initial reply to Ramus. The printed version began by mocking Ramus for misdating his own plea, which took place on the eighth of March but appeared in print with the date "5 Id. Mart.," that is, the tenth. "Thus the Royal Professor of Eloquence and Philosophy cannot number the days of the month of March in the Roman manner without making a

---

51. Estienne Pasquier, *Les Recherches de la France…* (Paris: Laurens Sonnius, 1621), 838.

52. Ramus, *P. Rami Actiones Duae*, cols. 1117–44. The first of Ramus's pleas, presented on 8 March 1566 (but erroneously dated "5 Id. Mart." in the printed version), takes up less than a column of text.

mistake, which in a boy would be shameful."[53] Charpentier found several occasions to twit his learned opponent in the course of his defense, perhaps most tellingly on Ramus's religious views which were already viewed with suspicion.[54]

Charpentier's central defense was that he held letters patent from the king appointing him to the chair. The will of the king was everything, and "the most Christian King wishes Charpentier to be not professor of mathematics alone but of philosophy in general."[55] The most cogent statement of this line of defense appears in Charpentier's third oration before Parlement, where he argued against Ramus's claim that transfer of royal chairs by their holders was previously unknown: "Let it be however great a novelty, if the method pleases the King. Or are you questioning the power of the King?"[56] Charpentier had other arguments available: that there was no set number of professors, that other royal professors of mathematics were ignorant of Greek and even of Latin, and that it was none of Ramus's business anyway. On top of that, six of the seven current royal professors had already accepted him as one of their number.[57] Still, the main point was that Charpentier had been appointed by the king himself, and no self-described dean had the right to challenge him.

---

53. Charpentier, "Oratio Prima," in *Ia. Carpentarii, Claromontani Bellovaci, Regii Professoris, Orationes Tres: pro iure professionis suae, in Senatu ex tempore habitae, contra importunas Rami actiones: Ad illustrissimum Cardinalem & principem Carolum Lotaringum* (Paris: Gabriel Buon, 1566), f. A3r: "Sic Eloquentiae & Philosophiae Regius professor, dies Mensis Martii non potuit ex Romana consuetudine numerare sine errore, qui in puero esset flagitiosus." I for one find it rather comforting than shameful that one of the best Latin writers of the sixteenth century could become so muddled about Roman dates. Walter Ong, *Ramus and Talon Inventory* (Cambridge: Harvard University Press, 1958), 357, mistakenly accepts Ramus's dates for the hearing.

54. See below, chapter 4, on Ramus's growing reputation as a heretic in the 1560s. Charpentier managed to insert a not-very-subtle reminder of this in his oration. In his demonstration of the utility of mathematics, Charpentier recalled, Ramus had suggested that Noah foresaw the flood by mathematical observations, and cited Josephus as his authority. That, said Charpentier, might be tolerable for a Jew. "But for a Christian, in a most Christian Parlement, in a most Christian realm, who would propose that, if not someone of little faith who wished to pervert the foundations of our religion?" Charpentier, *Ia. Carpentarii*, f. F4v: "Addis vero Noeum Mathematicis observationibus futuram inundationem praevidisse, qua peritura essent omnia: idque videris Iosepho in Antiquitatis Iudaicis ascribere. Quod si hic ullo loco scriberet, esset fortasse in Iudeo tolerabile. At in Christiano, apud Senatum Christianissimum, in regno Christianissimo dicente, quis feter hoc, nisi qui pari pietate religionis nostrae fundamenta velit pervertere?"

55. Charpentier, *Ia. Carpentarii*, f. 4r: "Rex Christianissimus Carpentarium non Mathematicarum artium modo sed universae etiam philosophiae professorum esse voluit."

56. Charpentier, "Oratio tertia," in *Ia Carpentarii*, f. E1v: "Sit quantumvis novum, si modo Regi placuerit. An etiam in Regis potestatem inquires?"

57. Charpentier was quite right that neither the number nor the fields of the royal chairs were established once and for all; Charpentier, *Ia. Carpentarii*, f. C1r–v, for Charpentier's discussion of the history of the royal chairs and their varying subject matters. The king was always free to create a professor in any subject he wished, and Charpentier claimed that Ramus himself, "by the death of Caligny, professor of Hebrew and Arabic, was nominated professor of eloquence and philosophy." Ibid., f. E2r–v: "Dixeram neque professorum numerum ulla lege definitum esse, neque professiones distinctas, sed mortuis, vel sua sponte cedentibus, Graecis aut Hebraeis, Regi semper fuisse liberum pro illis instituere Latinos Medicinae

Ramus's response, in his summary speech on the last day of the hearings, met Charpentier's challenge head on. Cardinals, kings, emperors, and popes could give Charpentier his various titles, "but of these not one can make you worthy of the royal chair of mathematics and philosophy."[58] Charpentier could not change the facts, and Ramus promised to proclaim them again and again: "in the royal college no chair of philosophy is vacant, but only a chair of mathematics."[59] Therefore, Ramus concluded, "I declare and affirm that you are most unworthy of the royal chair of mathematics and philosophy; and if you were worthy, you would undergo the public examination."[60]

---

aut Philosophiae professores, vel alterius cuiuscunque artis…teque de mortuo Calignio linguae Hebraicae & Arabicae professore, Eloquentiae & Philosophiae professorem esse nominatum." Cf. ibid., f. C3v, where Charpentier brought up the same claim to argue that since Ramus replaced Caligny without knowing Hebrew or Arabic, it was unreasonable to demand that he know Greek. The claim that Ramus was appointed to the chair vacated by Caligny was false, but Charpentier's point was nonetheless valid.

Not content with a defence which simply avoided the issue of his competence, Charpentier answered Ramus's charges more specifically. He admitted his ignorance of Greek, but two previous royal professors of mathematics had been equally ignorant of the language, and the current one, Etienne Forcadel, could not even speak Latin; ibid., f. G1v. Neither Finé nor Du Hamel knew Greek, according to Charpentier. On Etienne Forcadel, see Natalie Zemon Davis, "Sixteenth-Century French Arithmetics on the Business Life," 35–36. It was Ramus himself who had nominated Forcadel to the royal chair, despite having described him as "sine literatura, sine philosophia, solo ingenio atque uso quodam mathematicis…." Ramus, *P. Rami Arithmeticae Libri Duo*, f. 2r. The appointment had stirred up considerable controversy.

Finally, what gave Ramus the right to prescribe the qualifications for a royal chair? No one but Ramus was demanding an examination; indeed, a recent meeting of six of the seven current professors had proclaimed "with one voice "that Charpentier had been tested by many years of teaching and did not need further examination; ibid., f. D2v: "At in Carpentarium ut doctrinae examen decerneretur, nemo adhuc praeter Ramum nominatim postulavit. Imo duo inter eos nobilissimi, Lud. Duretus & Leod. a Quercu, ne totius collegii nomine causa haec ageretur, semper impediverunt. Reliqui sunt professores septem: de quibus Mercerus, Lambinus, Auratus, Forcadellus cum Dureto & Leod. a Quercu, nudius tertius in Regia schola Cameracensi congregati, Ramo absente, Salignaceo autem ex vetere collegii consuetudine, pro Decano sedente, una voce declaraverunt Carpentarium sic esse notum in Academia docyis omnibus, ut eum amplius probari non oporteat qui multorum annorum professione est probatus." It is worth noting that three members of the group, Duchesne, Dorat, and Duret, had a vested interest in helping Charpentier avoid an examination, as all three were eventually to yield their chairs to sons or sons-in-law. The timorous Lambin, of course, would have gone along with the majority in any case.

58. Ramus, *Actiones duae…*, cols. 1131–132: "Cardinales, Reges, Imperatores, &, si quid majus hic esse arbitraris, Pontifices, te variis beneficiorum titulis exornare possunt: At istorum nemo, regia philosophiae & mathematicae professionis cathedra te dignum potest efficere."

59. Ramus, *Actiones duae…*, col. 1129: "At moneo, & contenta voce, quod jam monui, iterumque iterumque monebo, in regio collegio philosophiae cathedram nullam vacuam esse, sed mathematicam solum."

60. Ramus, *Actiones duae…*, col. 1125: "Dico & affirmo, te regia & philosophiae & mathematicae cathedra indignissimum esse; & si dignissimus esses, tamen publicum tibi examen esse subeundum." Ramus of course had other arguments as well. Much of his closing address to the Parlement was taken up with a plea that mathematical teaching in Paris be preserved because it was so useful to the merchants, navigators, and others to whom the city owed its prosperity; "even its architecture is nothing other than

The two academics were arguing past one another, on totally different assumptions. Ramus assumed that the issue was merit, while Charpentier staunchly defended his privilege. Their disagreement was more than a courtroom tactic. It was a reflection of a dramatic change in the society of France taking place in the 1560s, as the ideal of merit faded and the elite oligarchy of the Old Régime took its place. The outcome of the lawsuit was almost a foregone conclusion, since it was the venal Parlement of Paris which decided it. Ramus lost, and Charpentier kept the chair in mathematics.

Ramus was to make one more attempt to institute the selection of professors by merit, one which would long outlive him. In his testament written on 1 August 1568, before his trip to Germany, Ramus left 500 livres to endow a public professorship in mathematics, which was to be held by a candidate chosen in a public concourse on the basis of merit. The successful candidate was to hold the chair for three years, at which time another concourse would be held.[61] On the thirteenth of March, 1573, the Parlement of Paris, arguing that the king was already paying a royal professor of mathematics, diverted the income from his bequest to Jacques Gohorry to support him while he completed his history of France.[62]

---

geometry in stone and wood"; ibid., col. 1123, "Architectura enim nil nisi in lapidus & lignis Geometria est." The defense of mathematics runs from col. 1120 to col. 1125.

61. Ramus's testament of 1568 has been published several times. See the facsimile copy and transliteration in François Bonnardot, ed., *Registres des délibérations du Bureau de la Ville de Paris*, vol. 7, *1572–76* (Paris: Imprimerie Nationale, 1843), 34–37.

62. Du Boulay prints the Parlement's verdict in full, *Historia Universitatis*, 6:732–33. Ramus's bequest was later recovered to support a chair in mathematics. See L. Am. Sédillot, "Les professeurs de mathematiques," 410–11.

CHAPTER 4
Deligere Aureum Saeculum

IN LATE 1569, DURING A VISIT TO HEIDELBERG, Ramus participated in a Reformed celebration of the Lord's Supper for the first time.[1] It was his first public profession of the Protestant faith, but no one was particularly surprised. His Protestant sympathies had been notorious for a long time, and many believed that he had secretly embraced the Reformation years or even decades earlier. His reputation as a heretic was the reason he was in Germany to begin with, since the renewed outbreak of religious war in France in 1568 had made Catholic Paris too hot to hold him. Everyone had expected that he would openly announce his conversion sooner or later.[2]

What is remarkable is that almost everyone was pleased when he finally did. Friends and enemies, Protestants and Catholics alike, all found reasons to celebrate his conversion. For the Huguenots, it meant a new and valuable recruit, a man of upright morals, immense prestige, and proven mettle. For Ramus's foes, it meant yet another stick with which to belabor the presumptuous royal professor. They had attacked him as an upstart peasant, a dangerous innovator, and an ignorant babbler, but now they could add a new and far more serious charge. Ramus was a self-avowed heretic.[3]

The rejoicing over Ramus's conversion was not quite universal, however. There were some who would have preferred for him to remain docilely within the Catholic fold. These were not, as might be expected, pious Catholics who regretted the loss of

1. In a letter to the cardinal of Lorraine, 22 October 1570, in *Collectaneae praefationes, epistolae orationes...* (Marburg, 1609), 212, Ramus explained his decision "to choose the golden age" as a model for his religious belief—that is, to embrace Protestantism: "de quindecim a Christo saeculis, primum vere esse aureum, reliqua, quo longius abscederent, esse nequiora atque deteriora. Tum igitur cum fieret optio, aureum saeculum delegi...."

2. Théophile de Banos, *Petri Rami Vita*, introduction to Ramus's *Commentariorum de Religione Christianum Libri Quatuor* (Frankfurt: A. Wechel, 1576), unpaginated: "Nam cum Heydelbergae una apud D. Immanuelem Tremellium anno septuagesimo viveremus, Gallicis concionibus semper interfuit, & sacrae Coenae, edita primum fidei suae confessione, cum magno Dei timore & cultus divini reverentia non semel communicavit."

3. Protestant hopes that Ramus would be an ornament to their cause are summed up in Bullinger's letter to Beza of 4 December 1571; *Correspondance de Théodore de Bèze*, vol. 12, 1571 (Geneva: Droz, 1986), 243–52. Bullinger praises Ramus's learning and faith and adds the hopeful comment (244) that

a soul to heresy. Most of them had already written off Ramus's soul as lost in any case. Nor were they close friends who feared for his safety when he returned to France. Ramus had few enough friends of any sort, and his only close one, Omer Talon, had died a decade earlier.[4] Instead, it was among his new Protestant brethren that many wondered whether the Reform really stood to gain by accepting Ramus into fellowship. No one doubted it more than Theodore Beza, Calvin's successor in Geneva and the most dynamic leader of European Protestantism.[5]

Beza had a variety of reasons for believing that Ramus's adherence would do the Reformed cause more harm than good. As an aristocrat by birth, breeding, and outlook, he was suspicious and contemptuous of vulgar social climbers like Ramus, whose disregard for the established hierarchies marked them as troublemakers and rebels. It was easy for Beza to conclude that Ramus was "always ready to upset what is best ordered."[6] If he ignored the laws and boundaries of French social status, was he likely to abide meekly by the rules of the French Church? His attacks on the great sages of the past convinced Beza that the answer was an emphatic "No." Any man who could insult Aristotle as Ramus had could not be expected to hold anything sacred, even the authority of Beza and Geneva. "A man to whom Aristotle is a sophist, Cicero ignorant of how to teach rhetoric, Quintilian unlearned, Galen and even Euclid unmethodical—who can believe that he would be satisfied with anything that came from us?" In short, Ramus was bound to cause as much trouble in the church as he had in the University. Beza had guessed as much as early as 1561, when he first learned that Ramus was leaning toward the Reform. "Already then I predicted," he

---

"his example is influential among the learned of Paris and among many of the foremost men [At pollet is authoritate apud studiosus Lutetianos et apud viros principes plurimos]." The attitude of Ramus's enemies, that he finally stood revealed as a heretic, is exemplified by Jean Dorat's epigram "De Ramo": "In fleeing the false and returning to real dangers / he has proven a known and true heretic [Nam dum falsa fugit, rediens se in vera pericula / Coniecit, verus cognitus Haereticus]," Jean Dorat, *Ioannis Aurati Lemovicis poetae et interpretis Regii Epigrammatum: Liber I* (Paris: Guillaume Linocer, 1586), 36; French translation in A. Maurat-Ballange, *Ramus et Dorat* (Limoges: Imprimerie et Librairie Limousines Ducourtieux et Gout, 1913), 24. Dorat is referring to Ramus's return to Paris after his two-year sojourn in Germany and Switzerland.

4. Talon died in 1562. See Charles Waddington, *Ramus (Pierre de la Ramée): Sa vie, ses écrits et ses opinions* (1855; reprint, Dubuque, Iowa: Brown Reprint Library, n.d.), 308.

5. On Beza in general, see Paul-F. Geisendorf, *Théodore de Bèze* (Geneva: Labor et Fides,1949). On his role in the French Reform, Robert Kingdon's *Geneva and the Consolidation of the French Protestant Movement, 1564–1572: A Contribution to the History of Congregationalism, Presbyterianism, and Calvinist Resistance Theory* (Geneva: Droz, 1967) is authoritative.

6. Beza, *Correspondance XIII (1572)*, 145. On Beza's general attitude toward the lower orders, see Kingdon, *Geneva and the Consolidation*, 18: "A possible further consequence of Beza's relatively high social standing, may have been his almost pathological hatred of religious groups which threatened to break the unity of the Reformed churches. The lower-class origins of some of these groups may well have provided a social reinforcement to his theological revulsion against them."

later wrote, "and would to Heaven I had been wrong! that in the future the spirit of discord would enter the churches of France along with him."[7]

Beza was not far wrong. During Ramus's brief career as a Protestant, from his conversion in 1569 to his death in 1572, the spirit of discord flourished in the French churches as never before. Ramus was not entirely responsible for that spirit. It had found its way into the churches long before him and without his assistance. The debates over lay versus clerical control of the church, and between the supporters of a centralized national church and the congregationalists were already in full swing by the time Ramus entered the quarrel, as was the conflict over the proper interpretation of the Eucharist. Ramus's contribution was to unite the dissenters on all of these issues into a coherent faction within the French Reform, and to provide them with a political program and an ideological platform. In brief, that platform was the original Lutheran message of the "priesthood of all believers," with all of the potential for anarchy and dissent such a program implied, but also with all the opportunity for each man to realize his own vocation that had been the hallmark of Ramus's life and career. Ramus's aim in joining the struggle for control of the Reformed churches of France was to return both church and society to a vanished golden age; the age of the Apostles, to be sure, but also the freer and fairer age of Francis I as he remembered and imagined it.

According to Ramus himself, it was through reflecting on the nature of Christianity in the Apostolic Age that he came to appreciate the merits of the Reform. The speech of the cardinal of Lorraine at the Colloquy of Poissy in 1561 inspired him to compare the practices of the primitive church with those of his own day, and he found the modern church wanting. As he later recalled, the cardinal had proclaimed: "Of the fifteen centuries since Christ, the first was truly golden, while the rest, the more time passes the more worthless and corrupt they are. Therefore [Ramus added], having the choice, I chose the golden age...."[8] Lorraine's speech had set Ramus thinking about religious matters and convinced him of the need to return to an earlier and purer faith. Still he did not make up his mind that the Reform was the answer until years later. In 1563, he still proclaimed that his only desire was to live as a good and true Catholic.[9]

---

7. Beza to Bullinger, 14 January 1572: "Cui enim Aristoteles est sophista, Cicero tradendae rhetorices ignarus, Quintilianus indoctus, Galenus ipseque adeo Euclides αμεψodos, quis putet placere quenquam nostrum posse?...Itaque quum ante decennium in Gallia essem, eumque nostris partibus nonnihil favere cognovissem, jam tum praedixi, utinam falsus vates, futurum ut cum hoc homine spiritus discordiae in Ecclesias Gallicas introiret." Beza, *Correspondance*, 13:31.

8. See n. 1. above.

9. In testimony, during his attempt to recover his office at Presles from Antoine Muldrac before the Parlement of Paris. A.N. $X^{1a}1605$, fol. 138 v (Parlement de Paris, Conseils, 12 mai 1563): "qu'il [Ramus] n'a oncques eu et n'a aucune aultre intention que de vivre et gouverner ledict college [Presles] paisiblement et catholiquement...."

By his own account, then, Ramus remained a loyal son of the Catholic Church until the middle of the 1560s. His biographers thought that he was not merely a good Catholic, but a particularly scrupulous one. Theophile de Banos described him as "observantissimus Pontificiae religionis" (Banos, *Petri Rami Vita,* unpaginated), and by the standards of the time he was indeed "most observant" of Catholic rites and practices. He attended Mass daily, a practice few of his contemporaries would have cared to emulate. Outside the chapel, he devoted additional hours to reading in his breviary, while his pupil Nancel remembered him praying in private.[10] Together with his austere mode of life and upright morals, Ramus's punctilious observance of religious duties earned him an almost saintly reputation among his friends. Omer Talon went so far as to claim that slander could never touch his friend, since "the integrity of his morals and religion remains intact, even according to those who accused him."[11]

While his friends praised Ramus's Catholic zeal, his students recalled his pious principles less fondly. They were the ones who had to suffer its consequences. Ramus held his charges to the same high standards of devotion he imposed on himself, and when they forgot their religious duties he reminded them with a beating. Failure to attend Mass earned the truant a pounding, while a whipping was the reward for lack of respect toward the Host. There is nothing remarkable about a college principal's use of thrashings to teach piety in the sixteenth century, but Ramus's lessons seem to have been particularly memorable. Even in old age, his former pupils remembered that he was as eloquent with his fists as with his tongue.[12]

Despite his blameless manner of living, his observance of ritual, and his zeal for the propagation of the faith among his students, Ramus's opponents were never convinced that his orthodoxy was sincere. Even his friends had their doubts, and Nancel himself allowed that he was never sure about his master's faith. Was his scrupulosity the sign of heartfelt belief or a cover for heretical or even atheistic ideas?[13] Nancel's

---

10. Nicolaus Nancelius, *"Petri Rami Vita*: Edited with an English Translation," *Humanistica Lovaniensia: Journal of Neo-Latin Studies* 24 (1975): 236: "Ut hoc tamen intelligas, secum preces meditari solitum, sed eas, ut judico, perbreves; nisi forte matutinas ex breviario, dum missae adesset quotidie, preduceret longius. Ita enim illi moris erat, quo tempore apud illum vixi, quotidie sacro ad horam sextam interesse...." Nancel's qualifications in this passage hint at his doubts about Ramus's religion, which are expressed more fully elsewhere (see below, n. 17.).

11. Omer Talon, "Audomari Talaei admonitio ad Adrianum Turnebum, regium gracae linguae professorem," in *Audomari Talaei, quem Petri Rami Theseum dicere jure possis, Opera, Socraticae Methodicaeque Philosophiae Studiosis pernecessaria...* (Basle: Waldkirch, 1584), 592–614, at 604: "tamenquoties publice caussa acta est, morum integritatem & religionem sartam tectamque, vel praedicatione eorum, a quibus accusabatur, habuit."

12. Nancel, *"Petri Rami Vita,"* 238.

13. Nancel, *"Petri Rami Vita,"* repeatedly points out that he could never be sure of his master's sincerity, and refuses to take a stand one way or another. In discussing Ramus's punishments for students who missed Mass, he comments (238), "quod ille faciebat vel ex animo, vel ut adversariis omnem occasionem

uncertainty is not difficult to understand. In many ways, Ramus's zeal seemed superficial. He attended Mass daily, to be sure, but once in the chapel he did not pay much attention to the service. Instead he spent the time in more secular meditations, which he would record in a notebook he carried about with him. He read in his breviary, perhaps, but aside from the breviary his large library contained only one other religious work. That was a New Testament, and not the sort of New Testament a Catholic was supposed to own. It was a French translation, and the translation was by the Protestant Castellio.[14]

The strict religious discipline Ramus imposed at Presles might have been evidence of his orthodoxy, but then again it might not. Even after his conversion he continued to insist on respect for Catholic rites. Only a few days before his death, he had a boy whipped, "publicly and excessively," for failing to show respect for the Host as a priest carried it past in the street.[15] The incident suggests that his treatment of his students reflected a desire for discipline and a dislike for insolence as much as or more than any real Catholic zeal. As for Ramus's private devotions, there is no reason to doubt that he spent time alone in prayer. Private prayer is no guarantee of orthodoxy, however. Who knows how he prayed, or what he was praying for?

Ramus's private life suggested to Nancel and to others that he was not so zealous a Catholic as he tried to appear. His public life created the same impression, even among those not acquainted with the contents of his library or his behavior during divine services. In the increasingly polarized religious atmosphere of France in the 1550s and 1560s, Ramus's opposition to the Sorbonne, to the Jesuits, to the monks of Saint-Germain-des-Prés, and even to Aristotle was interpreted as hostility to the church. On the principle that whoever was not always with them must be against them, the defenders of Catholicism in France concluded that Ramus's faith was, at best, very weak. At worst, it was perverse or even nonexistent.

Nothing did his reputation among the Catholics more damage than his repeated attacks on Aristotle. To the doctors of the University, an attack on the Philosopher was a repudiation of Philosophy itself. It was a denial of man's ability to

---

calumniandi circa religionis cultum amputaret." Elsewhere (250) he reports that Ramus was accused of being a Lutheran, "jure nescio an injuria."

14. Nancel, *"Petri Rami Vita,"* 208: "Atque in tota ejus bibliotheca longe instructissima amplissimaque, ne bibliis quidem sacris locus fuit, praeter unicum novum Castalione interprete testamentum et Breviarium Romanum, in quo quotidie dum sacris et missae interesset, legebat pauca quaedam, cum codicillis, quos circumferebat, etiam inter sacra audienda semper aliquid interim meditatum ex tempore adscriberet, et stylo induceret appingeretque."

15. The story is told by Walter Ong, "Père Cossart, Du Monstier, and Ramus' Protestantism in the Light of a New Manuscript," *Archivum Historicum Societatis Jesu* 23 (1954): 151. It was recorded by François du Monstier in an attempt to prove that Ramus never converted to the Reform. According to the text, the Parisian Adrien Perrier remembered Ramus having him whipped: "six jours....auparavant la journée apellée vulgairement St. Barthelemy il lui avoir fait bailler le fouet publiquement et excessivement pour l'avoir veu ne s'estre mis a genoux devant un prebtre qui portoit le sacrement a un malade...."

know any rational truth. Ramus's rejection of Aristotle therefore marked him as a skeptic, or an epicurean, or an academic, all of which is to say an atheist. Such at least was the reasoning of Pierre Galland, Ramus's early rival. Galland considered Aristotle an essential pillar of the Christian faith, without whom morality and virtue would disappear. "If students do not learn the doctrine of the Gospels from the philosophy of Aristotle...then by what means will we raise the minds of youths in the classroom to humanity and virtue?"[16] Galland's attitude was typical of the view held by many educated Catholics. It was easy to equate an attack on Aristotle with an attack on Christianity itself, and to conclude that Ramus was, if not an atheist, then at least a most notorious heretic.

To the theologians of the University of Paris, Ramus would have been suspect even if he had never said an unkind word about Aristotle, simply because he was a royal professor. The Sorbonne had opposed Francis I's project for a humanist college in Paris from its very inception, and with good reason. It was no secret that the royal chairs were established in order to promote the subversive ideas of Erasmus and his ilk. Erasmus himself had been invited to run the new college! The faculty of theology was bound to abhor such an institution. By establishing Erasmian humanism in Paris, it opened the door to even worse heresies. A disproportionate number of royal professors did in fact end up Protestants, and it would be hard to deny that the suspicions of the theologians were well founded. Insofar as Ramus stood for the ideals which inspired Francis to create the royal chairs, his orthodoxy and loyalty to the church were in doubt, and Ramus stood for those ideals more ardently than anyone else.

If Ramus's attention to the formal aspects of Catholicism was intended to allay suspicions raised by his attacks on Aristotle and his royal professorship, he would have done well to avoid other compromising activities. Instead, he continued to take the wrong side in disputes involving the church. A case in point is the affair of the Pré-aux-Clercs in 1557 referred to in the previous chapter. The Pré-aux-Clercs, an area of waste ground west of Paris, had been for centuries a favorite playground and promenade for University students. For just as long, it had been coveted by the monks of the nearby Abbey of Saint-Germain-des-Prés. Since at least 1215, the University and the powerful abbey had quarreled over ownership of the Pré-aux-Clercs, both in the courtroom and in pitched battles between students and monks. The students were always ready for a good scrap, and as a rule the monks were happy to give them one.[17]

16. Pierre Galland, *P. Gallandi literarum latinarum professoris Regii, contra novam academiam Petri Rami oratio: Ad illustrissimum Cardinalem & Principem Carolum a Lotharingia* (Paris: Vascosan, 1551), fol. 36v: "Quod si quia evangelii doctrina ex Aristotelis philosophia non cognoscatur...quibus in scholis ad humanitatem & virtutem puerorum ingenia excolamus, retinendum censebis?"

17. The story is told in César Egasse Du Boulay, *Historia Universitatis Parisiensis,* vol. 6 (1665–73; reprint, Frankfurt: Minerva, 1966), 491–518; and in Jean Baptiste Louis Crevier, *Histoire de l'Université de Paris depuis son origine jusqu'en l'année 1600,* vol. 6 (Paris: Desaint et Saillant, 1761), 28–56. Crevier blames Ramus for stirring up the students on this occasion as well as a decade earlier in July 1548. See ibid., 5:424–26.

The age-old dispute flared up once again in 1557 with a violent clash between students and monks, and the king decided to put a stop to the conflicts once and for all. Henry issued a series of decrees intended to punish the University and to ensure that in the future it would enforce stricter discipline on its charges. Several students were condemned to death, and all students who lived outside the colleges were banished.[18] Had the decrees taken effect, it would have been a devastating blow to the University, and many feared they would destroy it altogether. In this extremity, a commission was formed to plead for clemency. Naturally Ramus was chosen as a member, both because he was the University's finest orator and because he had powerful friends at court. It was a good choice. Ramus's mission led the king to rescind the harshest of his edicts and even to confirm the University in possession of the Pré-aux-Clercs. Ramus was lionized by his colleagues and invited to describe his triumph to the University as a whole, which he did in an oration in June 1557.[19]

As we have seen, his speech for the most part reflected his traditional concerns, such as praise for the cardinal of Lorraine and concern for students too poor to live in the colleges. It also included suggestions calculated to offend the monks even more than they had been already. He proposed for example that revenues from some of the abbey's buildings be diverted to provide support for University professors, a suggestion which raised the threat of a royal takeover of monastic property.[20] What was even more damaging to Ramus's religious reputation, however, was a consideration that appeared neither in his speech nor in the official documents of the case. By preventing the monks from taking over the Pré-aux-Clercs, Ramus made it possible for Reformed assemblies to continue to use it as a meeting place. A year later these gatherings were attracting as many as 4,000 Protestants, who congregated almost in the shadow of the Abbey to chant psalms.[21] Ramus may not have intended such an outcome, but intentionally or not, he served the interests of the Huguenots as well as the University in his appeal to the king. To his enemies, it was clear that he was both a foe of the regular clergy and a patron of heretics.

The idea that Ramus had been an enemy of the church since early in his career was naturally popular among his many academic rivals and opponents, and his philosophy and activities offered at least some support for it. If he was not a sincere Catholic, however, what was he? It was not easy to guess exactly what he did believe. Many thought him a hypocritical Huguenot, a secret agent of the powerful Protestant heresy. Others claimed that he was not a Christian of any kind, even the most perverse. His skepticism had led him to reject religion altogether, they charged, and

18. Du Boulay, *Historia*, 6:41, prints the terms of the edict.

19. Waddington, *Ramus*, 117.

20. Ramus, *Harangue*, fol. 8v: "Parquoy l'Université requiert, que le revenu de chasque année de ces edifices…s'emploient aux gages des lecteurs des quatres facultés.…" He repeats the suggestion on fol. 10r.

21. Jean Delumeau, *Naissance et affirmation de la Réforme*, 3d ed., Nouvelle Clio, 30 (Paris: Presses Universitaires de France, 1973), 148: "L'année suivante [1558], pendant quatre jours (13–16 mai), quelque 4,000 Huguenots se réunirent chaque soir, au Pre-aux-Clercs, face au Louvre, en chantant des psaumes."

to become an atheist. Separately or in combination, such accusations were standard in the polemics of Ramus's foes. Had there been any real evidence to support them, things might have gone badly for the royal professor of philosophy and eloquence. There was not, however, and so it sometimes became necessary to invent some.

Such apparently was the course adopted by Florimond de Raemond, counsellor of the king in the Parlement of Bordeaux and a former student at Paris. Late in life, he recalled having seen Ramus studying a "detestable" book in his college of Presles "bearing the title *Of the Three Imposters*, etc." For years this work had circulated clandestinely, spreading its mockery of "the three great religions, which alone recognize the true God: the Jewish, the Christian, and the Mohammedan." Mere possession of the book was blasphemy, since as Raemond added, "the title alone showed that it came from Hell...."[22] If Ramus was actually reading it, then clearly he was an enemy of all religion, an atheist. Despite Raemond's testimony, however, we can state with complete confidence that he never saw Ramus with the damnable book he described. The reason is that for all its notoriety, the book *Of the Three Imposters* did not exist. Only the title was passed on for generations until finally in the seventeenth century someone wrote a book to go along with it.[23] Whatever unorthodox beliefs Ramus may have harbored in his heart, he could never have revealed them to the world by reading that particular legendary work.

During Ramus's lifetime, his accusers generally did not bother fabricating evidence to support their claim that he was an atheist. They simply asserted it. Adrien Turnèbe, the royal professor of Greek, charged Ramus with "sacrilege" and "epicureanism" as well as "atheism" in the course of their debates over Cicero without troubling to adduce any evidence at all. It is unlikely that he expected anyone to take him seriously in any case. Sixteenth-century literary debates were full of charges and countercharges of atheism, and no one seems to have taken them literally. For the most part they were simply stylistic flourishes, rhetorical insults on a par with Turnèbe's description of his rival as a "baby," a "magician," and an "Augean stable."[24] Such name-calling was de rigueur among the humanists, who maligned their opponents with as much verve and imagination as they employed to praise their friends.

---

22. Florimond de Raemond, *L'Histoire de la naissance, progrez et decadence de l'heresie de ce siecle...* (Rouen: Jean Berthelin, 1623), 236: "en mon enfance i'en veu l'exemplaire au college de Prele entre les mains de Ramus, homme assez remarqué pour son haut & eminent sçavoir; qui embroüilla son esprit parmi plusieurs recherches des secrets de la Religion, qu'il manioit avec la Philosophie. On faisoit passer ce meschant livre de main en main parmy les plus doctes, desireux de le voir! O aveugle curiosité, que tu a fait trebuscher d'ames aux gouffres eternels."

23. D. C. Allen, "Appendix: De Tribus Impostoribus," *Doubt's Boundless Sea: Skepticism and Faith in the Renaissance* (Baltimore: Johns Hopkins University Press, 1964), 224–43; and François Berriot, chap. 3 of *Athéismes et Athéistes au XVIᵉ siècle en France* (Lille: Editions du Cerf, 1984), 305–576, for an extensive discussion of the *De Tribus Impostoribus*.

24. Omer Talon, "Audomari Talaei admonitio ad Adrianum Turnebum," 613, quotes Turnèbe's accusations, which include calling Ramus "tarditate & inscitia Epicuro similem,...sacrilegum,...& ne

It was all part of the game, and the insults did not often lead to enduring hostility.[25] By the time of his death in 1565, Turnèbe was on friendly terms with Ramus, not because he had decided that atheists were not so bad after all, but because he had never really believed that Ramus was an atheist to begin with.[26]

Nancel claimed that Ramus was above the sort of rhetorical mudslinging practiced by his opponents, and further that he did not deign to reply to their extravagant charges.[27] There was at least one occasion, however, when he struck back. His most persistent opponent, Jacques Charpentier, called him a "Diagorus" in the course of one of their many quarrels, and for once Ramus dropped his pose of haughty disdain to teach his adversary a lesson. The Athenian philosopher Diagorus of Melos was outlawed for his mockery of the gods and the mystery cults, and his name became a byword for atheism in the works of Aristophanes, Cicero, and others.[28] Why Ramus found this insult more offensive than Turnèbe's more explicit slanders is unclear. Perhaps his patience had been exhausted by Charpentier's constant sniping. In any case, he had Charpentier hauled into court and convicted of

---

infinita persequar, quae nova semper habes, ut atheum accusas." In all Talon counts sixty-one different insults hurled at Ramus by Turnèbe, including "Augiae stabulum, Magum, infantem." The list also includes "arrogantissimum," "indoctissimum," "nugatorem," "elephantis coriotectum," "stupidum," "aratorem," "rusticum," "insanum," "ventilatorem," "sceleratum," "fanaticum," "insolentem," "pestem," and my favorite, "simian tragicam." "Aratorem" and "rusticum" are of course pointed references to Ramus's less-than-distinguished birth; Turnèbe's family was certainly noble, although, like Ramus's, it had fallen into poverty and obscurity.

25. On the prevalence of such abuse between rival scholars and humanists, see Lucien Febvre, *Le Problème de l'incroyance au XVIe siècle: La Religion de Rabelais* (Paris: Albin Michel, 1968), 35–37: "D'où, pour nous historiens, une première règle de critique: ne jamais prendre au tragique ces invectives de magnificence; d'autant qu'une querelle ne profite point qu'aux seuls adversaires....Et donc, second précepte: ne jamais lire un seul poète pour juger d'une accusation lancée contre lui ou par lui...." The advice is as appropriate for royal professors as for the poets about whom Febvre wrote.

26. Nancel, *"Petri Rami Vita,"* 256, writes that both Galland and Turnèbe were reconciled with Ramus shortly before they died and became his friends; "et Gallandius et Turnebus, uterque paulo ante mortem, Ramo reconciliatus, factus est plane familiaris." If Nancel is correct, the reconciliation with Turnèbe must have occurred when he was very close to death indeed. He died in 1565, and in March of that year Hubert Languet wrote that the two men were still battling over Aristotle: "Contendunt inter se Turnebus et Ramus. Hic Aristotelem oppugnat, alter defendit"; Hubert Languet, *Viri Clarissimi Huberti Langueti Burgundi, ad Joachimum Camerarium patrem, & Joachimum Camerarium filium, Medicum, Scriptae Epistolae...* (Groningen: Johannes Nicolas, 1646), 41, ep. 16, Lutetiae Cal. April 1565.

27. Nancel, *"Petri Rami Vita,"* 246, praises Ramus's courage for holding his tongue in the face of scurrilous attacks: "Fortitudo animi maxima fuit in illo, ita ut Socratem provocare potuit, praecipue in ferendis injuriis, et calumniis hostium dissimilandis." Ramus was quite as capable of calumny as his foes when the fancy took him, however. Walter Ong, *Ramus and Talon Inventory* (Cambridge: Harvard University Press, 1958), 377, paraphrases one of his attacks, on the Tübingen philosopher and physician Jacob Schegk in 1569: "Ramus's next letter [to Schegk] begins with the remark that until he came to Germany, he had never heard of Schegk, and that even in Germany he had not heard much of him. He remembers the moths perching on Schegk's books in a Strasbourg library."

28. "Diagorus" in *Oxford Classical Dictionary,* 2d ed. (1970).

libel. Nancel recorded that he was imprisoned until he agreed to "sing a recantation."[29] While I cannot discover any evidence beyond Nancel's word that this incident actually took place, there is nothing intrinsically unlikely about it, and it may be confirmed in part by Talon's assertion that even Ramus's adversaries eventually had to admit his orthodoxy.

Neither Talon's assurances nor Charpentier's example kept those adversaries from calling Ramus an atheist. In some cases the charge was mere rhetoric, in others perhaps a more considered effort to undermine his reputation. At least a few scholars honestly believed, like Galland, that Ramus's philosophy undermined Christianity and led to atheism. After all, Ramus and some of his allies, including Talon, did profess what they called the "academic" philosophy.[30] Both Ramus and Talon upheld the academic doctrine that philosophers must be "free to judge and evaluate things…without being restricted as regards opinion and inclination."[31] Carried to its logical conclusion, such an attitude would indeed threaten the foundations not only of Aristotelianism but of Christianity as well. As it happens, Ramus did not carry his academic skepticism anywhere near so far. Charles Schmitt's careful study of the academic philosophy in sixteenth-century Paris found "little indication that academic skepticism was a very important factor in [Ramus's] overall worldview." Even in Talon's study of the *Academica*, the role of skepticism was "small indeed."[32] Ramus and Talon endorsed academic philosophy as a manifesto of philosophical freedom, not as an intellectual basis for religious skepticism.

There is no real evidence that Ramus was an atheist. There is a much more plausible case to be made that he was a Protestant who for years hid behind a mask of conformity to the established cult. Admittedly, Ramus was not the sort to hide his light under a bushel. On the contrary, he usually found it difficult to keep his mouth shut, even on the most delicate of matters. He was just not cut out to be tactful, much less hypocritical. Among the Huguenots themselves, however, it was not considered particularly scandalous for an adherent of the Reform to attend Mass and observe the rituals of the Roman Church. It may not have been a heroic way to behave, but it was an eminently sensible one. It was also the only way for most French Protestants to gain access to the sacraments, especially marriage and baptism, at a time when few Protestant ministers were available and few Reformed churches

29. Nancel, *"Petri Rami Vita,"* 250–52.

30. Omer Talon, *Audomari Talaei Academia, ad Carolum Lotharingia*, in *Audomari Talaei*, 330–43. Charles Schmitt says this work "seems to represent the first serious study of the *Academica* to appear in print"; *Cicero Scepticus: A Study of the Influence of the Academica in the Renaissance* (The Hague: Martinus Nijhoff, 1972), 82.

31. Talon, *Academia*, 331. He had written the work, he said, "nam ut homines pertinaces…liberarentur intelligentque verum philosophandi genus judicio & aestimatione rerum liberum esse, non autem opinione & affectione constrictum.…"

32. Schmitt, *Cicero Scepticus*, 79, 82.

organized.[33] Calvin repeatedly castigated his French coreligionaries for their failure to make a clean break with the Catholic Church, calling them "Nicodemites" and proclaiming that it would be better for them all to move to Geneva rather than to participate in Catholic rites.[34] Nonetheless "nicodemism" remained common among the Huguenots until at least the late 1550s. In such an atmosphere even Ramus might have learned to curb his tongue and to keep his beliefs to himself. Could he have been a crypto-Protestant in the 1550s?

Many of those who knew him best suspected as much. Nancel was not sure if Ramus's opponents were right to call him a "Lutheran," but he knew very well "that from Presles a great many learned men went out who thereafter professed the religion called 'Reformed.'"[35] One of those learned men was Ramus's old student Jerome Wolf, who told the English logician Roger Ascham that Ramus had admitted his secret conversion to him. The Protestant Ascham, in exile in Halle in 1551, wrote to Johann Sturm that Ramus "believed rightly about Christian doctrine," but could not say so publicly in ultra-Catholic Paris.[36] Nancel suspected, and Wolf was sure, that Ramus's attention to Catholic propriety was merely a front for his Protestant beliefs.

On the face of it, their testimony seems compelling. Certainly it deserves more careful attention than the accusations of Galland, Turnèbe, and Ramus's other academic enemies. Neither Nancel nor Wolf stood to gain by labeling Ramus a Protestant, and they knew their man far better than his adversaries did or would have wished to. Besides, the idea that Ramus was a Protestant is less intrinsically unlikely than the claim that he was an atheist. Atheists were, if not nonexistent, then at least few and far between in the sixteenth century.[37] Crypto-Protestants were numerous, at least in France. Finally, there is no doubt that Ramus did eventually convert to the Reform, and it is tempting to view his public profession of faith in Heidelberg as ex post facto

---

33. Thus as Émile Léonard comments, "Le succès du 'luthéranisme' français était d'autant plus remarquable que ses adhérents n'avaient point rompu avec leurs cadres naturels, famille, voisinage, milieu professionnel—et Église"; *Histoire générale du Protestantisme*, vol. 2, "L'Établissement (1564–1700)" (Paris: Presses Universitaires de France, 1961), 87. Delumeau, *Naissance et affirmation*, 147, explains that the French Protestants, "obligés à une semi-clandestinité,...continuaient parfois à suivre les cérémonies catholiques et à recevoir les sacrements de l'Église romaine."

34. Delumeau, *Naissance et affirmation*, 147–48; Steven Ozment, *The Age of Reform, 1250-1550: An Intellectual and Religious History of Late Medieval and Reformation Europe* (New Haven: Yale University Press, 1980), 356, n.12.

35. Nancel, *"Petri Rami Vita,"* 250: "et hoc scio, e schola Praella permultos exiise viros quidem doctissimos, eosdemque religionem deinceps habitam et dictam reformatam professos."

36. J. A. Giles, ed., *The Whole Works of Roger Ascham...* (1864: reprint, New York: AMS Press, 1965), 319, Letter CXXXV, 19 January 1552: "quum putarem Ramum recte sentire de Christi doctrina, et hoc modo, his temporibus et eo loco, suum consilium tegere...; et hoc meum de Ramo judicium, postea Augustae, noster Hieronymus Wolfius, qui Lutetiae fuit, verum esse confirmavit."

37. On the problem of atheism in the Renaissance, see Febvre, *Le Problème de l'incroyance*, passim; and Paul Oskar Kristeller, "The Myth of Renaissance Atheism and the French Tradition of Free Thought," *Journal of the History of Ideas* 6 (1968): 233–43.

evidence of a secret conversion earlier. In hindsight, the circumstantial evidence that he was already a Protestant in the 1550s, scant as it is, seems more convincing.

The strongest evidence against such a conclusion comes from Ramus himself. In a letter to the cardinal of Lorraine in October 1570, he explicitly stated that it was the cardinal's speech at Poissy that awakened his doubts about Catholicism. The cardinal's praise of the Apostolic Age, Ramus wrote, prompted him to reconsider his religious beliefs,

> and since then I have not ceased reading the writings of excellent theologians and whenever possible meeting with them face to face, and for my own instruction putting together commentaries on the main points of religion.[38]

The result of his studies was his conversion to the Reform. If Ramus's account is to be trusted, he was still a Catholic in 1561 and only gradually left the faith during the following decade. By 1570, when he wrote the letter, he had nothing to lose by telling the truth, since by then everyone knew that he was a Protestant anyway. If he had already converted before the Colloquy of Poissy, there would be little point in denying it at that late date.

On the other hand, Ramus might well have misrepresented his religious development in his letter to Lorraine for reasons besides self-protection. He might have decided that blaming the cardinal for his conversion would be a good way to pay back his old patron for abandoning him. In October of 1570, Ramus had just returned from two years of exile in Germany, and he badly needed help to reestablish himself in Paris. Twice he appealed to Lorraine, and twice his letter went unanswered.[39] It was in the second letter that he suggested that Lorraine was responsible for his conversion. His old patron must have winced when he read Ramus's account. He knew very well that he had strayed from the Catholic line at Poissy in an effort to lure the Lutherans back to Rome, and thereby isolate the Reformed in France.[40] If Ramus wished to embarrass his former Maecenas, a prince of the church and a leader of the ultra-Catholic Guise clan, he could hardly have done better than to portray him as a propagandist for the Reform. The letter, which Ong described as "petulant,"[41] must have seemed insolent to Lorraine. Ramus may have been less interested in historical accuracy than in cardinal baiting.

The question remains, then, whether Ramus was already a Protestant in the 1550s. As it happens, there is another document composed by Ramus himself which

---

38. Ramus to Lorraine, 22 October 1570, *Collectaneae*, 212: "posteaque non destiti scripta excellentium theologorum legere, cumque ipsis Theologis (ubicunque licuit) coram agere & communicare, & ad me ipsum privatim erudiendum commentaria praecipuorum capitum conficere." The commentaries Ramus was composing were to be published posthumously; see below, chapter 5.

39. *Collectaneae*, 210–13.

40. See esp. David Nugent, *Ecumenism in the Age of the Reformation: The Colloquy of Poissy* (Cambridge: Harvard University Press, 1974).

41. Ong, *Ramus*, 28.

makes it clear that he was not. The document is a will dictated by him in November 1559, and deposited in the same notarial archive as his later and more famous testament of 1568.[42] Historians have not paid as much attention to the earlier as to the later will. Neither Waddington nor Ong mentions it at all, and it is still unpublished. It is not, however, unknown. In a 1980 study, Jean Dupèbe analyzed it along with the wills of Ramus's colleagues Talon and Péna for evidence of Reformed beliefs, and concluded that none of them revealed any particularly Protestant characteristics. He found them all "moderate and equivocal" in confessional terms.[43] If we turn Dupèbe's question around, however, and look for evidence not of Protestant but of Catholic beliefs in Ramus's testament, we find little equivocation.

According to the text of the will, the "venerable and learned [sientifficque] person Pierre de la Ramee" came before the notaries Lamiral and Crozon in a solemn and reflective state of mind, "considering in himself that the days of every human creature were and are brief" and with his thoughts therefore "disposed to the health of his soul."[44] As a "good and true Catholic," he commended his soul to Jesus Christ, to the Virgin Mary, "advocate between him and all sinners," and to "all the saints [saintz et saintes] of Paradise," in the hope that they might conduct him to heaven after his death.[45]

The preamble to Ramus's testament proclaims his continued loyalty to the Catholic faith at the end of 1559. His prayer to Mary and all the saints to intercede for him is a clear mark of Catholic belief, since no Protestant would expect to find help from either quarter. The question is whether the preamble provides an accurate reflection of Ramus's real beliefs. There are two possibilities which would nullify the will as evidence of his continued Catholicism. The first is that the preamble might have been merely formulaic, a standard invocation added by the notaries with or without their

42. Archives nationales, Minutier central des notaires, Étude XLIX, liasse 63, fols. 545v–546v, dated 3 November 1559.

43. Jean Dupèbe, "Autour du Collège de Presles: Testaments de Ramus, Talon et Péna," *Bibliothèque d'humanisme et renaissance* 42 (1980): 137. Dupèbe adds, "Si nous avons pu déceler dans ces textes quelques touches d'évangélisme, rien ne nous permet d'aller plus loin."

44. Archives nationales, Minutier central des notaires, Étude XLIX, liasse 63, fol. 545v: Fut present ven^ble et sientifficque personne Mre Pierre de la Ramee lecteur ordinaire du Roy nostre S^r M^re et prin^al du College de presles fonde en l'université de paris.…Considerant en luy que briefz estoient et sont les jours de toute vie humaine…sa pensee despose au salut de son ame.…"

45. Archives nationales, Minutier central des notaires, Étude XLIX, liasse 63, fol. 545v: "comme bon & vray catholicque a recomande & recomande son ame a dieu notre createur saulveur et redempteur Iesus christ a la benoiste glorieuse et tressacree vierge marie sa mere ad^cate envers luy de tous pescgeurs…et a tous les benoists saintz et saintes de paradis en les priant et requierant treshumblement que quand son ame departira de son corps leur plaisir et vouloir soit prendre et icelle mener et conduire au benoist Royaume de paradis." After this preamble, Ramus proceeded to practical arrangements. He divided his property between his mother Jehanne and his uncle Honoré and forgave the debt owed him by the college of Presles, which at that time totaled some 9,000 livres (according to the accounts of the college, A.N. H³2874², "College de Presles 1546–1572," unpaginated). Finally, he named Omer Talon as his executor to make sure his wishes were honored.

clients' approval. The other is the possibility that Ramus was a crypto-Protestant, a "Nicodemite," who adopted the protective coloration of Catholic practices in his will as in the rest of his life, without believing that they were valid or efficacious.

Neither possibility stands up to analysis. Even if Ramus was secretly a Protestant in 1559, he could easily have dictated a will that was confessionally neutral, not so Catholic in tone as the actual document, but not especially Protestant either. Such a course would have guaranteed his safety without sacrificing his principles. We know that he could have done so because later, in 1568, that is exactly what he did. His later will began with the phrase, "In the name of the Father, the Son, and the Holy Spirit," and continued:

> I recommend my soul to God, who made it, praying Him to admit it into Heaven in the communion of saints; I leave my body to the earth from which it came, until the day of judgment.[46]

This was all that Ramus had to say on religious matters in his 1568 testament. The rest of the will is purely a business document, devoted mainly to establishing the new royal chair of mathematics. It was deposited in the same office, and signed by one of the same notaries, as his earlier will.[47] In 1568, Protestants in general and Ramus in particular were no more popular than they had been a decade earlier, and Ramus had not yet openly embraced the Reform. The inference is that if he had wanted to write a less Catholic-sounding will in 1559 he easily could have. Therefore the sentiments expressed in the earlier will were probably sincere, and Ramus was still a Catholic in 1559.

Unless of course the preamble was not Ramus's composition at all, and was added by the notary acting on his own. Certainly there are strong similarities between Ramus's will and Talon's in the expressions of religious faith they contain.[48] Even if it were the case that the preamble to Ramus's will was merely formulaic, however, there is other evidence in the will that Ramus still believed in the cult of saints and in their power to intercede for the souls of sinners. His legacies to his uncle and to the college of Presles were explicitly intended to ensure that Honoré and the students of the college would pray for the salvation of his soul after his death.[49] To a Protestant, such prayers would be pointless. Reformed theology clearly

---

46. Ramus's will of 1 August 1568 has been published numerous times, as in the biographies by Nancel, Desmaze, and Waddington. I am using the facsimile of the original published in Bonnardot, *Histoire générale de Paris,* 34–37. The preface reads "Animum Deo a quo factus est, in celestem Beatorum familiam adoptandum commendo; corpus terrae, unde ortum est, in judicii diem committo."

47. The earlier will was witnessed by the notaries Lamyral and Crozon; the later, by Lamyral and Chappelain.

48. Dupèbe, "Autour du collège de Presles," 137, quotes a substantial portion of the preamble to Talon's will.

49. Archives nationales, Minutier central des notaires, Étude XLIX, liasse 63, fol. 546r: "affin de prier dieu pour son ame," "prie dieu pour luy."

taught that all the prayers in the world would not avail to alter God's judgment on Ramus's soul. To a Catholic, on the other hand, the possibility of escaping purgatory through the good offices of the saints was open, and the prayers of survivors might convince them to intercede. It seems safe to say, then, that as of 1559 Ramus had not yet abandoned the Catholic faith.

What made him change his mind? Walter Ong suggested that the death of his friend Omer Talon in 1562 might have been a major factor in his decision to leave the Catholic Church, but it is hard to see why Talon's death would have such an effect.[50] Waddington believed that Ramus's hostility to Aristotle helped to estrange him from the Catholic establishment, which it certainly did. It could hardly have made the Reform any more attractive to him than Rome, however, since by the 1560s both Calvinists and Lutherans were once again as committed to Aristotelian orthodoxy as the Catholics.[51] Besides, Waddington's hypothesis does not account for the timing of Ramus's conversion. He had been an opponent of Aristotle since the early 1540s. Why would he have waited so long before breaking with Aristotle's great defender, the Catholic Church?

Ramus's own account of his reasons for converting, as expressed in his letter to Lorraine in 1570, deserve serious consideration.[52] Ramus may have misrepresented the role of the cardinal's address at Poissy in his religious evolution, but the reason he offered for leaving the Catholic Church rings true. His desire to revive a lost golden age, so prominent in his other endeavors, played a major role in his religious thought as well. To a great extent, his conversion was the product of a typically humanist return to the sources, in this case the sources of Christianity. Not surprisingly, he envisioned his religious development as a basically intellectual process, to be achieved through study, reflection, and debate, by "reading the writings of excellent theologians and meeting with them face to face." No great spiritual crisis led him to embrace Protestantism, and no sudden revelation showed him the truth of the

50. Ong, *Ramus*, 28, writes, "How far the upset of losing Talon had to do with Ramus abandoning his Catholic religion for Protestantism in this latter period of his life, we shall never know," but does not explain why it should have had any such effect at all.

51. Waddington, *Ramus*, 126–27. Waddington also mentions the ignorance of the Catholic clergy (127–28) and the influence of Ramus's Protestant students (130) as possible reasons for his conversion. On the return of Aristotle to favor among the Reformers, see e.g. Beza to Ramus, 1 December 1570, where Beza tells of his "firm resolution to follow the sentiments of Aristotle without the least deviation, both in the teaching of logic and in the rest of our studies" at the Academy in Geneva; Beza, *Correspondance*, 11:295. More generally, see Ozment, *Age of Reform*, 309–13, on Luther's attempts to eliminate Aristotle from the university curriculum and on the "new popularity of Aristotle in Protestant universities during the second half of the sixteenth century" (313).

52. Whatever Ramus's motives for embracing the reform, his opportunity may well have come from the settlement of his longtime lawsuit with Le Puy, which provided him a windfall of 3,000 livres in the fiscal year 1560–61 (A.N. H^{3}2874^2, "College de Presles 1546–72," unpaginated). On this settlement see above, chapter 2. Financial considerations might otherwise have kept him tied to the patronage of Lorraine, which he lost as a result of his conversion.

Reform. His religious quest was a thoroughly humanist and intellectual affair. It was also, as we shall see, more than a little influenced by his social aspirations and ideals.

Ramus's letter to Lorraine places the beginning of his conversion in the early 1560s, and the date is supported by his activities in that period. After the Colloquy of Poissy, it quickly became clear that Ramus was no longer the "good and true Catholic" of 1559. A series of well-publicized events in 1562 made his orthodoxy more suspect than ever. The most notorious was the "affair of the statues" in January of that year. As Ramus told the story, his mathematics classes, which met in the chapel of Presles, had grown so large that it was necessary to remove some of the statues of the saints to make more room. As the students maneuvered the heavy and cumbersome images out of the way, several of them fell and were shattered. Rumor had it that Ramus had deliberately destroyed the statues, and he was widely denounced as an iconoclast by the Catholics, while the Protestants praised his zeal for the Reform. Nancel refused to venture an opinion on the matter, and a University commission failed to reach a conclusion on what exactly had happened and why.[53] In popular opinion, any lingering doubts about whether Ramus was a heretic were nonetheless dispelled by the affair. The public did not need an official investigation to decide who was Catholic and who was not.

Shortly after the incident of the statues, Ramus's *Advertissements sur la réformation de l'Université de Paris* appeared to supply more evidence of his unorthodox beliefs.[54] His antagonism toward the regular clergy emerged clearly in the suggestion that the king divert revenues from wasteful uses, such as supporting monks, and employ them instead for the salaries of University professors.[55] Ramus even specified that two of the prebends of Notre Dame should be suppressed and their revenues turned over to the faculty.[56] This was an even more direct endorsement of secularization of church property than had appeared in Ramus's speech after the Pré-aux-Clercs affair, and it earned Ramus even more antagonism from the Catholic Church and its defenders.

this was not unusual in medieval universities

The *Advertissements* went even further than that. Ramus took it upon himself to criticize not only the wealth of the church, but its theology as well. He recommended that the faculty of theology at Paris be ordered to drop scholastic authors from the curriculum entirely and to teach only the Old and New Testaments. Furthermore, the Old Testament should be taught in Hebrew and the New in Greek. If theology were taught in this manner, Ramus asked disingenuously, "what perverse opinions could result from

---

53. The incident is reported in Nancel, "*Petri Rami Vita,*" 262; Du Boulay, *Historia*, 6:549–50; Crevier, *Histoire*, 6:130–31. Crevier claims that Ramus added "moquerie au sacrilège, disant qu'il n'avoit pas besoin d'auditeurs sourds et muets." I cannot find a source for Crevier's quotation.

54. The *Advertissements* appeared anonymously in 1562 in both Latin and French versions, the Latin being the original, according to Ong, *Ramus and Talon Inventory*, 351.

55. Ramus, *Advertissements*, 123, 128; *Prœmium*, cols. 1066–67, 1070.

56. Ramus, *Advertissements*, 132; *Prœmium*, col. 1073.

those who heard both Testaments interpreted by great and holy teachers?"[57] All of Europe knew the answer to that question. Luther, Zwingli, and Calvin had shown clearly the kinds of opinions that might result from the study of Scripture alone.

Such teaching was not in any case compatible with orthodox Catholicism. According to Nancel, Ramus attended Mass for the last time at Easter of 1562, and thereafter he not only stayed away himself but encouraged his students to do likewise.[58] He also sought to "abolish prayers for the dead and the invocation of saints" at Presles.[59] Ramus's religious beliefs had changed a great deal since he had requested just such prayers and invocations for himself a little more than a year earlier, and all of Paris knew it. His position there was becoming dangerous, and when civil war broke out after the Massacre of Vassy in March he had to flee the city to avoid being murdered as a heretic.[60] After the peace, he returned to Paris and resumed his anti-Catholic activities. He was among the most vocal opponents of the Jesuits when they sought to establish a college in the University.[61] In the same year, he actively promoted the creation of a Protestant academy in Orleans.[62]

---

57. Ramus, *Advertissements*, 159–60; *Prooemium*, col. 1098: "quaenam pevrersa [sic] de religione opinio ab iis, qui utrumque Testamentum e sanctis illis & eximiis doctoribus intellexissent, posset existere?" Ramus also urges that Charles institute royal professorships in the Old and New Testaments; ibid., col. 1061 [by error: 1091].

58. Nancel, *"Petri Rami Vita,"* 264: "Ac nisi fallor, postremo Paschate, quod apud illum versabar, cum domus quam plurimus et discipulis et magistris abundaret, nemo sacris aut communioni adfuit, praeter ipsum Ramum, et Jacobum Goupylum regium medicinae professorem, qui eo forte convenerat, et me tertium ejusdem mensae sacrae convivam. Ab eo autem tempore, Ramus aut in totum abstinere aut clam sacris participare instituit." The last Easter Nancel spent at Presles may have been as late as 1568. But Goupyl died in 1564, while Nancel was away teaching at the University of Douai (from 1562 through 1564). Apparently the Easter Mass to which he refers took place in 1562. Also according to Nancel (262), Ramus thereafter favored those students who, like him, avoided the Mass: "imo iis favere potius, qui abstinerent."

59. Nancel, *"Petri Rami Vita,"* 262, says Ramus sought "et memorias mortuorum et invocationes sanctorum abolere."

60. Waddington, *Ramus*, 150–53. This first flight from Paris gave rise to Ramus's first conflicts with Muldrac over the office of principal of Presles. See Victor Carrière, "Pierre de la Ramée et la principalité du collège de Presles," *Revue d'histoire de l'église de France* 26 (1940): 238–42.

61. Estienne Pasquier, *Le Catechisme des Jesuites: Ou examen de leur doctrine* (Ville-Franche: Guillaume Grenier, 1602), fols. 29v–30r. He identifies Ramus as the one who pled the case against the Jesuits, but denies that it was because Ramus was a Protestant. Indeed, "ny Ramus ny Mercerus ne s'en remuerent en leur particulier, bien furent ils de la partie tout ainsi que leurs autres confreres Professeurs du Roy, pour ne se separer du corps de l'Université." Cf. Du Boulay, *Historia*, 6:592. In general, see the account of the lawsuit in Charles Duplessis d'Argentré, *Collectio judiciorum de novis erroribus, qui ab initio duodecimi seculi post incarnationem Verbi usque ad annum 1632 in Ecclesia proscripti sunt & notati…Tomus Secundus…* (Paris: André Cailleau, 1728), 349–57, which makes Ramus's role in the whole affair seem minimal.

62. The chronicle of the Bordeaux student Claude de la Grange credits Ramus's repeated requests with convincing Odet de Châtillon to support 100 students in the new Protestant academy; N. Weiss, "Une des premières écoles de théologie protestantes en France (Orléans 1561–68)," *Bulletin de la Société de l'histoire du Protestantisme Français* 60 (1911): 218–24.

Meanwhile, his published works continued to attack Catholic practices. Both the "Scholae Physicae" of 1565 and the "Scholae Metaphysicae" of 1566 argue against the display of religious images, while the latter also urges a return to the Gospel in theology.[63] Not surprisingly, the renewed outbreak of religious war in 1567 once again forced him to flee Paris, this time to take refuge with the Protestant army of Condé at St.-Denis.[64]

The events of the 1560s made it clear that Ramus was no longer a loyal Catholic but had become an enemy of the church. Does that mean he had joined the French Reform? His contemporaries thought so, but then they always had. Ramus himself denied it. In 1564, he still bridled at the suggestion that he was a Huguenot, while his will of 1568 gives no explicit indication of adherence to the Reformed movement. Moreover, he did not participate in a Protestant Lord's Supper until the end of 1569. Ramus had abandoned the Catholic Church, and his religious ideas were clearly moving in the direction of Protestantism. They were not, however, moving in the same direction as the doctrine and practices of the Reformed churches of France. In fact, French Protestantism was developing in a manner Ramus found extremely distasteful, and it is that development which explains Ramus's long hesitation to join in organized Protestant worship.

The traditional source for the early history of the French Reform is the *Histoire ecclésiastique des Églises reformées*, attributed to Beza and published in Antwerp in 1580. As a source, the work has the advantage that it is roughly contemporary with the events it describes, and was composed by a man (or men) close to and involved in them. Of course these "advantages" are also possible sources of bias and partiality. Beza and his colleagues were most emphatically partial, as is evident in the following passage. It is taken from an account of the foundation of the Reformed Church of Paris in 1555 along Genevan lines:

> Satan then truly began to be assaulted and attacked, more closely than he ever had been in France before, where there had not yet, properly speaking, been any Church established in all its parts, there being merely believers taught by reading good books, and as it pleased God to instruct them sometimes by particular exhortations, without there being regular administration of the sacraments, or an established consistory. But they consoled each other as well as they could, gathering as the opportunity presented itself to pray, without there being properly speaking other preachers than

---

63. Ramus, "Scholae Metaphysicae" in *Scholae in Liberales Artes*, and "Scholae Physicae" in the same collection. In the former (col. 996), Ramus urges theologians not to rely on Aristotle, but instead "sanctum Christi Evangelium Christianae juventuti proponite."

64. Nancel, "*Petri R ami Vita,*"264, denies that Ramus's flight to Condé meant that he had joined the Protestant cause. He sought only safety, "non militando, non feriendo, sed observando, sed historiam meditando scribendeque...."

martyrs, aside from a small number of monks, and others preaching less impurely than the others.[65]

Clearly the French Reform was in a sorry state before 1555! The lack of preachers must have been particularly burdensome if the faithful had to rely on martyrs to preach to them. Geneva's determination to "take the French Reform in hand" must have been an enormous relief to the Huguenots.[66]

Beza certainly thought so, and in all fairness most French Protestants seem to have welcomed direction from Geneva. Still, the passage above says more about Geneva's attitude toward the indigenous French Reform than about French Protestantism itself. It is important to note that the passage does not say there were no churches, preachers, or sacraments before 1555. What it asserts is that there were not proper ones, and that preaching and the administration of sacraments were not regular, that is, according to rule. These conclusions are judgments and not statements of fact, judgments that depend entirely on who decides what is proper and who makes the rules. If Beza found the state of the French churches inadequate, it was in part because he considered Geneva the unique model of church organization. Any church not patterned after that of Geneva was ipso facto deficient. In the first half of the sixteenth century, however, French Protestants had other models before their eyes.

The earliest inspiration of the French reformers was Martin Luther himself. Jean Delumeau specified that it was the Luther "of before 1525, the one who resolutely put the accent on the interior dialog of the soul with God and neglected the exterior organization of the Church." French Protestants looked for direction to the early Luther, who promoted the priesthood of all believers and considered the outward form of the church a matter largely indifferent. What this meant for the organization of the early French Reform is summed up in another passage from Delumeau:

> it was a matter of pious communities, without a strict hierarchy and without solid links between them. It was a Protestantism of free congregationalism. In their meetings, there was little preoccupation with the sacraments, but the Scriptures were read with fervor.[67]

In factual terms, Delumeau's description of the early French Reform is essentially the same as that of the *Histoire ecclésiastique*, but the difference in point of view is striking. One shows us a vision of piety, egalitarianism, and zeal, while the other reveals chaos, deprivation, and anarchy. It is idle to ask which is the more accurate account. Even at the time, there was no agreement on whether "free congregationalism" was an

---

65. G. Baum and E. Cunitz, eds., *Histoire ecclésiastique des Églises réformées au royaume de France*, vol. 1 (1580: reprint, Paris: Librairie Fischbacher, 1883–89), 117.

66. The phrase is from Delumeau, *Naissance et affirmation*, 148: "C'est surtout à partir de 1555 que Calvin…prit en mains les Églises réformées du royaume."

67. Delumeau, *Naissance et affirmation*, 147.

ideal to be achieved or a disease to be cured. As we shall see, Ramus fervently believed the former and Beza the latter. What is important is that the French Reform in the first half of the century was characterized by a basically congregational organization under the control of laymen, in which each congregation enjoyed wide discretion in the interpretation of Scripture and the establishment of discipline. All of this was to change when the French churches came under the tutelage of Geneva, with its centralized, hierarchical, and clerical ideal of church government.

Huguenots who were dissatisfied with the fragmented condition of the early Reform sought a model of church polity abroad, but Geneva was not the first place they looked. They rejected the later Lutheran pattern of territorial churches under the control of the secular authorities as unattractive and unworkable in Catholic France and turned instead to Strasbourg and its reformer, Martin Bucer. As Lucien Febvre pointed out long ago, "for the churches of France, the mother church is not that of Geneva. It is the church of Strasbourg as it was from 1540 to 1542."[68] Strasbourg offered a model closer to the experience of French Protestants than either Wittenberg or Geneva. Although Bucer had been converted by Luther, he had come under the influence of Zwinglian theology and ecclesiology, with the result that the church of Strasbourg practiced a "freer evangelism" than either Luther or Calvin allowed.[69] French congregations sought pastors (Tournai, 1544) and instruction on discipline (Meaux, 1546) from Strasbourg long before 1555, when according to Beza the first real church was founded.[70] Through the influence of Bucer and of Heinrich Bullinger, Zwingli's successor in Zurich, Zwinglian ideas of church polity, eucharistic theology, and the relationship between church and society gained an early foothold in France.[71] Backed by the example of Zurich and the southern German cities, Zwingli's vision of the Reform proved a powerful rival to the Genevan program for organization of the Reform in France.

Nonetheless, from the middle of the 1550s on, Calvinist doctrine and practice made steady progress in France.[72] Some modern historians seem to regret the spread and eventual triumph of Genevan doctrine and discipline among the Huguenots in the 1560s. In their accounts, Geneva appears as an aggressively imperialist foreign

---

68. Lucien Febvre, "Crayon de Jean Calvin," in *Au coeur religieux du XVIe siècle* (Paris: Livre de Poche, 1983), 337–67, at 351.

69. Léonard, *Histoire générale*, 83.

70. Febvre, "Crayon de Jean Calvin," 351–52.

71. See esp. André Bouvier's excellent *Henri Bullinger, le successeur de Zwingli: D'après sa correspondance avec les réformées et les humanistes de langue française* (Paris: Delachaux & Niestlé, 1940), which details the influence of the Zurich *antistes* within the French churches. Delumeau, *Naissance et affirmation*, 329, emphasizes the importance of Zwingli and Bullinger for the Reformation not only in France but in Europe as a whole, and especially for the Reformed churches: "Pourtant le Protestantisme de type suisse doit peut-être autant à Zwingli qu'à Calvin. C'est donc une véritable réhabilitation qui s'opère sous nos yeux."

72. See above all Kingdon, *Geneva and the Consolidation*, passim.

power bent on replacing the pure French experience of the Reform with alien ideas and practices. Thus Émile Léonard referred bluntly to Geneva's "conquest" of French Protestantism.[73] It is easy to share the preference for the original French tradition of congregational autonomy and lay participation in the government of the church, and to regret the triumph of clerical hierarchy sponsored by Geneva. At the same time, it is important to realize that Geneva did not "conquer" the French Reform. On the contrary, Huguenot leaders actively sought Calvin's and Beza's guidance in organizing the church and codifying doctrine, while most rank-and-file Huguenots embraced Genevan practices willingly and even eagerly. There were dissenters, of course, and vocal ones at that. Still, French Protestants in general welcomed the leadership of Geneva for a variety of reasons. The desire for pure doctrine and for solidarity with the rest of the Reform was strong, and so was the need to present a united and coordinated defensive front to the threat posed by the Catholic majority in France.[74]

The Huguenots did not adopt Genevan practices all at once. Rather, the acceptance of Calvin's and later Beza's views on doctrine and discipline took place gradually, a bit at a time, in the acts of successive national meetings of the French Reformed churches. The first national Reformed synod, which met at Paris in 1559, endorsed Calvinist ideas in general terms but refused to adopt certain important parts of the Genevan model. The role of the laity in the election of pastors was affirmed in the decision that congregations could veto the selections of their consistories, while regular pastoral synods, as established by Calvin's *Ecclesiastical Ordonnances*, were explicitly forbidden. The assembly at Paris also stopped short of a blanket condemnation of nicodemism. Despite Calvin's remonstrances, the synod voted to tolerate members of the Reform who were baptized or married in the Catholic Church, a concession to a situation in which the Reformed could not always perform those essential functions for themselves.[75] As a general rule, the synod made modifications in the Genevan program to adapt it to French necessities and traditions. The clandestine existence of Protestantism in France made lay initiative, congregational autonomy, and relatively lax discipline essential.

In the course of the 1560s, thanks to the success of Protestant arms in the first three wars of religion and the concessions made to Protestant worship by the crown, the Reformed churches were able to elaborate a more permanent national organization which adhered more closely to Genevan guidelines. Already at Poitiers in 1561, the synod affirmed the exclusive right of pastors to administer baptism while restricting the lower ranking deacons to a purely social role in the churches. The same

---

73. Léonard, *Histoire générale*, 83.

74. Delumeau, *Naissance et affirmation*, 150: "Tout naturellement [the French Reformed churches] accueillerent avec sympathie le message et les consignes de celui qui parlait leur lange et était l'un des leurs."

75. John Quick, *Synodicon in Gallia Reformata: Or, The Acts, Decisions, Decrees and Canons of those Famous National Councils of the Reformed Churches in France...* (London: T. Parkhurst and J. Robinson, 1692), 2–4.

assembly ruled that laymen must not outnumber clerics at meetings called to discuss matters of faith.[76] The result was stronger clerical control of church affairs, and the power of the pastors was further augmented by the synod of Lyon in 1563, which ruled that neighboring pastors were to have a role in selecting new ministers for churches in their vicinity.[77] In Paris in 1565, it was affirmed that only representatives of regional synods, rather than members of each church, should have the right to attend national synods. Since the synod of Poitiers had decided four years earlier that pastors would always outnumber laymen at the regional level, this decision ensured that the clerics would control the national assemblies. It also established a firm hierarchy of authority within French Protestantism, descending from national to regional synods and finally to individual churches.[78] Hierarchical order was prescribed within the individual churches as well at the synod of Verteuil en Angoumois in 1567, which prohibited election of consistories by congregations and required instead that the places of departing members be filled by co-optation.[79]

The transformation of French Protestantism from a vaguely defined movement embracing numerous autonomous congregations dominated by laymen into an articulated hierarchical organization controlled by the clergy culminated in 1571 with the decrees of the synod of La Rochelle. The decisions of that synod, over which Beza himself presided, will be treated in the next chapter. Even a decade earlier, however, it was clear that French Protestantism was evolving in a direction of which Ramus could not approve. His suspicion of institutional authority in general, and of oligarchy in particular, led him to reject the Genevan model of the church, and to prefer the Reform as it had been in the time of Francis I. At the time of his conversion, the French Protestant movement had already begun its metamorphosis to the Genevan model, and Ramus naturally shied away from a strong commitment to it. Ramus was unwilling to participate in the increasingly Genevan church of the 1560s in France, and as we have already seen, he had become estranged from the Catholic Church as well. He had not become altogether disillusioned with religion, however; there is no evidence that he was either an atheist or a skeptic. The evidence suggests that he had decided to embrace Protestantism in the 1560s, but had not yet found the particular Protestant sect whose views on doctrine and discipline matched his own.

His opportunity to investigate the alternatives came in 1568, when renewed religious conflict in France forced him into exile once again. His farewell letter to the University of Paris in August of that year noted, with some understatement, that "the conditions of the times have come to oppose my former studies here."[80] Therefore, he went on, he had to beg leave to journey abroad. He probably did not have to

---

76. Quick, *Synodicon*, 15–16.
77. Quick, *Synodicon*, 33.
78. Quick, *Synodicon*, 56–58.
79. Quick, *Synodicon*, 71–79.
80. Ramus, "P. Ramus Rectori & Academiae Parisiensi," in *Collectaneae*, 175: "Jam vero cum status temporum studiis et exercitationibus pristinis tam adversis incidisset." Ong, *Ramus and Talon Inventory*,

beg very hard. His colleagues were glad to be rid of him, and after he had gone they went to some lengths to make sure he would not come back.

Ramus's letter stated that the plan of his sabbatical was "to visit the famous academies of the Christian world and greet the men most eminent for learning and intelligence."[81] That is exactly what he did, although his letter did not mention that the famous academies were those of the Reformed cities of Germany and Switzerland, and that the eminent men he greeted were for the most part committed to the Reform.

Ramus's itinerary took him to all of the great cities of the upper Rhine. Between August 1568 and August 1570, he visited in succession Strasbourg, Basel, Berne, and Zurich, Heidelberg and Frankfurt, with an excursion eastward to Augsburg and Nuremberg, and finally came to the French-speaking cities of Geneva and Lausanne before returning to Paris after the peace of Saint-Germain.[82] Wherever he went, his activities followed much the same pattern. In each city, he put himself forward as a candidate for a teaching position in the local university or academy while approaching the local leaders of the Reformed Church for instruction and advice. Being the sort of man he was, he also managed to stir up trouble at nearly every stop along his route.

Ramus had finally come to the realization that Paris was not the best place for him to live and work. It was hard to be comfortable and productive there when every year or so saw another outbreak of civil war and another period of exile. In 1562, 1567, and 1568, Ramus had to run for his life, and the situation did not seem to be improving. Besides, there was always the possibility that at some point he might put off his departure until too late, and suffer worse consequences than a sojourn in the provinces. Although he had always claimed that his loyalty to Lorraine, to the king,

---

suggests that this letter was printed in a limited edition as a sort of handbill to be distributed among Ramus's friends before his departure from Paris.

81. Ramus, "P. Ramus Rectori...," 175: "impetravi a Christianissimo Rege veniam peregrinationis annuae, tanquam liberae legationis ad nobiles Christiani orbis Academias invisendum, praestantesque ingenio, doctrina, homines salutandum." Waddington, *Ramus*, 190, writes that the safe conduct given to Ramus by the king was all that saved him from being executed as an emissary of Condé. It was on his journey out of France that he encountered a force of German mercenaries on their way to assist the Huguenot forces. As their wages were in arrears, the troops threatened to mutiny and return home, but Ramus so charmed them with his eloquence that they decided instead to proceed to the aid of their coreligionaries. The story is told most fully in Jacques-Auguste de Thou, *Histoire universelle de Jacques-Auguste de Thou...*, vol. 4, 1567–1573 (The Hague: H. Scheusleer, 1740), 41–42. Neither De Thou nor any of Ramus's other biographers indicates how Ramus was able to make himself understood, in Latin or in French, to the German-speaking soldiers.

82. Ramus's travels in Germany are described by Waddington, *Ramus*, 190–217; Freigius, *Petri Rami Professio regia, hoc est septem artes liberales in regia cathedra per ipsum apodictico docendi genere propositae...* (Basel: Henricpetri, 1576), 510–13; and most fully by Banos, *Petri Rami Vita*. Nancel, "*Petri Rami Vita,*" 264, refers his readers to Banos's account of the journey.

and to France made it impossible for him to take a job abroad, his travels in Germany were to a great extent a series of job interviews.

At first he must have been optimistic about his chances. Universities all over Europe had offered him positions in the past, from as far afield as Italy, Poland, and even Transylvania.[83] Bologna had offered him a chair in mathematics at the munificent salary of 1200 ducats, but Ramus had refused, because, as he later wrote, Lorraine had not permitted him to go. (Nancel remembered Lorraine's reaction a bit differently. In his account, the cardinal told Ramus to go, saying "you will certainly free France from great care, worry and dread; but your coming and your teaching will stir up all of Italy—perhaps not without serious danger for you, unless as you cross the sea you have a change of character as well as a change of air.")[84] Whatever Ramus's reasons for declining, it was too late to reconsider. Bologna's offer had come in 1563, and was not likely to be repeated now that Ramus's true religious colors were becoming apparent.

The problem was to find a post at a Protestant school, and suddenly none of them seemed to have room for the renowned royal professor. He offered his services to the Strasbourg academy and was rebuffed despite a recommendation from Johann Sturm, the school's founder. The elector palatine himself promoted Ramus's candidacy for the chair of ethics at Heidelberg, but to no avail. The faculty would not have him.[85] Ramus was even reduced to seeking a position at Geneva from Beza. Given Beza's opinion of Ramus, his rejection there was a foregone conclusion.

Why was it so difficult for a scholar of Ramus's reputation to find a job? The main reason was his treatment of Aristotle. Even Sturm had to admit that his friend was a "heretic" where Aristotle and Euclid were concerned, while the senate of the University of Heidelberg branded him an enemy of the truth and of Aristotle, which in their eyes came to much the same thing. Beza voiced the same objection:

> Two things only oppose our now doing that which you hope and which earlier our professors very much desired. The first obstacle is that there is presently no vacancy in the academy....The second obstacle consists in our

83. On the offer of a chair in Transylvania, see Lajos Rácz, "La Logique de P. de la Ramée en Hongrie," *Revue des études hongroises et finno-ougriennes,* 2/3 (1924): 199–201.

84. Ramus to Lorraine, 22 October 1570, *Collectaneae,* 211–12: "Parisiensem vero professionem accepta Bononiensi professione Romuli Amasaei (qui mille & ducentis ducatis docuerat) si permisisses...." Nancel, "*Petri Rami Vita,*" 254, reports Lorraine's comments as follows: "Vade (inquit ille paucis omnino verbis), magna quidem cura et molestia atque formidine Galliam liberaturus; sed Italiam totam tuo adventu tuaque doctrina plurimum perturbaturus. Ac forsan non sine tuo gravi discrimine, nisi cum coelo motes animum, qui trans mare curris." Sharratt identifies the quotation from Horace, *Epistolae,* 1, 11, 27.

85. Moritz Cantor, "Ramus in Heidelberg," *Zeitschrift für Mathematik und Physik* (Leipzig) 3 (1858): 133–43, details the opposition of the University to Ramus's appointment.

firm resolution to follow the opinions of Aristotle, without deviating an inch, either in the teaching of logic or in the rest of our studies. [86]

Ramus's apostasy concerning Aristotle was enough to sink his chances of employment anywhere in Germany and Switzerland, but there were other reasons why Ramus was not a good candidate for a permanent teaching post. Word had gotten around that he was a chronic malcontent and troublemaker who sparked discontent and discord wherever he went, and his reputation was abundantly confirmed by the events of his two-year tour. In Strasbourg, the students disrupted a dinner given in his honor. In Heidelberg, they attempted to shout him down when he rose to speak. Even in disciplined Geneva, Ramus stirred up the students, at least indirectly. During his stay in Calvin's city, he had been invited to teach a public course on Cicero's Catiline letters. The rector of the Geneva academy, Jean le Gasgneux, and Beza himself objected to his methods and asked him to teach in a different manner. As Beza reported to the Geneva Company of Pastors,

> It was thought that he would not agree, believing that he knew as well as anyone else the proper method to follow. So he did not lecture any longer, but gave it up entirely. At that some of the students were upset and posted certain verses in honor of Ramus and blaming those who they thought had forbidden him to continue to teach. [87]

In Geneva as elsewhere, Ramus's visit was marked by the appearance of factions and the outbreak of minor riots. No one wanted to find out what would happen if he settled in their town permanently.

Ramus's attempts to find a teaching position outside of France came to nothing. All he accomplished was to antagonize Beza, and Beza had not been overly fond of him to begin with. He had only slightly more success in his relationships with the theologians and churchmen he met, but the successes he did achieve were of crucial importance to his later career.

Ramus spent the greatest part of his stay abroad in Basel, from October 1568 to October 1569, partly in order to take advantage of the city's great publishing industry

---

86. Beza to Ramus, 1 December 1570, Beza, *Correspondance,* 295. The letter refers to Ramus's approach to Beza through a third party and, while professing affection and esteem for Ramus himself, emphatically dismisses the possibility that Ramus might teach at Geneva.

87. Olivier Fatio and Olivier Labarthe, *Registres de la Compagnie des Pasteurs de Genève,* vol. 3, *1565–1574* (Geneva: Droz, 1969), 26 (fol. 40r): "M. de Bèze et le recteur parlerent à M. Ramus de changer sa façon qu'il tenoit à enseigner et faire leçons en l'auditoire publiq. Ce qu'on pense qu'il n'approuva pas, comme estimant savoir aussi bien q'ung aultre la manière qu'il faloit suivre. Tant y a qu'il ne poursuivit plus à lire, ains desista du tout. Dont aucuns escoliers furent marris et afficherent certains vers en l'honneur dudit M. Ramus et blasmant ceulx qu'ils pensoyent luy avoir defendu de continuer ses leçons."

and to see several of his works through the presses.[88] While there, he also obtained leave to attend the lectures of Simon Sulzer and Ulrich Köchlin for his first real training in theology. In his published panegyric to the city of Basel he praises these two instructors lavishly, claiming that he had "no greater consolation than to follow their lessons regularly, the first explaining the Old Testament in Hebrew and the second the New Testament in Greek."[89]

Ramus spoke highly of Sulzer in public, but in private he sang a different tune. In July of 1569, he wrote to friends in Zurich warning them of Sulzer's treachery and urging them to rise up against him. The "hypocritical wolf" Sulzer had blocked the formation of a French church in Basel, Ramus claimed, and had accused those who sought to form one of "anabaptism." He had done so because he was secretly a traitor, a Lutheran in Reformed clothing. Ramus took it upon himself to spread the word that Sulzer was a devious, dangerous enemy of Christianity. Ramus was especially angry at Sulzer's attempts to insinuate a Lutheran view of the Eucharist into the Reformed Church, and he refused to take communion in Sulzer's church.[90] Ramus had already rejected the doctrine of Christ's real presence in the sacrament in favor of the more spiritual view of the Helvetic confession. The issue was one that was to arise again when he eventually returned to France.

88. Ramus's stay in Basel has attracted a good deal of attention from historians. Among them, A. Bernus, "Pierre Ramus à Bâle," *Bulletin de la Société de l'Histoire du Protestantisme français* 39 (1890): 508–23, is the most informative on Ramus's involvement in religious issues there. Peter G. Bietenholz, "Pierre Ramus," chap. 8 of *Basle and France in the Sixteenth Century*, 153–63, is excellent on Ramus's involvement with the great printing establishments of Basle, while arguing that Ramism per se exerted little long-term influence in that city; but see Joachim-Otto Fleckenstein, "Petrus Ramus et l'humanisme bâlois," *La Science au seizième siècle: Colloque International Royaumont, 1-4 juillet 1957* (Paris: Hermann, 1960), 119-133, who suggests that his influence on mathematics there extended to and laid the groundwork for the Bernoullis and Euler: "Ramus represente le point culminant de la transition de la Renaissance philologique à la Renaissance mathématique; comme prophete d'une nouvelle méthode dialectique, il est devenu le précurseur de Descartes" (120).

89. Petrus Ramus, *Basilea* (Lausanne: Probus, 1571). A. Bernus, "Pierre Ramus à Bâle," prints a French translation of this quotation from the *Basilea*: "J'ai assidûment écouté Simon Sulzer et Ulrich Koechlin; et au milieu des misères de ces tempêtes civiles je n'ai pas eu de plus grande consolation que de suivre régulièrement leurs leçons à tous deux, le premier expliquant l'Ancien Testament hébreu, et le second le Nouveau Testament grec. Alors je voyais se réaliser le voeu qui avait failli me coûter la vie, lorsque, dans mes *Advertissements sur la réformation de l'Université de Paris* je souhaitais que nos théologiens puisent à ses veritables sources la pure doctrine de la parole de Dieu et instruisent leurs disciples à l'y puiser." Paul Roth, "Petrus Ramus et l'Université de Bâle," *Mélanges offerts à M. Paul-E. Martin par ses amis, ses collègues, ses élèves* (Geneva: Comité des Mélanges P.-E. Martin, 1961), 271–77, provides a summary of the contents of the *Basilea*, and points out that it was never delivered publicly, and in fact appeared in print only after Ramus had returned to Paris.

90. Ramus's letter to Gwalter and Lavater, dated 22 (or 31) July 1569, appears as an appendix to Bernus, "Pierre Ramus à Bâle," 524–30, with extensive notes and a French translation. The autograph of the letter is in the Stadtbibliothek Zurich, MS. B. 31, fol. 28. On his criticisms of Sulzer, and on Sulzer's character and career, Bernus, "Pierre Ramus à Bâle," 515–21.

In Heidelberg, Ramus found a French church already established, and there he finally joined in a celebration of the Lord's Supper after so many years of abstaining. There he also found Thomas Erastus and quickly picked a quarrel with him. Ramus remembered the meeting in dry and neutral terms: "When I was in Germany I discussed church discipline with Erastus, who attributed all authority in that sphere to the Christian prince, an opinion I could not approve."[91] Ramus did more than simply disagree, however. According to Beza, his differences with Erastus led to a nasty and personal altercation. Ramus even seems to have published a polemical tract against Erastus, which unfortunately has not survived.[92]

Ramus's quarrels with Erastus and Sulzer pale beside his long struggle with Beza and Beza's views on the Eucharist and church government, which will be the subject of the next chapter. He disagreed with these three leading figures in the Reform, but he learned from them as well, and throughout his exile he continued to compose his own theological studies with the benefit of their teachings. And he finally did meet a theologian with whom he could agree.

Late in the summer of 1569, Ramus left Basel for a brief trip to Zurich, the home of the Swiss Reformation. He had been eager to visit for some time, and his expectations were not disappointed. The city mounted a splendid reception for him, and he met and became fast friends with Rudolf Gwalter and his relative Louis Lavater. His correspondence with these two is one of the most important sources we have for Ramus's religious activities during the last two years of his life. Ramus also claimed that his conversations with the theologian Josias Simler had a great effect on his religious development. Most important of all was Ramus's meeting with Heinrich Bullinger himself, a meeting which was to have crucial implications for the course of the Reform in France.

Bullinger's role in the spread of the Reformation, and the authority he exercised over its adherents, has not always been sufficiently recognized. This "great bishop of the Reform" was the most influential and respected Protestant leader of his time. Only Calvin rivaled him in authority, though Calvin himself used to wait impatiently for the opinions and advice of his colleague. Beza treated the Zurich minister with kid gloves. There was no better counterweight to Beza and Geneva than Bullinger and Zurich, and it was Ramus's good fortune that he found the Zwinglians there to hold opinions congenial to his own.

Bullinger liked Ramus. His biographer suggests that the two became good friends, and while the evidence does not seem to support such a strong relationship,

91. Ramus to Gwalter, 23 July 1571, Bibliothèque de la Société de l'histoire du Protestantisme français, MS. 730, pièce 1, 5–7, at 5: "De disciplina Ecclesiastica dum in Germania essem, sum collocutus cum Erasto, qui principi christiano totam hanc provinciam attribuebat, quod sane probare non potui...."

92. Beza to Bullinger, 13 November 1571, Beza, *Correspondance,* 215–27, at 221. The letter is discussed in Kingdon, *Geneva and the Consolidation,* 104 and appendix 2. Erastus himself thereafter referred to Ramus as a "Pest aller Wissenschaft"; Jurgen Moltmann, "Zur Bedeutung des Petrus Ramus für Philosophie und Theologie im Calvinismus," *Zeitschrift für Kirchengeschichte* 68 (1957): 295–318, at 302.

there is no doubt that the two men impressed each other favorably.[93] Ramus had brought his own theological writings with him to Zurich, and Bullinger had approved of them, as he recorded in his diary under the date 28 August 1569: "Professor Petrus Ramus of the famous University of Paris exhibited for my judgment some books he had written on the subject of religion and especially on the sacraments. They pleased me."[94] It is not surprising that they did. Ramus had come to hold Zwinglian ideas on the sacraments and church discipline, as we shall see, and one authority considers him "more Zwinglian than Bullinger" himself.[95]

The importance of Ramus's visit to Zurich for his later career cannot be overestimated. Aside from confirming him in a basically Zwinglian view of church doctrine and discipline, it gained him the best possible allies in the struggle with the Geneva-backed leadership of the French Reform which was to come. More than any other single part of his journey abroad, it set the terms for his challenge to the Huguenot establishment. Whether the particular issue was sacramental theology, appointment of pastors, or determination of doctrine, the fundamental character of Ramus's fight with Beza and his supporters was a conflict between the Genevan and the Zwinglian paradigms of the Reformation. The next chapter describes Ramus's mature religious views as set out in his *Commentaries* and follows his efforts to revive an open, congregationalist, participatory church within the French Reform.

93. Bouvier, *Henri Bullinger,* 378.

94. Bullinger, *Diarium,* ed. E. Egli (Basel, 1901), 377: "28 Augusti [1569] d. Petrus Ramus clariss. academiae Parisiensis professor. Exhibuit mihi iudicandos aliquot libros suos de causa religionis scriptos et potissimum de sacramentis. Placuere."

95. Bouvier, *Henri Bullinger,* 405: "Si nous ne craignions le paradox, nous dirions que Ramus est plus zwinglien que Bullinger."

CHAPTER 5
Nemo Nisi Vocatus

RAMUS WAS IN LAUSANNE WHEN HE LEARNED, in August of 1570, that the war in France was over.[1] "At last by the grace of God peace has been restored to us!," he exulted.[2] Immediately he began to prepare for his return to Paris. To his friends in Zurich, he wrote that he regretfully had to postpone a planned second visit to their city: "the desire to enjoy the peace, to see my homeland again, and no longer to be a pilgrim in this region, calls me home quickly."[3] By early September he was ready to leave Lausanne. On the fifth of the month he appeared, along with a score of other French expatriates, to take his leave of the city council.[4] By the beginning of October, he was back in Paris after two years of exile.

It was not a pleasant homecoming. Ramus had been eager to see Paris again, but Paris had no desire to see him. The University in particular had taken steps to prevent him from resuming his former pursuits. Both his college and his royal chair had been taken over in his absence, usurped, he wrote, by "rabid and famished wolves" who were in no mood to yield their prey to a returning heretic. Even worse, the "ululations" of these "wolves" were arousing other beasts—"even lions and leopards"—to join in a clamorous and slanderous chorus of vilification. It was as if Ramus were "some sort of magician or enchanter, who if he were seen or heard in

---

1. The full phrase is "ut nemo nisi vocatus doceat in Ecclesia," "that no one may teach in the church unless he be called," from a letter of Theodore Beza. See below, note 52..

2. Ramus to Tremellius, 27 August 1570, in A. Sterne, "Deux lettres de Ramus à Tremellius," *Revue critique d'histoire et de littérature*, n.s. 13, no. 15 (10 April 1882): 295–96, at 295.

3. Ramus to Gwalter, 5 September 1570, Bibliothèque de la Société de l'histoire du Protestantisme français, MS. 730, pièce 1, 3–4 [copy of the original in Staatsarchiv Zurich], 3: "Sed desiderium fruendae pacis et revisendae patriae nos celerius domum revocat, neque sinit in his regionibus diutius peregrinos esse."

4. E. Chavannes, "Liste de réfugiés français à Lausanne de juin 1547 à décembre 1574," *Bulletin de la Société de l'histoire du Protestantisme français* 21 (1872): 463–78, at 472, citing the records of the Lausanne city council: "1570, 5. sept. Plusieurs seigneurs de France se sont présentés…pour autant ilz ont entendu publication de la paix avoir esté partout en France faicte, se veuillans retirer en leurs maisons; Prenans, causant ce, congie. Desquels sont escriptz: assavoir Monsieur maistre Pierre de la Ramée, lecteur du roy à Paris, appellé monsieur Ramus…." The list continues with another two dozen names of French exiles preparing to return home.

public, the Catholics would be annihilated."[5] Homeless, unemployed, and confronted by a hostile Paris, Ramus was as much an exile in his own city as he had been in Germany.

The University had worked hard to achieve such a result, and with the help of the Parlement of Paris and of Charles IX it had succeeded, at least for a while. The University owed its success to the continued hostility between the warring religious camps, which the treaty of Saint-Germain had done little or nothing to resolve. Despite Ramus's optimism, Saint-Germain had not really restored peace at all. It had done no more than bring about a temporary and uneasy truce between the Catholics and the Huguenots. In Paris, the steadfastly Catholic population remained openly hostile to the Protestants, and Reformed worship was still forbidden.

The University's desire to protect its purity from returning heretics like Ramus was in accord with the mood of the city and the tone of the treaty. It was also in accord with the policy of the king, who acted at the urging of the "oldest daughter of the Church" to prevent his capital from becoming once again a nursery of heresy. On 8 October 1570, shortly after Ramus's return, Charles issued an edict against "several Principals, Lecturers, Regents, Masters and Pedagogues" who were "instructing boys in their so-called religion" and "corrupting our University." To prevent the corruption from spreading further, Charles prohibited all those who were not "known and approved Catholics, holding the Catholic and Roman religion," from keeping "little Schools, Principalities and Colleges, or reading in any Art or Science whatsoever, either in public or in private." By the terms of the edict, Ramus was barred from his college and from his royal chair, wolves or no wolves. Not lions and leopards, but the king of France was to blame.[6]

Charles's edict was couched in general terms, but Ramus was not mistaken in believing that it was aimed at him in particular. Fear of Ramus prompted the University to send a special delegation to the king in mid-December to ensure that the

---

5. Ramus to Zwinger, March 1571, in Charles Waddington, *Ramus (Pierre da la Ramee): Sa vie, ses écrits et ses opinions* (1855; reprint, Dubuque, Iowa; Brown Reprint Library, n.d.), 430–31, at 430: "Lupi duo famelici et rabidi occupaverant alter gymnasium Praelleum, alter professionem eloquentiae et philosophiae, quibus molestissimum erat tam suavem bolum eripi e faucibus. Itaque luporum istorum ululatu reliquae nostri nemoris bestiae commotae, leones etiam et pardos in me unum concitarunt, tanquam P. Ramus voce quin etiam vultu quidam magus et incantor esset, qui si in publica cathedra audiretur vel conspiceretur, subversus esset protinus romanam gentem."

6. César Egasse Du Boulay, *Historia Universitatis Parisiensis*, vol. 6 (1665–73; reprint, Frankfurt: Minerva, 1966), 712–13, prints the text of the edict against "plusieurs Principaux, Lecteurs, Regens, Maistres & Pedagogues [qui] se sont retirez en ladite Université, instruisans les Enfans en leur pretendue Religion, lesquels par ce moyen sont une pepiniere de ladite pretendue Religion, corompans nostredite Université...disons, declarons, ordonnans, voulons & nous plaist que defenses soient faites à toutes Personnes de tenir petites Escholes, Principautez & Colleges, ny lire en quelque Art ou Science que ce soit en public, ny en privé en chambre, s'ils ne sont connus & approuvez Catholiques, tenans la Religion Catholique & Romaine."

royal professor's powerful friends at court would not use their influence to have him reinstated.[7] Their concern was well founded, insofar as Ramus's first reaction to the edict was to apply to his old patron Lorraine for assistance. As it turned out, they need not have worried. The cardinal had abandoned his protégé and did not even bother to reply to his pressing appeals for help.[8] Lorraine's influence had made Ramus's career, and without his support the future seemed bleak indeed.

Nonetheless, by the following spring Ramus was firmly established in Paris once again, in circumstances even more comfortable than those he had enjoyed in the 1550s. "At last, thanks to the great insolence of the envious and wicked," he wrote to Zwinger in March of 1571, "a dignified ease is established for me, such an ease as I could barely wish, much less hope for, in a time of peace and tranquility."[9] Ramus was held to the terms of Charles's edict, but that did not keep him from settling back into his college of Presles and enjoying his royal stipend. How did he achieve such a favorable result?

As far as Presles was concerned, his success was due to the loyalty of his students and to the terms of the college's charter, laid down by Raoul de Presles two and a half centuries earlier. Raoul had specified that the college would support two chaplains, one for the Holy Virgin and the other for Saint James, and that whoever held the chaplaincy of Saint James would serve as principal of the college as well. Furthermore, only a scholar of Presles could serve as chaplain or, ipso facto, as principal.[10]

The "wolf" who had usurped Ramus's position as principal had relied on the founder's wishes to gain control of the college. Antoine Muldrac had been appointed chaplain of Saint James by the bishop of Paris in 1563, during Ramus's first flight from Paris, and Ramus was forced to appeal to the Parlement of Paris on his return to dislodge his rival.[11] Muldrac was waiting in the wings, however, and when Ramus fled once again in 1568 he convinced Parlement to reconfirm his appointment. Between

7. Du Boulay, *Historia*, 6:713: "Iuxta hocce Decretum & literas Regias [of 8 October 1570] Rector die 2 Decemb. cum Deputatis egit de lite prosequenda adversus Petrum Ramum & alios Academicos fidei desertores. Et quia ille solebat apud Regem habere Patronos, delecti die 15 eiusdem mensis Vigor & Carpentarius qui Regem adirent, curarentque denuo confirmavi obtentas ab ipso literas contra fidei Desertores."

8. See Ramus's two letters to Lorraine in *Collectaneae praefationes, epistolae, orationes…*(Marburg, 1609), 210–13, and the discussion in chapter 4.

9. Ramus to Zwinger, March 1571, in Waddington, *Ramus*, 431: "Denique perspicis maxima invidorum et malevolorum importunitate otium nobis cum dignitate comparatum esse, et quidem otium, quale tranquillis et pacatis temporibus vix optare, nedum sperare potuissem."

10. See above, chapter 2.

11. A.N. X^{1a}1605 ff. 138v–139r, Parlement of Paris, Conseil, 12 May 1563: "pendant son [Ramus's] absens necessaire maistre Anthoyne Muldrac s'est soubz faulz devis a faict commettre par provision ala principaute dudict college…de laquelle toutesfoys il s'est fort mal et scandeleusement porte." The court decided in Ramus's favor.

Parlement's decree and Charles's edict, Muldrac might have retained control of Presles permanently for all that Ramus could do about it.[12]

Muldrac's downfall resulted, oddly enough, from his own academic success. By completing his degree as doctor of philosophy in 1569, Muldrac made himself ineligible to be a scholar at Presles or principal of the college. The conflict might have been ignored had not Muldrac made himself unpopular with his students, who challenged his right to run Presles in a suit before Parlement in April 1570. Despite its sympathies, Parlement could not escape the logic of the students' case. If Muldrac could not be a scholar, he could not be a chaplain; and if he could not be a chaplain, he had no claim to be principal of Presles.[13]

In itself, Parlement's decision could not help Ramus, who was after all banned from running Presles by his religious beliefs. The students elected one of their own, Claude Serain, to administer the college. Serain, a pupil of Nancel, became principal de jure, but he refused to use the title as long as Ramus was alive. Instead, he yielded control of Presles to Ramus on an informal basis. Ramus was thus able to enjoy his old quarters as well as the revenues and direction of the college for the rest of his life, thanks to the loyalty of his students and the niceties of the college's charter.

Ramus recovered the substance of his old position at Presles, even if he had to forgo his old title. His efforts to reclaim his royal chair met with just the opposite result. As Hubert Languet explained to Camerarius in June 1571: "Although Ramus is not permitted to teach publicly, nevertheless the King not only pays his salary which he enjoyed from teaching, but even adds to it six hundred livres a year."[14] Ramus's own words confirm Languet's report. "Thus to honor or console my retirement from service, my salary was doubled," which since he had previously been earning 600 livres a year comes to the same thing.[15] Barred from teaching, Ramus was allowed to keep his title and salary and even to add to it.

Clearly, Ramus had found a new friend at court to take the place of his old schoolmate Lorraine. Waddington speculated that his new patron was Charles of Bourbon, another old acquaintance who had studied with Ramus and Lorraine at the college of Navarre and who had, like Lorraine, taken a shine to the poor scholar from

---

12. On Muldrac and his long-term effort to take over the college of Presles, see Victor Carrière, "Pierre de la Ramée et la principalité du collège de Presles," *Revue d'histoire de l'église de France* 26 (1940): 238–42, the result of careful and extensive investigations in the archives of the Parlement of Paris.

13. Nonetheless, Muldrac did not give up after his defeat in 1570. After Ramus's death, he immediately challenged the new principal in an appeal to the Privy Council; A.N. M186, no. 66, "Extrait des registres du Conseil privé du roi, 3 octobre 1572"; and Carrière, "Pierre de la Ramée," 241.

14. Languet to Camerarius, 19 June 1571, in Hubert Languet, *Viri Clarissimi Huberti Langueti Burgundi, ad Joachimum Camerarium patrem, & Joachimum Camerarium filium, Medicum, Scriptae Epistolae...* (Groningen: Johannes Nicolas, 1646), ep. 56, 137–38: "Ramo quidem non permittitur ut hîc publice doceat, sed tamen non tantum numerat ei Rex stipendium, quod ob professionem habuit, sed etiam id illud addit sexcentos francicos annuos."

15. Ramus to Zwinger, March 1571, in Waddington, *Ramus*, 431: "Itaque ad emeritae militiae vel honorem vel consolationem stipendium nobis conduplicatum est."

Picardy. Bourbon had been made chancellor of the University in September of 1570, upon the death of Jean du Tillet, bishop of Meaux, and according to Waddington, he took advantage of his position to bolster Ramus's sagging career in late 1570.[16]

Waddington's theory is attractive on several counts, especially since the political and religious situation in France in 1570 and 1571 made an alliance between Bourbon and Ramus a natural one. But the evidence for such a relationship is weak. Aside from their boyhood acquaintance, there is only a comment by Du Boulay in his history of the University to support it. Bourbon's position as chancellor is of no real significance, as the chancellor had no special role in the choice or oversight of the royal professors. If Bourbon had wished to assist Ramus, he could have done so just as well with or without official standing at the University.

Besides, if Bourbon did take on the not inconsiderable burden of defending and advancing a client as troublesome as Ramus, he had little reward for his pains. Lorraine's efforts on Ramus's behalf had been repaid in numerous dedications and orations praising his generosity, lineage, learning, and character. In the context of the sixteenth century, this was only right and proper: the writer looked after his patron's fame, while the patron attended to his client's fortune. If Bourbon was Ramus's guardian after his return from Germany, then Ramus showed himself strangely ungrateful. He did not dedicate a single work to Bourbon or compose a single address in his honor.

Ramus's dedications are a useful source for investigating his relationships with his patrons. Up to 1560, most of Ramus's works were dedicated to Lorraine. Of the twenty-five published between 1550 and 1560, seventeen were dedicated to the cardinal, while the remainder were addressed to "the reader" or bore no dedication at all. After 1560, however, Ramus ignored his old patron entirely, another indication that the two had broken their ties around the time of Ramus's conversion. Of the fourteen works published from 1560 to the time of his death, eight either bore no dedication or addressed themselves to the anonymous reader.

The remaining publications are more interesting, as five of them are dedicated not to powerful courtiers but to members of the royal family itself; one to Charles IX, one to the duke of Anjou, and three to the queen mother, Catherine de' Medici.[17] Having cut his ties to Lorraine, Ramus apparently decided to go straight to the top. His decision to concentrate on flattering the queen mother was a wise one. It seems that the king and queen mother accepted Ramus as a client after 1560. They certainly looked out for him. It was the king who sent him out of Paris and then

---

16. Waddington, *Ramus*, 230–31. In fairness, it should be noted that Waddington advances this argument only tentatively, relying on a brief note in Du Boulay, *Historia*, 6:928.

17. The sixth work, the *Actiones duae mathematicae* of 1566, was dedicated to Christophe de Thou. This was a transparently political maneuver on Ramus's part, since the work contains Ramus's pleas against Charpentier in the matter of the royal chair of mathematics, and De Thou was hearing the case as a president of the Parlement of Paris.

sheltered him at Fontainebleau during the first religious war, and the king again who arranged his safe conduct out of France at the outbreak of the third. Catherine and Charles also seem to have commanded that Ramus be spared in the Saint Bartholomew's Day Massacre. No doubt they were also responsible for reinstating him in his title and stipend in 1570 or 1571. Ramus himself gave them the credit. In his previously cited letter to Zwinger, he wrote that he had appealed to them, and especially to Catherine, by reminding her of how he had sung her praises in his *Præmium mathematicum* of 1567. "This oration pleased the king and queen," he wrote, with very favorable results.[18] In theory, a scholar who had the king and queen mother of France as patrons was in the best of all possible worlds.

In practice, however, Charles IX and his mother were not the most stable of supports. They were caught between the powerful forces of the Catholics on one side and the Huguenots on the other, and obliged to shift their policies constantly to maintain a precarious balance between them. In this great game, Ramus could be no more than a pawn, to be advanced or sacrificed when the need arose. His death in 1572, whether as a victim of royal policy, royal neglect, or royal weakness, shows just how uncertain the position of a royal favorite could be in the era of religious wars.

Still, for the time being, Ramus was in a comfortable and even enviable position. Secure in his college and his stipend, he could devote his time and talents entirely to the Reform. That his opinions were no more welcome among the French Protestants than they were among the Parisians did not daunt him in the least. Nor was he discouraged because a national synod of the church was busily rejecting his most cherished doctrines just as he prepared to expound them. In his typically dogged and disrespectful manner, he set about to reverse the developments of the past two decades, and to return French Protestantism to its pristine condition, despite the opposition of the Reformed leadership in France and in Geneva.

The extent to which Ramus had developed a clearly formulated theology and ecclesiology before mounting his challenge to the established church in France is important, if only because some historians have suggested that his doctrinal stands were merely opportunistic, adopted on the spur of the moment to exploit one or another weakness in his opponents' position.[19] It seems clear, however, that Ramus's stands on the Eucharist, on church government, and on most of the other contested issues were not merely tactical maneuvers but parts of a coherent religious

---

18. It seems likely that Ramus's appeal to the king and queen appeared in print as the preface to Ramus's *Grammaire* of 1572. While the preface does not make a direct appeal for reinstatement, it does request that Ramus be permitted to continue his task of translating the arts into French, and in words identical (with allowance for translation into Latin) to those used in the letter to Zwinger previously cited.

19. See for example Robert Kingdon, *Geneva and the Consolidation of the French Protestant Movement, 1564–1572: A Contribution to the History of Congregationalism, Presbyterianism, and Calvinist Resistance Theory* (Geneva: Droz, 1967), 105.

viewpoint. The strongest evidence to that effect lies in his *Commentariorum de Religione Christiana.*[20]

This work, Ramus's only venture into the realm of theology, did not appear until after his death. The posthumous edition, prepared by his disciple Théophile de Banos, seems to have been an immediate success. Banos reported to Sir Philip Sidney, to whom he had dedicated the work, that at least 2,000 copies were printed in the first edition, and demand was such that a new printing was required the next year. Two more editions appeared before the end of the century, which suggests that while the *Commentaries* were not one of the sixteenth century's best-sellers, they did attract a good deal of attention in the closing decades of the 1500s.

The posthumous publication of the *Commentaries* makes it difficult to determine when they were completed. On the one hand, Ramus had a manuscript available in 1569 to show to Bullinger in Zurich, and Waddington believed that he had substantially completed his work by the time he wrote to Lorraine in October of 1570. On the other hand, if he had finished the manuscript, it is hard to understand why he did not publish it. Ramus was not one to keep his thoughts from the world any longer than he had to; his habit was to rush into print as quickly as possible. Besides, Ramus wrote to Gwalter in September of 1570, saying that he was still working on the book.[21]

We will probably never know the complete history of the composition of the *Commentaries*, but the problem of when Ramus finished composing them is in some ways a false issue. In fact, he never finished composing them. What he had planned to write and what has come down to us under the title *Commentariorum de Religione Christiana* are two very different things. His plan had been for a work that would embrace all of theology, with the subject divided into two distinct areas, Christian doctrine and Christian discipline. The first part was to cover faith and works of faith, while the latter was to prescribe church discipline and polity.[22] As published in 1576, however, the *Commentaries* contained only the part of theology subsumed under the heading "doctrine." Ramus's writings on discipline, if any existed, never appeared in print.[23]

---

20. *Petri Rami Veromandui, Philosophiae et eloquentiae Regii professoris celeberrimi, Commentariorum de Religione Christiana, Libri quatuor...* (Frankfort: A. Wechel, 1576).

21. Ramus to Gwalter, 5 September 1570, Bibliothèque de la Société de l'histoire du Protestantisme français, MS. 730, pièce 1, 3: "Communicavi vobis cum commentarios quosdam de religione, de quibus amplius etiam communicare cupiebam, quia si qua tanti boni facultas nobis a Deo concessa sit, statuo diebus Dominicis istam nobis Theologicam praelectionem futuram."

22. Ramus to Lorraine, 22 October 1570, in *Collectaneae*, 213: "Saeculum nostrum doctissimis in omni lingua scientiaque hominibus beatum est, quos tu potes unius de tam multis tuis abbatiis impensa tibi adjungere,...ad conficiendum indicem, qui praecepta atque exempla cujusque partis, vel ad doctrinam de fide, deque fidei actionibus in lege, precatione, sacramento, vel ad eorum omnium politiam disciplinamque artificiosa ratione ac via complectatur."

23. It is possible that Ramus did in fact write his projected work on church government, and that the establishment of the French Reform prevented its publication and dissemination. The records of the

Fortunately, sources on Ramus's view of proper church government do survive, in records of synods of the Reformed Church in France. These will be considered later. The doctrinal views laid out in the *Commentaries* as they were published are worth our attention, however, for their role in the struggle over the development of the French Reform was major. Ramus's opinions on matters of faith were the foundations of his views on church government, and it would be difficult to understand one without the other.

Opinions on the merit of Ramus's theological work vary widely. Walter Ong considered Ramus's work "a curious deformation of theology,"[24] while Jürgen Moltmann found in it "a new organic union of customary points."[25] In the only full-length study of Ramus as a theologian, Paul Lobstein delivers a mixed verdict, finding his work "vague" on some points, "insufficient and feeble" on others, but at the same time "an eloquent appeal to Christendom for unity in spirit through the bond of peace."[26]

Most descriptions of the *Commentaries* avoid any careful analysis of their theological content, emphasizing instead the extent to which purely methodological concerns determined their form and content. The tendency began as far back as Nancel, who viewed the work simply as Ramus's attempt to apply to theology "that certain method...to which he had already reduced the other arts."[27] Ong similarly saw the work as the product of the grinding "machinery of Ramist dichotomizing analysis," which, he added, "fails to engage dogma or practice effectively."[28] Even writers more sympathetic to Ramus, such as Graves, yielded to the temptation to concentrate on the organization of the *Commentaries* rather than on their substantive theological content.[29] The theology

---

synod of Nîmes held in 1572 relate that Ramus had prepared a "book" in defense of his position, but whatever might have been the nature of this "book," it has not survived. As the synod also ordered that the records of the synod of the Île de France held at Brie earlier in the same year be "razed," it is not unlikely that Ramus's work received the same treatment. Of course, the "book" which Ramus brought to the synod may have been no more than a sort of scriptural brief, and not the projected second part of his *Commentaries* at all. See Quick, *Synodicon*, 1:111–12; Kingdon, *Consolidation*, 108–9.

24. Walter Ong, "Ramus and the Transit to the Modern Mind," *The Modern Schoolman* 32 (1955): 301–11, at 303 [previously published as "Ramus et le monde anglo-saxon d'aujourd'hui," *Revue de littérature comparée* 28 (1954): 57–66].

25. Jürgen Moltmann, "Zur Bedeutung des Petrus Ramus für Philosophie und Theologie im Calvinismus," *Zeitschrift für Kirchengeschichte* 68 (1957): 304.

26. Paul Lobstein's *Petrus Ramus als Theologe: Ein Beitrag zur Geschichte der protestantischen Theologie* (Strasbourg: C.F. Schmidt, 1878), 36, 37, 47.

27. Nicolaus Nancelius, "*Petri Rami Vita*: Edited with an English Translation," *Humanistica Lovaniensia: Journal of Neo-Latin Studies* 24 (1975): 224: "Quamquidem Ramus cum ad certam illam methodum reducere studeret, ad quam et caeteras artes olim reduxerat...."

28. Walter Ong, *Ramus and Talon Inventory* (Cambridge: Harvard University Press, 1958), 391.

29. Frank Pierrepont Graves, *Peter Ramus and the Educational Reform of the Sixteenth Century* (New York: Macmillan, 1912), 173–203, esp. 189.

expressed in the work, however, is extremely revealing in the context of the French Reform in the later sixteenth century, and deserves a detailed analysis.

It is wrong to conclude, though, that the arrangement of the work is devoid of interest or significance. The general scheme of the work appears in Ramus's first letter to Lorraine in October 1570, and in more detail in the introduction as it appeared in print. Ramus divided the study of the Christian religion into matters of doctrine and matters of discipline, as we have seen, and further divided doctrinal issues into the categories of "faith" and of "works of faith." The latter subdivision was further broken down into two general subjects, "obedience and prayer" and "sacraments." This outline does indeed suggest Ramus's fondness for dichotomies, at least superficially, and Graves reprints a typically Ramist table showing the breakdown of the topic by a series of binary divisions.[30]

On closer inspection, however, it is clear that the *Commentaries* are organized on a fundamentally different principle, and that the "machinery of the Ramist dichotomizing analysis" was adapted to that principle, rather than the other way around. In fact, the work's organization reflects not Ramus's "method of nature," "by which that which is above all and absolutely most evident and well-known is placed first," but rather the "method of prudence, in which the first things [are] not above all and absolutely the best known, but those things most expedient to whoever is to be taught, and more likely to induce and lead him to the place we desire."[31] Ramus did not impose his own organization on the content of the Christian faith, but instead borrowed an organization already familiar to and accepted by Reformed Christians.

In fact, Ramus's work closely follows the traditional organization of the Christian catechism, in particular the one composed by John Calvin in 1542.[32] Like Calvin, Ramus began with an exposition of the Apostles' Creed, which he used to explain the main points of faith. In book 2, the Decalog served as a framework for his discussion of Christian law and duty, and in book 3, the Lord's Prayer was the outline for his commentary on worship. The system broke down in the fourth book,

---

30. Ramus lays out this scheme in the introduction to the *Commentariorum*, 3: "Quapropter subductis Theologis omnibus de quibus mihi nosse vel audisse licuit, Theologum methodicum fore statuo, qui legitimam methodi viam sequitur doctrinam praeposuerit disciplinae, quique in doctrina ipsa disserverit primo loco de fide, secundo de fidei actionibus in lege, precatione, sacramentis, qui postremo disciplinam, id est doctrina praxin & politiam declararit." Graves's table is on 190 of his *Peter Ramus*.

31. Michel Dassonville, ed., *Dialectique de Pierre de la Ramee, a Charles de Lorraine Cardinal, son Mecene* (1555; reprint, Geneva: Droz, 1964), 145: "Méthode est de nature ou de prudence.... Méthode de nature est par laquelle ce qui est du tout et absolument plus évident et plus notoire est préposé,..." and 150: "S'ensuyt la méthode de prudence en laquelle les choses précédentes non pas du tout et absolument plus notoires, mais néantmoins plus convenables à celluy qu'il faut enseigner, et plus probables à l'induire et amener où nous prétendons."

32. Ramus, in Moltmann's words, "folgt mit dieser Einteilung dem Aufriß der üblichen Katechismusmethode"; Moltmann, "Zur Bedeutung des Petrus Ramus," 304. See the brief account in Euan Cameron, *The European Reformation* (Oxford: Clarendon Press, 1991), 398; and the discussion in the *Oxford Encyclopedia of the Reformation*, vol. 1, s.v. "Catechisms."

which treats the sacraments, and Ramus was obliged to follow instead an almost scholastic method of definitions followed by refutations of his adversaries' positions. On the whole, Ramus followed the traditional three-part division of the Christian catechism into creed, code, and cult, and more particularly the organization of Calvin's catechism of 1542. In the context of his other works, this scheme reveals that the *Commentaries* were not intended as a scientific exposition of Christian doctrine but as a persuasive and popular appeal, written not to prove the truth of Ramus's views, but to convince his contemporaries that they were correct.

The same aims can be discerned in an examination of Ramus's methods in a less technical sense. Like the other Reformers, he claimed to draw his conclusions entirely from the Bible. Lobstein pointed out that while Ramus did mention Augustine and Peter Martyr with approval, he did not refer to any of the other French or Swiss reformers. "Ramus maintained resolutely the position of Reformed Protestantism in relation to the Holy Scriptures. He stated the axiom: 'de divinis rebus non aliter quam per divinas scripturas agendum est.' Holy Writ is the only rule in matters of faith...."[33]

Nonetheless Ramus did not live up to his own maxim. His desire to refer only to "sacred scripture, in which alone the foundation of faith is united," led him to slight the great religious writers of earlier times and of his own era, but not to omit citations from the greatest pagan authors of Greece and Rome. He warned his readers that he intended to season his work with borrowings from the classical poets, orators, and historians,

> not that any authority or approbation for religion can be derived from them, but so that it may be clear Christian theology is not so abstruse or so remote from the human senses that it cannot illumine all people with a certain natural light, and its very humanity invite and allure men to engage in divine studies with eagerness.[34]

Numerous quotations from the classics were intended in part to allure men to Ramus's version of divine studies by making his work more attractive than the dry catechisms and analyses with which it competed. They were a natural accompaniment to the "method of prudence," used not to prove Ramus's ideas right, but to make them more palatable. Far from seeking to produce an "art" of theology on the

33. Lobstein, *Petrus Ramus*, 35–36: "In denn Commentariis selbst wird keiner der schweizerischen oder französischen Reformatoren citirt; der einzige reformirte Theologe, den Ramus nennt, ist Petrus Martyr." Lobstein apparently missed the citations to Immanuel Tremellius and Martin Bucer in Ramus's discussion of the Eucharist (*Commentariorum*, 286, 341), which are significant in an evaluation of Ramus's overall theological position.

34. Ramus, *Commentariorum*, 2: "non ut inde ulla religionis vel authoritas vel approbatio repetatur, sed ut planum sit Christianam Theologiam non adeo abstrusam esse: vel ab hominum sensibus remotam, quin naturali quaedam luce populis omnibus illuceseat, hominesque ideo humanitas ipsa ad divinia studia capessendum invitet, atque aliciat."

model of his "arts" of logic, grammar, mathematics, and so forth, Ramus was engaged in propaganda for his own opinions on God, man, and the Church.

The passage quoted above also suggests two of Ramus's more substantive theological ideas. First and most obviously, it implies that every man is free to "engage in divine studies"; theology is not the exclusive preserve of those with a God-given call to interpret the Scriptures. Second, it stresses the humanity of the Christian religion, and points to Ramus's emphasis on religion as a human experience. As the very first line of the work maintains, "Theologia est doctrina bene vivendi." It was Christianity as a subjective experience which was important, not as "a reflected representation of God's self-knowledge," but as a mirror for man. In contrast to the orthodox Calvinist view, which saw the crux of the Christian faith in the decrees of an omnipotent and imperious God, "the traditional essential points of objective theology no longer stand in the center" in Ramus's religious thought. The struggle between Ramus and Geneva can only be understood on the basis of this fundamental difference in their approaches to the meaning of Christianity. What was to the Calvinists the realization and embodiment of God's eternal and incomprehensible decrees, was to Ramus the expression of man's subjective relationship with his creator and savior.[35] The observation holds true whether we investigate the general tone of the *Commentaries* or concentrate on Ramus's interpretations of specific points of doctrine such as the Eucharist and predestination.

Ramus's views on predestination are particularly interesting. To a man whose life was built upon the premise that "labor omnia vincit," the idea that God had preordained his eternal destiny without regard to his efforts on earth cannot have been an appealing one. Ramus was a simple and straightforward man, and in simple and straightforward terms, predestination is the antithesis of his fundamentally meritocratic worldview. On the other hand, the logic of Calvin's arguments for God's supremacy and man's helplessness to contribute to his own salvation was compelling. Faced with this dilemma, Ramus waffled on the issue.

He begins firmly enough in his chapter "De praedestinatione," with a definition of predestination that refers to the preceding chapter on providence: "Predestination is related to providence, in that God elects some to eternal salvation through his free mercy, and repudiates others to eternal perdition by his justice."[36] There follow numerous scriptural proofs to demonstrate both election and reprobation, but in the

---

35. The man-centered character of Ramus's approach to Christian theology was emphasized by Moltmann, "Zur Bedeutung," 304: "Im Mittelpunkt stehen nicht mehr die wesentlichen traditionellen Stücke der objektiven Offenbarung. Ihr neuer Beziehungspunkt ist der subjektive Glaube und desen Ausdrucksformen." Lobstein, *Petrus Ramus*, 38, notices the same approach in Ramus's treatment of the sacraments, when he concludes that "Es wird vorwiegend die subjektiv menschliche Seite des Sacraments hervorgehoben."

36. Ramus, *Commentariorum*, 28: "Providentiae praedestinatio germana atque affinis est, qua Deus alios as aeternam salutem pro gratuita sua misericordia delegerit, alios ad aeternam perditionem pro sua justitia repudiarit."

final analysis Ramus is evidently unable to convince himself, let alone the reader, that God's justice condemns so many to damnation. After all, God wills the salvation of all men, and commands that the Gospel be preached to all. How could He then also create vessels appointed to destruction (Rom. 9:22)? "These sentences," Ramus wrote in reference to Paul's parable, "appear to be repugnant to infirm human nature," but he went on to endorse them nonetheless.[37] Ramus refuses to resolve the evident contradiction between God's will that all men be saved and his creation of many for damnation. In the end, he simply counsels the "docta ignorantia" of the Christian philosopher, which allows him to avoid drawing any firm conclusion.

Lobstein finds here "a mitigation or shifting with respect to Calvinist principles, which is not neutralized or retracted through [Ramus's] condemnation of adverse doctrines," and he is quite correct. Ramus sought to soften the rigid logic of Calvin while remaining in harmony with the Reformed view of predestination, and the result is, to say the least, vague. Whether its vagueness justifies Lobstein's exclamation—"How insufficient and feeble this chapter seems in comparison with the bold and imposing presentations of a Zwingli and a Calvin!"—is another matter, and one to which we will return.[38]

In the matter of the Eucharist, Ramus explicitly stated that the words of Christ which instituted the sacrament were not intended literally, so the claim that Christ is substantially present in the Eucharist has no foundation—a position that put him squarely at odds with the emerging consensus of the French Reform. "Body and Blood are metaphors," Ramus asserted, and not the real body and blood of the savior at all, just as the water of baptism is not the blood of Christ, although it is so called.[39] Ramus devotes eight chapters of his fourth book—nearly a third—to refuting the doctrine of real presence on various grounds: "per repugnantiam primae Coenae, ex homogenia Baptismi, ex analogia Hebraei paschatis, per consensum primitivae Ecclesiae," and so forth.[40]

---

37. Ramus, *Commentariorum*, 32: "Hae sententiae, si quid humanae naturae infirmitati repugnantes esse appareant, credamus tamen...."

38. Lobstein, *Petrus Ramus*, 36–37; see Moltmann, "Zur Bedeutung," 306, who also emphasizes Ramus's vagueness without, however, condemning it or making invidious comparisons.

39. Ramus, *Commentariorum*, 287: "Corpus autem & Sanguis metaphorae sunt, non id ipsum quod dicitur, sed dicto simile significantes, ut in baptismo si dicatur Aqua est sanguis Christi, talis metaphora sit, non in verbis aqua, vel Est, sed in nomine, Sanguis."

40. The discussion of the Eucharist takes up chapters 8 to 18 of book 4 of the *Commentaries*, 284–343, beginning with a definition (ibid., "Quid sit Coena," 284–90), continuing with seven different refutations of the doctrine of real presence (ibid., chaps. 11–16, 305–35), and concluding with discussions of the Catholic Mass (ibid., "De Missa pontificia," 335–40) and of the exotic inventions of men in their descriptions of the sacrament and the libels to which they have given rise (ibid., "De Calumnia adversus Christianos propter [artolatreia], deque exoticis & ab homine excogitatis verbis in quaestione de coena," 340–43). In other words, about one-eighth of the *Commentaries* is devoted to proving the absence of Christ's body from the Eucharist.

Here again we may detect an emphasis on the human, subjective side of the sacraments, in that the Eucharist becomes a sign from God of His grace, and from man of his commitment, rather than the mysterious and miraculous presence of Christ's body in the elements themselves. Just as important in the present context, however, is Ramus's reliance on the German theologians Bucer and Tremellius in his discussion of the sacrament, for in mentioning these two he gives an important clue to the sources and affinities of his theological opinions.[41]

What were these sources, and how can we characterize Ramus's theology? Walter Ong's remarks can provide a framework for approaching this problem. While Ong did not make a detailed study of Ramus's religion per se, his familiarity with Ramus's life and works lends weight to his comments on the subject. Together these comments suggest that, fundamentally, Ramus was a Christian humanist, with a great deal more emphasis on humanism than on Christianity. In denominational terms, he was indeed a Protestant, but of a peculiarly shallow and insipid sort. His Protestantism was "singularly lacking in Luther's Angst and in Calvin's ruthless conviction, being somewhat farsed, like Erasmus's Catholicism, with humanistic yearnings...." Elsewhere we are told that Ramus's religion was not merely "farsed" with "humanistic yearnings" but founded upon them. His conversion, Ong wrote, is to be understood "in terms of personal and business associates, in terms of politics, national and university, in terms of the Golden Age myth implied in the complex of humanist doctrine and the pagan, nonevolutionary, cyclic view of history, and doubtless in other terms which will always escape us...."[42] Here secular considerations and humanist (even pagan!) ideals appear as prime determinants of Ramus's religious ideas, rather than the spiritual conviction and emotional commitment we might have expected. No wonder, then, that Ong found Ramus's *Commentaries* "a curious deformation of theology."[43] Little better could be expected of a man whose "lapse into Protestantism" was the result of reading not the Gospels but the Greeks, not the letter to the Romans but Roman men of letters.[44]

Ong's comments suggest the problems involved in characterizing Ramus's religious thought, largely because they reflect two common prejudices which must be exorcised before the significance of his position can be appreciated. The prejudices which impart an antagonistic slant to Ong's remarks are harbored by many other Reformation scholars, Protestant and Catholic alike. The first is the common tendency to

---

41. Ramus, *Commentariorum*, credits Tremellius for his definition of the sacrament (286) and Bucer as well as Peter Martyr for their rejection of such scholastic terms as "reale, carnale, corporale, substantiale, consubstantiale, transsubatantiale,..." "quare vocabula in sacris literis peregrina barbaraque penitus fugienda esse, duo singulares aetatis nostrae doctores verissime monuerunt: Bucerus in libello de usu sacramentorum. Martyr in epistola ad Anglum quendam episcopum" (ibid., 341).

42. Walter Ong, "Père Cossart, Du Monstier, and Ramus' Protestantism in the Light of a New Manuscript," *Archivum Historicum Societatis Jesu* 23 (1954): 156.

43. Ong, "Ramus and the Transit to the Modern Mind," 303.

44. Ong, "Père Cossart," 156.

make Luther's religious experience, and to a lesser degree Calvin's, the definitive standards against which all other reformers are to be measured. By defining Luther and Calvin as the "normative" Protestants, historians devalue the spiritual development and religious insights of other Protestant thinkers. Their opinions and beliefs are no longer analyzed as independent and authentic expressions of Christian faith but as more or less unsuccessful attempts to come up to Luther's (or Calvin's) mark.

In regarding Luther as the touchstone of true Protestantism, historians turn differences from his paradigmatic ideas into shortcomings. Gottfried Locher has shown how damaging this approach has been to efforts to understand Zwingli, and has further pointed out how it has discouraged efforts to deal with Zwinglianism as a coherent and unified system. No appreciation of Zwingli's thought can emerge from an analysis that isolates bits and drabs of his theological system to see if they agree with Luther's doctrines or diverge from them. Locher provides a parody of such an analysis which makes the point clearly:

> Zwingli, a Humanist, also became a Reformer, but without sharing Luther's cloister experience or his spiritual troubles. He agrees with Luther at most points, but there are the following differences etc. So these points of difference…are wrenched out of their context in Zwingli's thought and are overemphasized. While at the same time, as regards the points of agreement…his own characteristic arguments and aims are overlooked….[45]

Without suggesting for a moment that Ramus was even close to being Zwingli's peer in theology, it seems he deserves the same courtesy as the Zurich reformer, namely that of not being judged by standards alien to his own. While Angst and "ruthless conviction" are certainly absent from his religious thought, their absence would be "singular" only if he were Luther or Calvin. Since he was not, then there can be no question of a "lack" in his religious life. Similarly, his ideas on predestination may seem to Lobstein to be "far removed from the zeal, the logic and the unbroken belief of Calvin,"[46] and therefore to be "weak and feeble," but by this standard there is hardly any Christian confession which is not "weak and feeble." If Luther and Calvin are the sole standards of authentic Protestant faith, then Ramus was a bad Lutheran, a bad Calvinist, and a bad Protestant. If not, he might simply have been a Protestant of a rather different kind.

---

45. Gottfried Locher, "The Characteristic Features of Zwingli's Theology in Comparison with Luther and Calvin," in *Zwingli's Thought: New Perspectives* (Leiden: Brill, 1981), 142–232, at 149. In this connection, Bernd Moeller's comments deserve attention as well. Moeller laments the tendency of historians to reduce "the Protestant movement in the sixteenth century to one man—Luther," and deplores their expectation "that Luther's followers themselves could have become, as it were, little Luthers, that they should have set aside their own background and put on his"; *Imperial Cities and the Reformation*, trans. H. C. Erik Midelfort and M. U. Edwards (Durham, N.C.: Labyrinth Press, 1982), 11, 15.

46. Lobstein, *Petrus Ramus*, 37.

He might have been, that is, if it was possible to be a good Christian while continuing to maintain the tenets of sixteenth-century humanism. Quite a few historians seem to doubt that such a thing is possible, or at least to deny that humanism can ever be an integral and organic part of true Christian faith. They suggest that humanist ideas can only be adulterants, foreign intrusions that are essentially alien to Christianity. Humanistic Christianity, in this view, can only be a muddle of diverse tenets, jostling each other uncomfortably within what purports to be a unified system of values and beliefs. Thus Erasmian Christianity is not a synthesis of humanism and Catholicism, but only Catholicism with "humanistic yearnings" interpolated in a more or less inappropriate manner, and Ramist Christianity is the same sort of stew but with a Protestant stock.

Not only modern historians but also his own contemporaries accused Erasmus of creating just such a sterile hybrid. The same charge was leveled against Zwingli. Walther Kohler, one of the foremost Zwingli scholars of the twentieth century, suggested the problem to his students in the following terms, as related here by Locher:

> One day he [Kohler] praised, in the presence of his students, the well-known monument which stands behind the Wasserkirche in Zurich, which, in a most impressive way, represents the Reformer armed with Bible and sword. But then he added that one must think of the book as having the pages of the Greek New Testament interleaved with pages of Plato's Dialogues.[47]

Kohler's point, as Locher interprets it, is that an antithesis runs through Zwingli's work, a dichotomy between the classical and biblical elements in his thought. The image of the New Testament interleaved with Plato is appropriate to the idea, and forcefully recalls Ong's remark that Ramus's Christianity was "farsed" with humanism. The difference is that Kohler believed Zwinglianism to be a fruitful synthesis of the two strains and not a hodgepodge of incompatible elements. Zwingli himself undoubtedly believed that he had produced a unified and valuable expression of Christian faith. So did Erasmus, and so did Ramus.

Ong's remarks on Ramus's religion are bedeviled by prejudices against the possibility of a viable synthesis of Christian and humanist doctrine, and more generally against any form of Protestantism which does not mimic the patterns established by Luther or Calvin. Nonetheless, if we can abstract from the more judgmental of his comments, we discover a plausible account of the character of Ramus's religious

---

47. Locher, "How the Image of Zwingli Has Changed in Recent Research," in *Zwingli's Thought*, 42–71, at 43. Moeller, *Imperial Cities*, 15, comments aptly on the presumption of conflict between humanism and Christianity. Citing Dilthey, he urges that "we should also grant that the Protestant humanists represent 'an intersection of coherent tendencies.' As such, they had an internally coherent 'character.'"

ideas. His theology was inspired by both the Bible and classical antiquity, and developed not in response to emotional crisis but through study and contemplation. It sought a return to the Golden Age of the church in the Apostolic era and a revival of primitive Christian simplicity and charity. It was in short an intellectual, broadminded, and nostalgic sort of Christian humanism.

Most of these conclusions are implicit in Ramus's own account of his conversion addressed to Lorraine in 1570. What Ong added are explicit references to Erasmus and the hint that Ramus himself was an Erasmian. The hypothesis has much to recommend it. Like Erasmus, Ramus found in humanism the inspiration for a simpler and more humane faith unencumbered by the scholastic subtleties of the Sorbonne. Even before he abandoned Catholicism, he followed the great Dutch humanist in rejecting the cult of the saints, chastising the monks for their greed and idleness, and pleading for a return to pure Scripture as the basis of a purified Christian faith. The two humanists encountered similar hostility from orthodox Catholics, who regarded them as heretics, hypocrites, or skeptics for their efforts to reform Catholicism from within.

What spoils the comparison between Ramus and Erasmus is that Erasmus remained a Catholic while Ramus left the church and eventually converted to Protestantism. In general terms, Ramus was, like Erasmus, a Christian humanist, but he was more specifically a Protestant Christian humanist, and the difference is too important for us simply to label him an Erasmian, even in the 1560s. Ramus must instead be understood in the context of Protestant humanism and of its earliest spokesman, Huldreich Zwingli.

It is no coincidence that Zwingli's name has come up so often in the last few pages. The importance of Zwingli's humanistic training for his understanding of the Christian faith, and the deprecating attitude of some modern historians toward his theology because of it, recalls Ong's assessment of Ramus. So does Zwingli's departure from the Lutheran paradigm of the reformer, which has been seen as a weakness in his case as in Ramus's. Even more telling is the importance of Zwingli and Zwinglianism in the formation of French Protestantism before its "conquest" by Genevan Calvinism. It was the early Reformation in France, with its antihierarchical and antiauthoritarian structure, that Ramus took as a model in his quest to revive the church of the Apostolic Age. Ramus had come to hold Zwinglian ideas on the sacraments and church discipline, and by the time he returned to Paris, Ramus was a confirmed Zwinglian, as François Hotman wrote to Bullinger in 1573:

> You write to me that the excellent Ramus gave public testimony of your doctrine and church while with you. I am not surprised, and I tell you, as God is my witness, in all of France and in all our churches, there was no one who was more attached to you, who more openly held your church to

be his mother and nurse, and who more detested the Roman synagogue as a wolf and a daughter of Satan.[48]

Ramus saw the Zwinglian ideal essentially in congregationalist terms. For him, there could be no distinction between the church as the whole body of believers and the church as those who had been somehow called to the ministry when it came to matters of doctrine and discipline. While the surviving portion of the *Commentaries* does not suffice to explain Ramus's ecclesiology in detail, we can depend on other sources for a clearer explanation of his ideas of proper church government.

The previous chapter has shown how the Reformed churches in France were gradually transformed from a group of autonomous, lay-controlled congregations into an increasingly unified and hierarchical national church dominated by the clergy. The culmination of the process occurred at La Rochelle in April of 1571, during the seventh national synod of the French Reformed Church. This synod, which Kingdon calls "the most important synod of the century, perhaps of the entire history of French Protestantism,"[49] was noteworthy in several respects. The gathering of distinguished Huguenots of noble blood in itself constituted a spectacle; the queen of Navarre, the prince of Navarre, and the prince of Condé, the admiral Coligny, and even Louis of Nassau from the Netherlands were in attendance.

The meeting took place in the great bastion of French Protestantism and under the direction of the most dynamic Reformed leader in Europe, Theodore Beza of Geneva. Under Beza's guidance the delegates of the regional synods reaffirmed and tightened clerical control of the church and threatened those who resisted the new order. Churches in Languedoc which continued to allow lay involvement in questions of doctrine and discipline were censured and condemned, while a request from the church of Meaux that participation of the people in selecting ministers be reestablished was simply ignored. Presbyterian control was legally and actually in place, and the synod of La Rochelle was sufficiently confident of its strength to demand conformity from all the Huguenots of France.[50]

The issue on which the national church asserted its new authority was that of eucharistic theology. The synod sought to refine the church's interpretation of the sacrament and to make it uniform throughout France on the basis of Genevan doctrine,

---

48. Hotman to Bullinger, 2 March 1573, quoted in translation in A. Bernus, "Pierre Ramus à Bâle," *Bulletin de la Société de l'Histoire du Protestantisme français* 39 (1890): 523.

49. Kingdon, *Geneva and the Consolidation*, 96.

50. Quick, *Synodicon*, 89–101. See esp. chap. 6, art. 8, where "Monsieur Vercelle Deputy of Brie declareth unto this Synod, that the Elders and People of Meaux are dissatisfied with the first Article of particular Matters; and complain, that they be deprived of their Freedom and Priviledge in Elections. Whereupon it was advised, that inasmuch as they had been diverse times heard,...Letters should be dispatcht unto them from this Assembly, exhorting them to acquiesce in the Order of Discipline received in our Churches of France..." (95).

which itself was ultimately based on the thought of John Calvin. The Calvinist doctrine of the Eucharist became a test case, a clear issue dividing the presbyterian church establishment in France from the more independent congregations of the Île de France and Languedoc.

Calvin's conception of the Eucharist was in some ways closer to that of Luther than to that of the other Swiss reformers. In his teaching on the subject, he consistently referred to the "real presence" of Christ in the elements of bread and wine, and he obliged students at the Academy of Geneva to subscribe to a confession which declared Christ was "substantially" ["substantialiter"] present in the sacrament. The other Swiss churches, and Zurich in particular, held to the "sacramentarian" position which denied the presence of Christ's body in the elements and rejected the conception of the sacrament which made it a reenactment of Christ's sacrifice.

Calvin's preference for the doctrine of real presence did not, however, take the form of a rigidly held dogma. He was flexible on the matter and followed a policy of live and let live with the other Swiss churches, as is shown by his adherence to the Consensus Tigurinis of 1549. This common doctrinal statement of the Swiss Reformed cities did not admit the crucial terms "substance" or "substantial" in its definition of the Eucharist, yet Calvin endorsed it and even defended it against its Lutheran detractors.

After Calvin's death, his disciple and spiritual heir Theodore Beza moved toward a more strict definition of eucharistic orthodoxy in Geneva. Beza insisted that the Genevan churches accept Christ's substantial presence in the bread and wine of the sacrament, and used his immense influence and prestige among the Huguenots to bring all of the French churches into harmony with Geneva as well. The La Rochelle synod decreed that Beza's interpretation of the Eucharist was the only acceptable one.[51] The other Swiss churches were not at first disturbed by Beza's departure from the Helvetic norm. Nor did his attempt to impose his eucharistic views in France trouble his most influential coreligionary, Heinrich Bullinger. The Zurich *antistes* was more concerned to see the message of the Gospel spread abroad than to quibble over the fine points of its interpretation.

In France, reaction to the new hard line on the Eucharist was mixed. A vocal minority arose to protest Beza's heavy-handedness, especially when he attempted to use his authority to silence his sacramentarian opponents. The issue quickly moved beyond the problem of the Eucharist to embrace that of the organization of the French churches, which in its steady evolution toward presbyterianism seemed to some to be no more than a façade for the domination of Geneva and Beza.

A good example of how the interpretation of Christ's words instituting the Lord's Supper could become a focal point in the dispute over church government in

---

51. Quick, *Synodicon*, chap.2, art.7: "That the Synod…rejecteth their Opinion, who will not receive the word Substance…and therefore all Pastors, and the Faithful in general are required not to yield unto the contrary Opinions…" (92).

France comes from the city of Lyon in 1566. Two Reformed Italians, Lodoico Alamanni and Cappone Capponi, continued to practice and preach an extreme sacramentarian position despite the widespread agreement in the church leadership that
Beza's interpretation was the orthodox one. Beza himself took a hand in attacking
Alamanni and Capponi, describing them in a letter of 2 June 1566 as mere troublemakers who sought only to disturb the harmony of the church. He challenged not
only their particular teachings on the Eucharist, but even their right to teach at all:
"For such is the order established by the Son of God…that no one may teach in the
church unless he be called [...ut nemo nisi vocatus doceat in Ecclesia]."[52]

To Capponi and Alamanni, such an argument had no weight at all. To triumph
over opponents by denying their right to speak was simply to establish a new tyranny
in place of the old Catholic one, with Geneva and Beza in the roles of Rome and the
pope. They protested in a letter of 9 June against those who would

> band together to maintain certain persons who have written and taught in
> our time, wishing to make them and their writings an oracle, inferring and
> maintaining that they cannot err in anything, either now or in the future.

Beza and Calvin were the "oracles" who were being followed so blindly by the
French synods, and whose opinions were to be immune from challenge by mere
laymen.[53]

The Italians' defense of the "priesthood of all believers" against the claims of the
clerics who had been "called" to decide matters of doctrine and discipline failed to
attract many supporters, even from the church in Lyon. There and elsewhere the
ministers continued to increase their power in consistories, regional synods, and
national assemblies and to disregard the opinions and preferences of the laity.

Natalie Zemon Davis has investigated the effect of this trend in the Lyon
churches, where the triumph of oligarchy and hierarchy was enough to drive the
more humble members out of the Reformed movement entirely. The printers' jour-
neymen she studied found that the new church discipline only reinforced the work
discipline imposed by the master printers. As ecclesiastical oligarchy came increasingly to second economic oligarchy between 1566 and 1572, nearly all the journey-
men left the Reformed fold. Most of them returned to Catholicism, believing as
Davis suggests that "the only real alternative was the Mother Church."[54]

---

52. Henri Meylan, "Bèze et les Italiens de Lyon (1566)," in *Mélanges Augustin Renaudet*, Bibliothèque d'Humanisme et Renaissance (Geneva: Droz, 1952), 235–49, at 242; and idem, *D'Erasme à Théodore de Bèze: Problèmes de l'église et de l'école chez les Réformés* (Geneva: Droz, 1976), 175–89, at 182.

53. Meylan, "Bèze et les Italiens," 240; idem, *D'Erasme à Théodore*, 180: "qu'ils se perdent
aujourd'huy et s'amusent si opinionastrement et se bandent pour maintenir aucungs personnages qui ont
escript et enseigné de nostre temps, voulant faire et rendre eulx et telz escriptz com'ung oracle, inferer et
sustenir qu'ils n'ayent peu en rien errer, ores ny pour l'advenir."

54. Natalie Zemon Davis, "Strikes and Salvation at Lyon," in *Society and Culture in Early Modern
France* (Stanford: Stanford University Press, 1975), 1–16, at 15.

There were some, however, who attempted to create a third alternative between the increasingly hierarchical Reformed Church and Catholicism by challenging the leadership of the French Reform directly. The best-known case of resistance to Genevan ideas in the French churches was that of Jean Morély, sieur de Villiers, which Philippe Denis and Jean Rott have traced in detail.[55] Morély's ideas were summed up in his 1562 manifesto, *Traicté de la discipline & police chrestienne*, which embroiled him in a long-running controversy with Geneva and the Genevan party in France. The theory laid out in the *Traicté* contradicted Beza's ideal of a centralized, hierarchical church government at every turn. Christ's command, in Morély's eyes, was that all believers in Him were to share in creating and enforcing discipline in all its aspects: admonition, excommunication, absolution, and the selection and deposition of pastors. Robert Kingdon summarizes Morély's dream as that of an "ecclesiastical democracy of a pure and rather simple sort."[56]

As soon as it appeared, Morély's work was condemned by the French Reformed establishment (at the synod of Orléans in 1562), and Morély himself was summoned to appear before the Geneva synod in November of the same year. His refusal marked the beginning of a breach in the French Reform which persisted through the 1560s and beyond, despite numerous attempts on both sides to bring about a reconciliation (most of them, it seems, in bad faith). Morély's ability to spread his message, and even to convince some French congregations to accept him into fellowship despite his condemnation by both Swiss and French authorities, calls for some comment, especially since Ramus was later to adopt many of Morély's strategies in his own confrontation with the Genevan party in France.

Morély was able to recruit support from two important groups of Huguenots in his quarrels with the church establishment. The first group included many of the great Protestant nobles of France, whose influence could not be ignored by his opponents in France and Geneva. Concerned by the increasing clericalism of the French Reform, which left them without a voice in its councils, as well as by the prospect of foreign domination of their church, members of some of the greatest families in France intervened to defend and support the rebel Morély.

---

55. Philippe Denis and Jean Rott, *Jean Morély (ca. 1524–1594) et l'utopie d'une démocratie dans l'église* (Geneva: Droz, 1993).

56. Morély's *Traicté de la discipline & police chrestienne* (Lyon: De Tournes, 1562) was dedicated to Pierre Viret, whom Kingdon calls "probably the most popular single preacher using the French language in the Protestant cause"; Kingdon, *Geneva and the Consolidation*, 46. Viret did offer Morély advice, but he never read the entire manuscript of the work. Morély was concerned about what he called the "aristocratic" and "oligarchic" tendencies in the French Church, and urged, as Kingdon put it, that "all kinds of clerical and secular dictation must be done away with; all important decisions must be vested in the entire membership of the local congregations. This was the way, he [Morély] felt, that discipline had been established in the time of the Apostles" (ibid., 57). Morély's program had many similarities to Ramus's later reform efforts, but it would be going too far to say with Kingdon that Morély "attracted" Ramus to his cause (ibid.,15).

Morély's first noble patron was no less a figure than Odet de Coligny, the cardinal of Châtillon. Châtillon chose to see Morély as a victim of Genevan tyranny, and reportedly indicated to the regional synod of the Île de France in 1565 that

> it is not reasonable that two or three or a few people give the law to others, and that it is necessary that the discipline which one would want to have observed by all the churches should first be seen and approved by all the churches, indeed after long and mature deliberation.[57]

By hinting that the leaders of the Reform were acting tyrannically, Châtillon was justifying Morély's stand, and at least seemingly aligning himself with the supporters of democracy within the church. Even though the synod of the Île de France and the national synod of Paris later in the same year condemned Morély's opinions in accordance with Geneva's wishes, Châtillon's stand led them to permit Morély himself to remain in communion with the French Reform.

Châtillon did not persist in supporting the troublesome Morély. A year later he was convinced to abandon Morély by supporters of the Genevan party. It did not take long for Morély to find another patron, however, and by May of 1566 he had managed to convince Jeanne d'Albret to appoint him tutor to her twelve-year-old son, the future Henri IV. In that position, he could afford to maintain his views against any opposition from within the church. The Huguenots were even less willing to offend the House of Navarre than to offend the Colignys. Like Châtillon, Jeanne d'Albret eventually dismissed Morély from her service on the urging of Beza and other Reformed leaders, but by the time she did, a new civil war was imminent, and the Reformed leadership had more pressing concerns than Morély's dissenting opinions.[58]

Morély was able to attract the support of powerful lay patrons largely because the Huguenot nobility shared his fear of what he called "cruel and insupportable, even impious tyranny" on the part of Beza and Geneva. The sentiments voiced in Châtillon's letter to the Paris synod of 1565 reflected growing concern among lay leaders of the Reform, who saw their influence eroding as church government came increasingly under clerical control. Morély's tactic of stressing the spectre of Genevan and clerical tyranny was the best means available for recruiting noble support, and his experience provided Ramus with a valuable lesson in his later conflicts with the church establishment.

Aside from his noble patrons, Morély found an additional source of support in the Huguenots of the Paris region. The importance of the Paris congregations to the French Reform as a whole was great enough that their opinions carried weight out of proportion to their numbers. Morély attempted, with some success, to use Paris as a counterweight to Geneva in his struggle for a democratic church government.

---

57. Kingdon, *Geneva and the Consolidation*, 75.
58. Kingdon, *Geneva and the Consolidation*, 82–91.

The Île de France, including Paris, seems to have been relatively resistant to the spread of Genevan ideas. Between 1563 and 1572, the region did not receive any pastors from Geneva, while churches elsewhere in France continued to welcome Beza's protégés into their pulpits.[59] Perhaps also the Parisian churches felt the influence of Morély's noble patrons more strongly than did churches elsewhere. For whatever reasons, the Paris region proved to be Morély's strongest support after he was excommunicated by the Genevan church. Time and again, the churches of the Île de France agreed to take him back into fellowship despite his democratic views and the disapproval of Geneva. Each time, the regional synod insisted that Morély mend his ways and amend his book, and each time he promised to do so. Each time, he failed to keep his promise, but the churches continued to seek accommodation with him. At the synods of La Ferté-sous-Jouarre in April 1564, of the Île de France in February 1565 and again in July, and in the national synod held at Paris in December of the same year, the decision was to allow Morély to remain in communion. At the national synod, he seems even to have won support for his views from some local congregations.[60]

Morély's success with the Paris churches and his noble patrons kept him relatively safe from Beza's wrath and allowed him to maintain his resistance to the Genevan model of the church, but it was not enough to launch a broader resistance movement among the Huguenots at large. With the resumption of armed conflict between Catholics and Huguenots in France in 1568, Morély faded into obscurity. Still, Morély's resistance to Geneva set useful precedents for Ramus's later program of reform. It demonstrated the possibility of enlisting noble support for a congregational program and the potential of the Paris churches for providing a broad base of support. Ramus was to exploit both of these lessons during his campaign against Geneva, along with some refinements of his own. Morély may have been important in another respect as well. Without the threat which he posed to the Huguenot establishment, the synod of La Rochelle might not have taken such a strong stand against dissenters, and had it not, a crucial element of Ramus's strategy—recruiting Zurich to balance the influence of Geneva—might well have been impossible.

59. Kingdon, *Geneva and the Consolidation*, 33 and appendix 1.

60. For example, the records of the synod of La Ferté; Bibliothèque de la Société de l'histoire du Protestantisme français, collection Auzière, MS. 563[1], "Synodes Provinciaux: Procès-verbaux des Synodes tenus dans l'Ile de France, la Brie, la Champagne, le Pays Chartrin, en 1564, 1605, 1623,... etc.," 1–21, "Synode de la Ferté." The synod made it very clear that in its opinion, "le Gouvernement de leglise appartient et doibt appartenir au consistoire de leglise representant tout le corps pour gouverner selon la parolle de Dieu. Et ensemble que les eslections et cognoissance de la doctrine, excommunication et ses dependences corrections et discipline, appartiennent au consistoire de leglise pour la gouverner selon la police qui y est establye, conforme a la parolle de Dieu" (12). In response Morély was less than perfectly repentant, "suppliant la compagnie ne trouver mauvais si en la contenant en toute paix, il ne recepvoit si promptement en soy mesmes led. ordre et police ecclesiastique, attendant que Dieu luy ait plus amplement faict entendre et croire quil est plus approchant de la parolle de Dieu que celluy quil en a escript" (13). The synod found his response "assez ambigue," but nonetheless "a donne la main dassociation."

The La Rochelle synod played into Ramus's hands by explicitly rejecting the opinion of those who refused to allow the word "substance" to describe Christ's participation in the sacrament and requiring both pastors and laymen to shun such a view. Ramus saw the synod's decision not only as an affront to his own beliefs, but as a goad with which to awaken Bullinger from his easy acquiescence to Beza's plans for the French Reform.

Ramus began his campaign against the new order of the church in France by contacting his friends in Zurich and alerting them to the way in which apostolic church discipline was being undermined. On 23 July 1571, three months after the synod of La Rochelle, he wrote to Gwalter in Zurich of its decisions, with an appeal for help against the Genevan dominance. "I love modesty and peace," he claimed, "but in accordance with piety," and went on to explain why it was that he felt unable to keep the peace any longer.[61]

The report was spreading that letters from Zurich had reached La Rochelle endorsing and praising consistorial discipline, and Ramus was unwilling to believe it until he had heard it from Zurich itself.[62] The main points on which he sought clarification concerned the authority to decide doctrine, the mode of electing ministers, and the powers of moral correction and excommunication. The problem, he wrote, was graver than it might appear at first sight; the overthrow of one pope by so much effort would be vain if the reformers themselves became "popified."[63]

Ramus's letter was intended to do more than simply inform Zurich of what was going on in the French Church. Nor was he urgently in need of information on the structure of the Zurich church. He knew it well already. What he was really after was a document, or even better an emissary, from Zurich to support his side in the French struggle. Geneva had triumphed at La Rochelle in part because Beza, with his immense prestige, had dominated the synod's deliberations, and the only possible counterweight was definitive word from Bullinger that he was on Ramus's side. In mentioning to Gwalter that "the authority of the Zurich church is, for its singular merits, great among all the evangelical nations of the world," he was not flattering

---

61. Ramus to Gwalter, 23 July 1571, Bibliothèque de la Société de l'histoire du Protestantisme français, MS 730, pièce 1, 5–7, copy of the original in Stadtsbibliothek Zurich, MS F42, 234: "Modestiam amo et pacem, sed quae pietati congruant," a sentence which, coming from Ramus, seems particularly disingenuous. Ramus was rapidly advancing in the art of hypocrisy.

62. Ramus to Gwalter, 23 July 1571, Bibliothèque de la Société de l'histoire du Protestantisme français, MS 730, pièce 1, 5–7, copy of the original in Stadtsbibliothek Zurich, MS F42, 234: "Fama quaedam percrebuit vestras literas Rupellam pervenisse, quae consistorialem disciplinam laudarent et probarent,…respondi id mihi mirabile videri, meque id non ante crediturum, quam a vobis ipsis mihi confirmatum perciperem."

63. Ramus to Gwalter, 23 July 1571, Bibliothèque de la Société de l'histoire du Protestantisme français, MS 730, pièce 1, 5–7, copy of the original in Stadtsbibliothek Zurich, MS F42, 7: "Quaestio ista gravior est quam in speciem videatur: frustraque sit tot contentionibus et animorum et armorum papatum unum cervicibus nostris esse depulsum, si nos ipsi papaturimus."

his old hosts but stating a fact.[64] Bullinger was probably the only man in Europe who spoke to the Reformed with more authority than Beza.

Not only might Bullinger's word create support among the French for Ramus's faction; it might also bring pressure to bear directly on Geneva to stop meddling in the affairs of the Huguenots. And Bullinger could exert a great deal of pressure. Tiny Geneva was constantly under the threat of invasion by the stronger Catholic powers on its borders, France and Savoy, and relied heavily on the assistance of the Bernese to guarantee its security. But the Bernese followed Zurich's lead. If Bullinger was unhappy with Geneva, Bern would be, too, and for Geneva a hostile Bern would be a strategic disaster. Ramus's task was to keep Zurich up-to-date on what was happening in France and to hope for any of a variety of results; the appearance in France of a prominent Zwinglian minister, a letter of support from the church of Zurich, or a Bullinger suspicious of his Genevan associate's beliefs and motives and willing to rein him in.

The most effective way to do so was to go straight to the source, and to address Bullinger himself on the issues. This is precisely what Ramus did, in a letter dated 1 September 1571.[65] Without beating around the bush, he told Beza how the synod of La Rochelle had imposed the Genevan model of the church on France. The ministers had taken over completely, and the deacons, elders, and congregations had lost their voice in the churches. As a result, those who refused to use the term "substance" in describing the Eucharist were damned as heretics. "I recall," Ramus added coyly, "that in your book on these matters I read, and in your presence I learned, how this word appears unfortunate and of ill omen to you."[66] Since the synod of the Île de France was to meet soon, Ramus requested Bullinger's opinion on the question.

Ramus launched into a theological argument against the stand taken by La Rochelle, but he must have had a pretty clear idea already of what Bullinger would have to say. Bouvier concluded that "what Ramus wanted were clarifications, and what he said does not at all prove that there was within him a determined desire for trouble."[67] I suspect that Bouvier was being too kind. Ramus wanted a fight, and his repeated requests for a response from Bullinger to be used at the provincial synod, as well as his assurance that the authority of Bullinger and the Zurich church had the most weight in France, tip his hand.[68]

---

64. Ramus to Gwalter, 23 July 1571, Bibliothèque de la Société de l'histoire du Protestantisme français, MS 730, pièce 1, 5–7, copy of the original in Stadtsbibliothek Zurich, MS F42, 7: "Autoritas ecclesiae tigurinae pro suis singularibus meritis apud omnes nationes evangelium amplexas magna est."

65. Ramus to Bullinger, 1 September 1571, printed in Waddington, *Ramus*, 433–35. Discussions of this letter appear in Kingdon, *Consolidation*, 102; and Bouvier, *Henri Bullinger*, 396–98.

66. Waddington, *Ramus*, 433: "memini enim quae in vestris libris de his rebus legerim, quaeque a vobis praesens didicerim, quam vobis hoc nomen infaustum atque ominosum videretur."

67. Bouvier, *Henri Bullinger*, 397.

68. Waddington, *Ramus*, 435: "Authoritas enim et tua et tuae ecclesiae maximum apud nostras ecclesias pondus subitura est...." That Ramus was eager for a reply is evident from his letter of 3 September 1571 to Theodore Zwinger in Basle: "Mitto nunc epistolam ad D. Bullingerum, quam Tigurum

Over the next months Ramus waited anxiously for a reply from Bullinger that he could use to persuade the upcoming synod of Zurich's support for his plan.[69] Bullinger did not draft a reply until early in December, however, because before responding to Ramus's complaints he wanted to get Beza's version of the story. In clearly agitated letters to Beza he asked for an explanation of the synod's actions, which seemed to throw the Zurich church out of communion with its French brethren. In particular he questioned the condemnation of those who would not accept the word "substance" to describe what happened during the Lord's Supper. After all, even the Helvetic Confession avoided the use of the term. What was going on in France? "I cannot explain clearly enough," Bullinger wrote, "how this affair burns and tortures my heart."[70]

So far, Ramus's attempt to split Geneva and Zurich seemed to be going well. Two things, however, stood in its path. One was Bullinger's unwillingness to bring about discord in the movement, and the other was Beza's all-out effort to appease his influential colleague. The Swiss leaders had more experience holding the church together than Ramus did tearing it apart, and Beza's skill showed brilliantly in his long reply, which Kingdon calls "practically a small book."[71]

Beza began by conflating the ideas of Ramus and Morély in order to make Ramus's program of reform more odious in Bullinger's eyes. What the two sought, according to Beza, was "the most muddled and seditious democracy" in place of the aristocratic system of the consistory, "which they have always had and still have in common with us."[72] In historical terms, of course, Beza was simply wrong; consistorial discipline was a relative newcomer to the French Reform. But as we have seen, Beza did not believe that the history of the French churches before the arrival of Genevan discipline really counted.

It was not overly difficult to convince Bullinger that Ramus's ideas on church discipline were dangerous. Aside from the tactic of identifying them with Morély's

---

fideliter et diligenter perferendam curabis: ac si quid respondeat, fac ut responsum per fidelem tabellarium ad nos Lutetiam in gymnasium Praelleum perferatur." Waddington, *Ramus*, 436.

69. His letters continue to report on the status of his correspondence with Bullinger, as in a letter at the beginning of January 1572, where he mentions, a propos of nothing in particular, "De literis ad Bullingerum nihil adhuc audivi...." Ramus to Zwinger, 7 January 1572, in Waddington, *Ramus*, 437.

70. Bullinger to Beza, 24 October 1571, in Beza, *Correspondance de Théodore de Bèze*, vol. xxii, 1571 (Geneva: Droz, 1986), no. 868 (quoted in Bouvier, *Henri Bullinger*, 399, who prints much of the text of the letter on 549–51), and 4 December 1571, *Correspondance*, vol. xxii, no. 877.

71. Kingdon, *Geneva and the Consolidation*, 103, describing Beza to Bullinger, 13 November 1571; *Correspondance*, vol. xxii, no. 871. Kingdon prints the text of the letter in the same work (appendix 2) as well as providing a convenient summary of it on 103–4.

72. Beza, *Correspondance*, xxii:ccxx; and Kingdon, *Geneva and the Consolidation*, 212: "perturbatissimam & seditiosissimam Democratiam stabilire in Ecclesia recusarint," whereas in fact the French churches "habuerunt autem semper, et adhuc nunc habent in genere aristocratiam Consistorii nobiscum communem."

democratic program and claiming that French ecclesiastical tradition was against them, Beza could count on Bullinger's long-standing fear of anarchy in the church. Ever since the Anabaptist movement first took shape in Zurich, Bullinger had feared that it would spread and undermine good doctrine and discipline all through the Reform. Once he had it in his mind that Morély was an Anabaptist, and that the Anabaptists—"the enemies of truth, the opponents of God,…the greatest threat to the existing order, the state, and Christendom"—had been working on Ramus, he was not likely to side with the reformers against Beza.[73]

Beza was less successful in his attempt to explain away the decisions of La Rochelle regarding the Eucharist. While he insisted that the word "substance" was required only to quell Italian troublemakers in Lyon, the explanation had a hollow ring. Alamanni and Capponi did not pose much of a threat even in 1566, and that a national synod five years later would make such an important pronouncement merely because of them strains credulity. It did not completely convince Bullinger, in any case. While he found Beza's excuses convincing in most respects, La Rochelle's statements regarding the use of the word "substance" were too obviously hostile to Zurich to be explained away. Eventually Beza would be obliged to back down in order to restore harmony.

Ramus came close to driving a wedge between Zurich and Geneva and thereby opening up the French Church to his own reform program, but Bullinger's conciliatory character and Beza's adroit diplomacy frustrated the attempt. Zurich was not Ramus's only hope, however. Even while trying to recruit Bullinger's support, Ramus was opening another front against the Reformed establishment in France by seeking the support of the Reformed churches of Paris.

Ramus's most signal success was to convince the churches of the Île de France region to endorse his views of church government. The provincial synod of Lumigny en Brie, in March of 1572, seemed to point the way to a reconciliation between the Genevan and Zurich factions in the French Reform, and perhaps even to the triumph of Ramus's own theological and ecclesiological views. The official records of the synod itself were destroyed by the order of the synod of Nîmes later that year, but surviving accounts indicate that what took place at Lumigny was little less than a love feast.[74]

Two letters describing the synod survive, one from a supporter of the Genevans and the other from Ramus himself. Ramus wrote to Bullinger on the nineteenth of

---

73. The quotation is from Harold S. Bender, "The Zwickau Prophets, Thomas Müntzer and the Anabaptists," *Moravian Quarterly Review* 27 (1953), cited in Steven Ozment, *The Age of Reform, 1250–1550: An Intellectual and Religious History of Late Medieval and Reformation Europe* (New Haven: Yale University Press, 1980), 343, who goes on to describe the word "Anabaptist" as "a scapegoating epithet, sincerely believed by the radicals' persecutors, much like the term 'witch' in the sixteenth and seventeenth centuries."

74. Quick, *Synodicon*, 112, chap.7, art. 5: "The Colloquy of Lumigny shall be advised to get the Memoirs of their Synod to be razed, nor may they make any particular Canons of their own, but shall be governed by those of our Discipline."

March, the same day that Nicolas de Lestre sent off his account to Beza in Geneva. Between them, the two accounts provide the best evidence we have about Ramus's ideas on the proper organization of the church.[75]

Ramus's letter is the less informative of the two. He related that he had attended the synod at Bullinger's suggestion, and brought up the questions of decision on doctrine and discipline, including election of pastors and excommunication. He found what happened to be beyond his best hopes; a decree that "no ecclesiastical decree be promulgated, unless it be by the judgment and consensus of the whole Church determined and deliberated."[76]

Unfortunately Ramus does not describe the acts of the synod one by one, merely promising to explain them more fully later. Instead, he launches into the praise of God for shedding His light on the synod and of his "most beloved brethren" for showing themselves to be so benign and liberal: "And so by public prayers and thanksgiving these concords were celebrated."[77]

Not that all was love and concord, however; for a man of Ramus's stamp that would indeed have been a miracle. The second half of the letter was devoted to discussing the synod's resolution on the Eucharist and, concurrently, the arrogant and ill-informed opinions of Beza, "who so imperiously forces on France not only his opinions but even his very words."[78] The word in question was of course the vexing term "substance," which the synod of La Rochelle had attempted to require in the definition of the Eucharist. Ramus's party won its point on this as well:

> the remarkable consensus was, that if Beza was so charmed by his word, he could use it…still the opinion of Zurich and of Christians elsewhere, who don't wish to use such a captious and perilous word, is in no way to be rejected; but all are free to use it or not.[79]

75. Ramus's letter to Bullinger is printed in Waddington, *Ramus*, 438–40. De Lestre's letter to Beza is in *Correspondance*, vol. 13, no. 909. De Lestre was a minister of Paris who had served as president of the national synod of Verteuil in 1567 and was later often selected as a member of important commissions of the national church (at La Rochelle in 1571, Nîmes in 1572, and Sainte-Foy in 1578). Despite his apparently high standing in the Reform, little is known of his life and opinions.

76. Waddington, *Ramus*, 439: "totamque caussam de decisione doctrinae et disciplinae, de electione praefectorum Ecclesiae et gubernatorum, de excommunicatione fratrum proposui, et latius literisque explicavi. Noli putare quicquam unquam mihi tam praeter spem accidisse. Una omnium sententia ac vere decretum est, ut nullum Ecclesiasticum decretum diceretur, nisi quod sententia et consensu universae Ecclesiae statutum ac deliberatum esset." Whatever documents or writings Ramus used to explain his positions are unknown to me.

77. Waddington, *Ramus*, 439: "Itaque publicis et precibus et gratulationibus concordia haec celebrata est."

78. Waddington, *Ramus*, 439: "qui tam imperiose non solum opiniones suas, sed sua etiam vocabula Francis obtruderet."

79. Waddington, *Ramus*, 439: "ut si D. Beza suo vocabulo tantopere delectaretur, eo uteretur…; Tigurinorum tamen opinio et aliorum quorumvis Christianorum, qui tam captioso tamque periculoso verbo uti nollent, nequaquam rejiceretur; sed liberum esset omnibus uti vel non uti."

The reason for telling Bullinger all of this, Ramus wrote in conclusion, was that he feared Beza might otherwise misrepresent the conclusions of the synod. Because of that fear, he urged that Bullinger send someone from Zurich to the upcoming national synod at Nîmes, or at least an admonitory letter on the liberties of the church, and especially the freedom to use or not to use the term "substance."[80] He needed ammunition for his confrontation with Beza at Nîmes.

Ramus was perhaps more foresighted than his fellows at Lumigny en Brie, at least if De Lestre is a fair representative. His letter to Beza described the same tableau of peace, harmony, and concord as Ramus's, but he wrote with much more confidence. "Having assembled us these past days for the synod at Lumigny en Brie, God has given us the grace to bring our differences to a good accord."[81]

De Lestre began by distinguishing the position of Ramus and his followers from that of Morély. While acknowledging that the two were similar in many respects, De Lestre pointed out that unlike Morély, Ramus desired to see not ecclesiastical democracy, but a church government wherein everyone has a voice, but where "the opinions of some weigh more than those of others according to geometric proportions."[82] We will return in the next chapter to the question of just what Ramus's group meant by this curious proposal. For now, however, let it suffice to say that the essence of their position was that the whole church should have a say in matters of doctrine and discipline.

The letter moves on to specific solutions of problems raised by the conflict between the congregationalists and the supporters of the ministerial monopoly on church government. On the question of who might speak in the church, the synod suggested that those who had received a divine gift of prophecy, or "gifts acquired by study and diligence," might address special assemblies of the faithful after undergoing an examination by the pastors and elders of the church. Such assemblies would be under close clerical supervision, and no one would be required to attend, but "the door would be open to all who would like to be there." Finally, the synod of the province in which the church lay would retain the right to call a halt to such meetings if they gave rise to problems.[83]

It was a small enough concession to Ramus's party, but as the synod went on it became clear that it was only the beginning. De Lestre next reported the results of the synod's discussions on doctrinal decisions. While the pastors had complete control of these matters as a general rule, there were certain cases which required a

---

80. Waddington, *Ramus*, 439: "Itaque vehementer optarem, ut vestrum aliquis adesset, aut saltem epistola aliqua a vobis huc pervenerit, quae Ecclesiae libertate honestam admonitionem aliquam haberet, praesertim de vocabulo substantiae, ne quisquam ab Ecclesia rejiciatur, qui eo uti nolit."

81. Beza, *Correspondance*, xiii:xcvi.

82. Beza, *Correspondance*, xiii:xcvi: "Ramus et les autres, combien qu'ilz condamnassent en quelques points l'ataxie de Morély, toutesfois en approchoient bien fort. Seulement vouloient que les advis des uns poisassent plus que des autres selon les proportions geometriques."

83. Beza, *Correspondance*, xiii:xcvii.

broader consensus from the church as a whole. In such matters local pastors, or even the national synod, would still decide the matter, after hearing "all those who could help in making the decision." But their decision would be subject to lay approval, in that if "complaints and discontent" remained after it was announced, the whole matter would be deliberated once again. Effectively, this meant that, as Ramus had written to Bullinger, the whole church debated questions of doctrine and discipline. Curiously, De Lestre believed that Beza would agree with such a plan:

> Thus the second resolution, which we think is the intention of all our preced-ing synods, of Calvin, of you, and of all who have written; to moderate both the popular license desired by some, and the tyranny of the pastors....[84]

De Lestre continued with the synod's views on the election of pastors and on excommunication, claiming that "nothing was done on these matters except to clar-ify the articles of our discipline." He clearly implied the congregation's right to choose a pastor for itself, while refusing the laity a voice in the excommunication and absolution of church members.

The Eucharist was also a matter for discussion at Lumigny en Brie, but De Lestre seems to have realized that it was an especially touchy subject and he men-tioned it only briefly. His letter merely states that it appeared advisable to soften the stand taken at La Rochelle by permitting those who did not wish to use the word "substance" not to do so, "providing they confess and teach the thing" themselves. De Lestre was at pains to point out that all these decisions were "only memoirs to be reported to the next national synod," perhaps to stave off Beza's wrath.[85]

He quickly recovered his enthusiasm, however, and in the remainder of his report his conviction that the problems dividing the Reform in France had been solved is plain. Naively, he singled out Ramus for special praise:

> And I can tell you that Ramus and the others showed us great docility, bearing reverence towards the company and always protesting a holy sub-mission. Which gave all of us a grand occasion for praising God.... Now I believe that you will praise God for this along with us.[86]

84. Beza, *Correspondance*, xiii:xcvii: "Voila la seconde resolution laquelle nous pensons estre l'inten-tion de tous noz Synodes precedens [!], de Monsr. Calvin, de vous, et de tous ceux qui ont escrit: pour moderer et la licence des peuples desirée par aucuns, et la tyrannie des Pasteurs...."

85. Beza, *Correspondance*, xiii:xcviii: "Il a esté touché de ce mot de substanceen la matiere de la Cene. Et pour ce qu'aucuns (protestans neantmoins sentir une mesme chose avec nous) trouvent estrange qu'aux actes du Synode de la Rochelle, il y a qu'on rejette l'opinion de ceux qui ne veullent user de ce mot de subs-tance (mesmes les Suisses l'ayans ainsi escrit), on seroit d'advis d'adoucir cela, sans imposer necessité à aucun d'user d'un terme non accoustumé à l'Escriture, pourveu qu'il confessast et enseignast la chose."

86. Beza, *Correspondance*, xiii:xcvix: "Et vous puis dire que Ramus et les autres nous ont montré une grande docilite, portans reverence a la compagnie, & protestans tousiours d'une sainte submission. Qui nous a donné a tous une grande occasion de louer Dieu....Or je croi que vous en louerez Dieu ainsi avec nous."

De Lestre even suggested that Beza write Ramus a letter of congratulations for his role in the synod, especially since Ramus had proclaimed wholeheartedly his "love and reverence for you." De Lestre does not seem to have understood just how serious the breach in the French Reform had become, or how determined Ramus and Beza were to see their own factions prevail.

Beza did not find De Lestre's report an occasion for praising God, nor did he write a congratulatory letter to Ramus. On the contrary, Beza, like Ramus, saw the results of the synod not as the end of the problems which had divided the church but as a defeat for the Genevan cause. His reaction is recorded in the register of the Company of Pastors of Geneva:

> On Sunday the twentieth came news of the Colloquy of the Île de France held at Lumigny, which Ramus and some of his sect attended, and not only obtained audience to plead the case of Morély, but for the most part won it, certain articles being accorded them there which are against the Synod of La Rochelle and open the door to the overthrow of the whole discipline of the French Churches.[87]

Beza was certain that the Reformed of the Île de France would embroil the next national synod in disciplinary disputes, that they were spreading their ideas in writing all over the country, and that the result could be the ruin of the French Church. Immediate action was essential. Beza had planned to write to the Nîmes synod, but it was decided that more was needed. Geneva had to send a representative to Nîmes, and the situation was so serious that Beza himself was delegated to go.

The synod of Nîmes met on the sixth of May in 1572. Ramus does not seem to have attended, but his presence was nonetheless strongly felt. The deputies from the Île de France presented the positions taken at Lumigny, apparently in the form of "books" composed by Ramus and others.[88] They seem to have been given a fair hearing; exceptional freedom was given every man to express his opinion, "and to this purpose the Doors of the Synod shall be left wide open, and silence shall not be imposed upon any Man in this matter for this time." The synod was careful, however, to assert that such freedom should not become a precedent.[89]

The result of the debates was a complete victory for Beza and the Genevan party. It is true that Beza and the French Church retreated from their earlier insistence on the use of the word "substance,"[90] but as Beza reported to the Genevan pastors, the

87. *Registres de la Compagnie des Pasteurs*, vol. 3, *1565–1574*, 66.

88. Quick, *Synodicon*, 112.

89. Quick, *Synodicon*, 112, chap. 7, art. 3.

90. Quick, *Synodicon*, chap. 2, art. 2, 104: "Instead of these words extracted from the Acts of the National Synod of Rochel in the Year 1571: 'We reject their opinion, who will not receive the word Substance,' shall be put, 'Without prejudicing those Foreign Churches, who for reasons best known to themselves, do not use the word Substance...'" (punctuation added).

program of Ramus and his supporters was condemned "en tout et par tous," a "happy success" for Christianity.[91] The records of the synod itself report the same result:

> And as for those positions asserted by Monsieur Ramus, Morellius, Bergeron and others, (1) About the Decision of Points of Doctrine. (2) About the Election and Deposal of Ministers. (3) About Excommunication out of the Church.... And lastly about Prophesying, None of these shall be received among us, because they have no foundation in the Word of God, and are of very dangerous consequence to the Church....[92]

As for the authors of the subversive doctrines themselves, the synod ordered that they be corrected "gently and sweetly." Realizing that such a course might not suffice to convince a man like Ramus, the synod also decided what to do in case sweetness should prove ineffective: "And in case upon their appearance they should reject their Admonitions, they shall be proceeded against as Rebels and Schismatics, according to the Canons of our Discipline."[93]

The synod of Nîmes cut the ground out from under Ramus and his supporters. By modifying the stand of the French Church on the Eucharist, it reconciled Bullinger and Zurich to the French Reform, and by rejecting the proposals of the deputies from Paris after full discussion by all interested parties it undermined Ramus's accusations of tyranny. Of course, Ramus did not give up. Throughout the summer of 1572, he continued to agitate among his friends in Zurich, even though he seemed to be grasping at straws.

Ramus's last letters to Gwalter seem almost random, seeking any source of disharmony between Zurich and Geneva. He brought up Sulzer; he brought up excommunication; he brought up the question of "substance"; he brought up nearly everything he could think of, but he did not find the issue that could divide Zurich from Geneva once again.[94] Instead Bullinger sent him a flattering note which offered little hope for his program. "I see," Bullinger wrote, "that everything among you in France is settled," and he prayed for the preservation of the new harmony.[95]

This was not the response Ramus hoped to receive, but it may well be that he never received it. The Saint Bartholomew's Day Massacre broke out on the twenty-

---

91. *Registres de la Compagnie des Pasteurs*, vol. 3, *1565–1574*, 75: "Au reste Monsieur de Besze nous a faict entendre l'heureux succès du Synode auquel l'affaire de la discipline avoit estée vuidee, le livre de Morély, de Ramus et de Du Rosier examinez article par article et condamnez en tout et par tous...."

92. Quick, *Synodicon*, 112, chap. 7, art. 4.

93. Quick, *Synodicon*, 113, chap. 7, art. 12.

94. Ramus's last two letters to Gwalter are in Bibliothèque de la Société de l'histoire du Protestantisme français, MS 730, pièce 1, 8–11 (1 July 1572), and 15–16 (17 July 1572).

95. Bullinger to Ramus, 10 August 1572, Bibliothèque de la Société de l'histoire du Protestantisme français, MS 730, pièce 1, 17–18: "Video, Vir Clarissime idemque Domine honorande et frater carissime, omnia apud vos in Gallia sic esse composita....Oro itaque Dominum, ut nos omnes in sancta et syncera ad Verbis sui simplicitatem et puritatem concordia compositam conservet...."

third of August and brought an end to all of Ramus's dreams of reform. Ramus's death deprived the dissidents within the church of their most important spokesman, and the massacre in Paris eliminated many of the Protestants who had been his strongest supporters. It also gave the French Reformed Church more important problems to deal with than the selection of pastors and the nature of the Eucharist. The wars that followed left little time for internal squabbling.[96]

Ramus's efforts to reform the church, like his attempts to reform the University, ended in failure, and the principle which had prompted both reforms—a desire for French society to adopt open, participatory, and meritocratic institutions—all but disappeared from the scene. Ramus's death did not cause the collapse of meritocratic ideals, but it marked the end of their influence in the intellectual and social life of France. The meritocratic ideal of the Renaissance gave way to the hierarchical society and ideology of Old Régime France.

96. See Kingdon, *Geneva and the Consolidation*, 111–21, "The St. Bartholomew's Massacre Ends the Quarrel."

CHAPTER 6
Respublica Timocratia

LOOKING BACK ON RAMUS'S STRUGGLES with the Reformed establishment in France, historians have generally accepted Beza's claim that Ramus was a dangerous radical, in fact a democrat.[1] From Bayle through Michelet and on down to Jürgen Moltmann, they have concluded that he was the champion of ecclesiastical democracy, just as Beza had claimed.[2] Some have even suggested that his democratic zeal was not confined to the church, but eventually extended to the state as well. Guggenheim claims that "we may call [Ramus] the representative of democratic principles, first in the church, and then in politics."[3] A cursory view of Ramus's activism might support such a conclusion. But while Guggenheim is quite right to see in Ramus's principles political and social as well as ecclesiastical dimensions, he is wrong to label those principles "democratic."

In 1558, Ramus's old student Michel de Castelnau made a French translation of his master's *Liber de moribus veterum Gallorum*, "in the hope that I might do

---

1. The "timocratic republic," which will be defined in this chapter, represents Ramus's ideal for the organization of society.

2. See for example Pierre Bayle, "Ramus," in *Dictionnaire historique et critique*, 5th ed., vol. 4 (Amsterdam: P. Brunel, 1740), 25–31, at 29, col. 1, n. M; Augustin-François Thery, "Il cherchait à rendre démocratique l'administration des églises," *Mémoire sur l'enseignement public en France, au xvie siècle, et spécialement sur les écrits et la personne de Ramus* (Versailles: Montalant-Bougleux, 1837), 34; Jules Michelet, *Renaissance et Réforme* (Paris: Laffont, 1982), 580: "Le Fameux Professeur Ramus…voulait qu'on maintînt la démocratie de l'Eglise"; H. Schweizer, "Die Entwicklung des Moralsystems in der reformierten Kirche: Die Philosophie des Petrus Ramus: Untersuchen ihres Einflusses auf die reformierte Ethik," *Theologische Studien und Kritiken* 1 (1850): 69–78, at 71, n. B: "Beza bekämpfte auf einer Synode in Frankreich die Bemühungen des Ramus, statt der Consistorien eine reine demokratische kirchenverfassung einzuführern…"; Jürgen Moltmann, "Zur Bedeutung des Petrus Ramus für Philosophie und Theologie im Calvinismus," *Zeitschrift für Kirchengeschichte* 68 (1957): 313: "Immerhin trat Ramus für eine demokratische Laienkirche…und bekämpfte Bezas pastoralaristocratischen Kirchenbegriff als Despotie und Tyrranis…."

3. Guggenheim, "Petrus Ramus als Reformator der Wissenschaften" (Sonderabdrukt aus dem 18. Jahrgang des *Humanistischen Gymnasiums*, 1–11), 3: "Um Ramus schart sich, was wir die vertreter des demokratischen Prinzips, zünachst in der Kirche, dann im Staatsleben nennen können."

something agreeable for those of my countrymen who would like to be able to see in their own language the manners of their ancestors."[4] Castelnau took a few liberties with Ramus's text, generally in the interests of brevity, but among the changes he made one is particularly significant. In describing the government of the Gallic Hedvois, Ramus had concluded, "Ergo talis ac tanta Galliae Celticae civitas timocraticam illam Rempub. habuit." Castelnau either suspected that his readers would not know what a "timocratic" republic was, or else did not know himself. Whichever was the case, he chose to render Ramus's words as "Donques une telle et si grande cité de la Gaulle Celtique a eu ceste Republique Democratique."[5] The timocratic republic of the Gauls which Ramus had described became, in Castelnau's hands, a democracy.

Four hundred years later, in his master's thesis at St. Louis University, James John Nouws encountered the term "timocracy" in the text of another work by Ramus and faced the same problem as Castelnau: what did the strange word mean? Nouws had set himself the task of translating Ramus's six Ciceronian prefaces into English, and the result is a useful and generally accurate edition.[6] The word "timocracy" in Ramus's preface to the *De Legibus*, however, proved to be a stumbling block. Ramus had written that, according to Cicero, the well-organized state harmonizes the three true forms of government: monarchy, aristocracy, and timocracy.[7] Nouws not only followed the same course as Castelnau by translating "timocratic" as "democratic," but improved on his predecessor by altering Ramus's own text to read "democratico" instead of "timocratico." In Nouws's case, however, the motives for making the change are clear. A note alerts the reader that "Ramus has *timocratico*, a

4. Michel de Castelnau, *Traicte des façons et coustumes des anciens Galloys, traduit du latin de P. de la Ramée, par Michel de Castelnau* (Paris: A. Wechel, 1559), fol. 2v. This is Castelnau's translation of *P. Rami, regii eloquentiae et philosophiae professoris, Liber de Moribus veterum Gallorum, ad Carolum Lotharingum Cardinalem* (Parisiis: A. Wechelus, 1559). References to the Latin version are to the 1562 edition. On Castelnau (1520–92) and his diplomatic career see Gustave Hubault, *Michel de Castelnau: Ambassadeur en Angleterre (1575–85)* (Paris: V. Delin, 1856).

5. Ramus, *Liber de moribus*, 131; Castelnau, *Traicte des façons*, fol. 88v. Elsewhere, when Ramus terminated his discussion of the governments of Celtic Gaulle with the rather abrupt "Quamobrem timocratiam Gallicarum civitatum tam multis exemplis satis explicatum esse arbitror," Castelnau again modified the original. It became "par quoy je pense que le gouvernement des Republiques Gaulloyses a esté assez expliqué par tant d'examples...." In the first case Ramus's timocracy became democracy, and in the second simply government.

6. James John Nouws, "Six Ciceronian Prefaces by Petrus Ramus: Translated with Introduction and Commentary by James John Nouws, C.M., A.B." (Master's thesis, St. Louis University, 1957).

7. Petrus Ramus, *Petri Rami, professoris regii, et Audomari Talaei Collectaneae praefationes, epistolae, orationes...* (Paris: Dionysius Vallensis, 1577), 115: "Marcus Tullius Cicero, Mecoenas, sex libris de Repub. descripserat, non tantum e populi potestate & optimatum authoritate, sed tribus justis generibus, Regio, Aristocratico, Timocratico temperatam...." Nouws was working from the 1577 edition of the *Collectaneae* which has the same text.

word not in the dictionaries."[8] I can vouch for the truth of Nouws's observation: "timocratia" is not in fact in the standard Latin dictionaries. (Neither, for that matter, is "democratia.")[9]

The reason that it is not, of course, is that it is a Greek term, discovered by Ramus in the political writings of Plato and Aristotle. It was not any more familiar in Ramus's time than in ours, as the combined testimony of Castelnau and Nouws suggests. But it is easy enough to determine that it does not mean the same thing as "democracy," at all, and that in describing it as one of the three true forms of government and as the authentic basis of the republics of the ancient Gauls, Ramus was not endorsing democratic rule. What he was endorsing was a sort of meritocracy, as can be seen through an examination of the history of the word "timocracy" and an analysis of Ramus's use of it.

Both Plato and Aristotle used the term "timocratia," but in very different senses. Plato coined the word in the eighth book of *The Republic* to describe one stage in the natural life cycle of constitutions from the best, aristocracy, to the worst, tyranny.[10] In Plato's eyes, the downward path ran through timocracy, oligarchy, and democracy before reaching its nadir in tyranny, each step following the next as new types of men rose to prominence and power. In the first stage, the aristocrat, bred and trained to be the perfect governor, yielded place to the timocratic man, "the man who is contentious and covetous of honor," who is governed by "ambition and high spirit" and is therefore "haughty of soul and covetous of honor." The constitution he creates is accordingly "based on the love of honor." Since there is no common term for such a constitution, Plato has Socrates propose the names "timocracy" or "timarchy" (cf. "time," "honor.")[11]

Aristotle adopted Plato's term, but with some violence to its original meaning. He presented timocracy as one of the three true forms of government, along with monarchy and aristocracy, and as the worst of the three, although better than the three "perversions" of tyranny, oligarchy, and democracy. He explains the timocratic state as "that which is based on a property qualification" (cf. "time," "worth"). But Aristotle does not intend to equate timocracy with simple rule by the wealthy, which is more properly labeled oligarchy. Instead he suggests that "it is the ideal even of

---

8. Nouws, "Six Ciceronian Prefaces," 56, gives Ramus's text as "regio, aristocratico, democratico...," and explains why he altered it on 91, n. 56.4. Later when Ramus attributed "timocratic" power to the people (*Collectaneae*, 116: "regio consules imperio, aristocratica senatus authoritate, timocratica populi potestate,..."), Nouws again changed the text to read "democratica populi potestate..." (Nouws, "Six Ciceronian Prefaces," 58 and 91, n. 58.11). The question of why Ramus believed that Cicero considered timocracy one of the three true forms of government will be explored below.

9. Not at least in Charlton T. Lewis and Charles Short, *A Latin Dictionary* (1879: reprint, Oxford: Oxford University Press, 1980); or J. R. V. Marchant and Joseph F. Charles, *Cassell's Latin Dictionary* (New York: Funk and Wagnalls, 1945).

10. Plato, *Republic* VIII, 545–49.

11. Plato, *Republic* VIII, 549.

timocracy to be the rule of the majority, and all who have the property qualification count as equal," and later that in timocratic governments "the ideal is for the citizens to be equal and fair; therefore rule is taken in turn, and on equal terms."[12]

Aristotle's description of a state with both a property qualification for participation in government and the ideal of majority rule, with citizens ruling in turn, is more than a little ambiguous. It suggests that he either expects almost everyone to meet the property qualification eventually, or else that he is simply unconcerned with those who fail to qualify as citizens. Probably the latter explanation is closer to the truth. It is at least harmonious with the general Greek attitude toward noncitizens. If man is a political animal, then anyone who does not belong to a polis as a citizen is something less than a man and not worth worrying about, and presumably those who do not meet the property qualification are ipso facto noncitizens.

The competing definitions of timocracy from two such authorities caused a good deal of confusion among later scholars.[13] In the sixteenth century, Henri Estienne managed to preserve the distinction between the two usages in his *Thesaurus*, but Louis Le Roy became a bit confused, conflating Plato and Aristotle in his definition: "where regard is to estimation of goods, is not properly called aristocracy, but timarchie or timocratie, or ambitious republic, according to Plato...."[14]

The term was a perfect one for Ramus to employ in describing his own vision of the best society for France. It had an unimpeachable classical pedigree, but was neither widely used nor well understood, which allowed him to adapt it to his own ends. Furthermore, the references from Plato and Aristotle made it clear that whatever "timocracy" meant, it did not mean the same thing as "democracy," and it was a matter of some importance for Ramus to avoid the charge of being a dangerous democrat.

Plato's definition of the term was the more appealing to Ramus for more than one reason. Himself a professed Platonist and longtime foe of Aristotle, he preferred to follow the earlier philosopher on the grounds of consistency. In addition, Ramus's understanding of his own times fit well in the schematic chronology laid down by Plato for the degeneration of states. The timocracy of Francis I's time, which had allowed the ambitious and contentious Ramus to slake his thirst for honor by rising to fame and even a sort of power, was giving way to oligarchy, just as Plato had said it would. Certainly Ramus could not sympathize with the oligarchic implications of Aristotle's definition.

---

12. Aristotle, *Nicomachean Ethics* VIII, 10.

13. Franz Passow, in his *Handwörterbuch der Griechischen Sprache* (Leipzig: F. C. W. Vogel, 1857), clearly differentiates between the Platonic and Aristotelian senses of the word: "τίμοχρατία, Staatsverfassung, deren Princip die Ehre ist, Plat. rep. 8 p. 545 B.C.\ 2) Staatsverfassung, deren Princip das Vermögensverhältniss ist, Arist. eth. 8, 10 (12), 1."

14. Henri Estienne, *Thesaurus Graecae Linguae* (Paris: Didot, 1848–54), s.v. "timocratia." For Le Roy's definition, see Edmond Huguet, *Dictionnaire de la langue française du seizième siècle*, vol. 7 (Paris: Didier, 1967), s.v. "timocratie."

Plato's discussion of "timocracy" suggests the sort of character who would be successful in a timocratic state, but it does not say a great deal about how such a state might be organized. Ramus had to figure that out for himself, and he did so by seeking a model in history. The fullest expression of Ramus's timocratic ideal appears in his history of the ancient Gauls referred to at the beginning of this chapter. The term does not appear in his more strictly pedagogical writings, which offered less opportunity for a direct statement of ideological positions, but his commentaries on Cicero contain some valuable information on what Ramus conceived timocracy to be. Interpreted in the context of Ramus's educational and religious activities, the *Liber de moribus veterum Gallorum* and the Ciceronian commentaries provide an outline of Ramus's utopian ideal for France.

Throughout the *De moribus*, Ramus makes it clear that the ancient Gauls well deserve to be models for the France of his own time. They were the leaders in all the arts of civilization, having taught grammar, rhetoric, logic, physics, and theology to their own youth and—so Ramus proclaims—to Greece and to Rome as well. Gaul was the teacher of the ancient world, and even transmitted her alphabet to the Greeks, Caesar's mistaken belief that the Gauls used Greek letters notwithstanding. The Gauls taught the doctrine of transmigration to Pythagoras and mathematics and philosophy to the Greeks. In sum, Ramus wrote, "affirmo Graeciam Galliae non magistram, sed discipulam fuisse": Greece was not the teacher of Gaul, but her pupil.[15]

Such a claim reflects Ramus's pride in France and her glorious past, a common motive among French historians of the Gauls in the sixteenth century, but it serves a more important purpose in his argument as well. By claiming that the Gauls, and in particular the Druids, antedated Pythagoras and Plato and were their teachers, Ramus granted them a privileged place in the tradition of ancient wisdom labeled the "ancient theology" by D. P. Walker.[16] If in fact the Gauls were the teachers of Pythagoras and Plato, then they deserved at least some measure of the respect accorded Hermes Trismegistus, Moses, Orpheus, and the Chaldeans, all bearers of the ancient wisdom tradition.

In his work, Walker discusses Ramus's use of the tradition that religious insight was vouchsafed to pagans outside the Jewish and Christian traditions and handed down to the initiated few over the millennia. Like other French humanists, such as Symphorien Champier and Le Fevre de la Boderie, Ramus gave the Druids a prominent place in the transmission of the ancient theology, in particular for their teaching of the immortality of the soul. Still, Walker finds that Ramus's attitude toward the ancient theology is "peculiar to himself," in that he "reduces the Ancient Theology…to nothing more than a rhetorical decoration." In fact, Walker avers, Ramus would have ignored the ancient theology altogether had it not been for his love of

---

15. Ramus, *Liber de moribus*, 98.
16. D. P. Walker, *The Ancient Theology: Studies in Christian Platonism from the Fifteenth to the Eighteenth Century* (Ithaca: Cornell University Press, 1972).

rhetoric and dislike of Aristotle.[17] Walker may have been a bit hard on Ramus, for as we have seen and will see again, his ties to the ancient wisdom tradition were not limited to rhetorical flourishes, even if he was among the most prosaic of that tradition's interpreters.

Whether Ramus considered the ancient theology mere decoration or not, it helped to make the example of the Gauls doubly valuable; because it was ancient (and therefore pure), and because it was Gallic (and therefore French). What example did they set? According to Ramus, their liberty and their frugality were most to be praised. As regards the latter, the Gauls refrained from alcohol, were chaste in marriage, honored labor, and despised gold. All of this set them apart from the decadent Romans; all of it recalls Ramus himself. So also does their reported fondness for bragging. Ramus had re-created the ancient forebears of the French race largely in his own image.[18]

Ramus's account also reveals Ramist tendencies in the political and social organization of the Gauls. A taste for debate and for participation in public life reflected the vital individualism of the Gallic race, and not surprisingly they all sought to have their own views heard and respected. Claude-Gilbert Dubois echoes Castelnau and Nouws in suggesting that Ramus's portrait of the Gauls is that of a democratic people: "the word democracy is not used, but it is present throughout the description." And he goes on to ask,

> Is this not a utopian image of a regenerated people which is presented to us?… It is an ideal projection: that of the city regenerated by frugality and political liberty; a dream proper to a new party of liberal intellectuals.[19]

Here again Ramus's utopia is interpreted as a democratic one, and here again the term is inappropriate. He did not use the term "democracy" in his *De Moribus* because he did not believe that the Gauls were democratic in their government, as the text itself reveals.

According to Ramus, the Gauls were divided into three "estates," which bear a remarkable resemblance to the three estates of his own day. These were the Druids, the knights, and "the people."[20] In labeling the second estate "knights," Ramus was consciously recalling the social structure of Republican Rome, and his description of government among the Gauls follows a republican model. Magistrates elected annually or for longer terms were guided by a senate (of unspecified composition), but

17. Walker, *Ancient Theology*, 127.

18. Castelnau, *Traicte*, fols. 9v–15r, discusses the Gauls' characteristic virtues; their fondness for boasting is discussed on fols. 12v–13r.

19. Claude-Gilbert Dubois, *Celtes et Gaulois au XVIe siècle: Le Développement littéraire d'un mythe nationaliste: Avec l'édition critique d'un traité inédit de Guillaume Postel, De ce qui est premier pour reformer le monde* (Paris: J. Vrin, 1972), 110.

20. Castelnau, *Traicte*, fol. 77r.

both were under the ultimate control of the people themselves. The Gauls evidently enjoyed a perfect Polybian mixed government,

> in which all the just political forms were included: a sort of kingship in the annual (or longer-term) magistrate; aristocracy in the Senate; and finally timocracy in the full authority of the people, by which both Senators and Magistrates were created.[21]

Their experience became the model for the Greeks and Romans in the days of their liberty, and both Plato and Aristotle favored such a government, which Ramus named "timocratic."[22] If the forebears of the French practiced such a government along with the Greek city-states and the free Romans, and if the world's greatest minds praised it so highly, could there be any question that it was best suited to six-teenth-century France as well?

Ramus is short on details about how this government functioned, but what he does have to say is revealing.[23] The most important role in society was played, he suggested, by the Druids. They were the spiritual leaders of society, but in a sense rather different from that in which Christian clerics were the spiritual leaders of Ramus's France. They were first and foremost teachers of the arts and sciences, including but by no means limited to theology, and they owed their preeminence to their learning.[24] Society's leaders, according to Ramus, should be teachers, a claim that is ambiguous at least. Whether the history of the Gauls suggested that magis-trates should teach or that teachers should rule is not entirely clear.[25] In ancient Gaul, evidently, it was a distinction without a difference. The Druids supplied the magistrates for the society, and did an excellent job at it. Ramus was lavish in his praise of their judicial acumen.[26]

The importance of these professors was indicated in Ramus's account of how concerned the Romans were to oppress them. Tiberius deposed them, according to

---

21. Ramus, *Liber de moribus*, 121: "in quo justae politiae species omnes comprehenduntur: erat enim regium quiddam in annuo, aut longioris temporis legitimo magistratu: erat Aristocratia in Senatu, & denique, timocratia in summa populi authoritate, unde & Senatores & Magistratus existerent."

22. Ramus, *Liber de moribus*, 121, where Ramus specifically refers to the high esteem in which Plato and Aristotle, Greeks and Romans, held this model of government: "Haec Caesar, unde intelligitur Rei-pub. status timocraticus ille, quem Plato quemque Aristoteles tantopere comprobarunt, quemque libera Graecia Italiaque cupidissime tenuerunt...."

23. Having mentioned the knights and the people, Ramus says nothing about how they are to be fit into the political scheme.

24. Castelnau, *Traicte*, 52v–65v, discusses the teaching of the Druids at length, treating each of the arts in turn in their accepted order: "de la Grammaire,...Rhetorique, Logique, Mathematique, Physique, Theologie" (fol. 52v).

25. Castelnau, *Traicte*, fol. 78r–v. Ramus cites several Roman myths and examples to bolster his claim.

26. Castelnau, *Traicte*, fol. 77r, where Ramus relates that the magistrates were drawn from the ranks of the Druids, and 79v–81v, where Ramus describes and heaps praise upon the excellence of the Druids as judges.

Pliny, largely on account of their magical practices, and with their suppression the learning and liberty of their countrymen declined together.[27] The message in all this is clear. Learning is the measure of a man's worth and his value to society, and the most learned are the most fit to rule in politics and religion.

Within this meritocratic utopia, however, "the people" still have the final say on who shall rule. Ramus goes so far as to claim that they were entitled to depose their magistrates, an anticipation perhaps of the later Protestant resistance theories propounded by, among others, Ramus's own enemy Beza.[28] Nonetheless, the selection of magistrates is to be only from among the learned Druids. This is not quite democracy, nor quite pure meritocracy. It is simply timocracy.

How was it to work in practice? Here it seems we need to look more closely at one aspect of Ramus's venture into ecclesiastical politics. De Lestre described him as desiring that all members of the church have a say in matters of doctrine and discipline, but not an equal say. Their votes were to be weighted so that "the opinions of some weigh more than those of others according to geometrical proportions."[29] Ramus liked to give his ideas a scholarly air by inserting a snatch of Greek or a mathematical term into his speech and writing, but I suspect there was more to his use of the term "geometrical proportion" than mere rhetorical ornament.[30]

Ramus was not the only one who had become interested in the esoteric science of mathematics in the 1560s, or in its possible applications to politics. Among the others who shared his interests was another Parisian, the scholar Jean Bodin. Bodin's ideas can shed light on Ramus's social ideology, and may even have been derived in part from Ramus himself. Bodin had studied at the University of Paris for two years in his youth, probably between 1545 and 1550. He was a Carmelite brother, and according to his old colleagues in the order he stayed in the Carmelite monastery during his two years at the University.[31] The significance of this is that the monastery was located immediately across the street from the college of Presles, where

27. Castelnau, *Traicte*, fol. 79r.

28. Castelnau, *Traicte*, fol. 82v. A good bibliographical discussion of the rise of resistance theory in Reformation France is Robert Kingdon, "Pamphlet Literature of the French Reformation," in Steven Ozment, ed., *Reformation Europe: A Guide to Research* (St. Louis, Missouri: Center for Reformation Research, 1982), 233–48. The older studies by Allen and Church remain valuable, but the best account is now Skinner, "Calvinism and the Theory of Revolution," *The Foundations of Modern Political Thought*, vol. 2, 189–348.

29. De Lestre to Beza, 19 March 1572, in Beza, *Correspondance de Théodore de Bèze*, vol. 13 (1572) (Geneva: Droz, 1986), no. 909, 96.

30. Cf. his complaint in the *Advertissements* of 1562, that theologians want a geometrical and not an arithmetic relationship between their income and that of the philosophy teachers; Petrus Ramus, *Advertissements sur la réformation de l'Université de Paris* (Paris: A. Wechel, 1562), reprinted in the nineteenth century in L. Cimber and F. Danjou, *Archives curieuses de l'histoire de France*, vol. 5 (Paris: Beauvais, 1835), 124.

31. A. Ponthieux, "Quelques documents inédits sur Jean Bodin," *Revue du seizième siècle* 15 (1928): 57–58. Ponthieux's article confirmed J. A. de Thou's claim, in his *Historiarum sui temporis libri CXXX-VIII*, vol. 5 (Geneva: P. Roviere, 1626–30), 701, that Bodin had been a Carmelite in his youth.

Ramus had recently become principal. "If physical propinquity is an argument of any importance at all," Kenneth McRae wrote, "does it not suggest that the omnivorous young Carmelite from Angers was among the eager students, drawn from the entire University, who crowded the halls of the Collège de Presles to listen to Ramus?"[32]

McRae went on to analyze several of Bodin's works, including his *Methodus ad facilem historiarum cognitionem* of 1566 and *Les six Livres de la Republique* of 1576, and discovered in them substantial evidence of Ramist influence in organization and method. A few years later, he was even able to confirm Bodin's direct acquaintance with Ramus's thought through the discovery of a volume containing three works by Talon and Ramus's own commentary on the *De fato* with extensive notes in Bodin's hand.[33]

McRae concluded that "Bodin's general approach to social and political theory, embodied in his conception of a universal law to be derived from a systematisation of total human experience, was to a considerable extent inspired by Ramist attempts to organize other branches of knowledge in the same way."[34] Not only Bodin's general approach, but also some of the specifics of his political thought, are remarkably similar to Ramus's ideas.[35]

Bodin's mind was that of a sixteenth-century humanist intellectual, strongly influenced by Aristotle and by Italian Platonism. His political thought was at least in part founded upon mystical and spiritual beliefs, and especially on number mysticism. While most modern accounts tend to downplay the importance of such beliefs in their reconstruction of his ideas, or to ignore them altogether, such a course can be dangerous. The point has been made in relation to the history of science, with interesting results for our understanding of sixteenth-century astronomy; it needs to be more widely recognized in the analysis of political theory in the same era.

At issue here is not a reevaluation of Bodin, however, but a particular aspect of his work which connects him to Ramus, the description of how office in the state should be awarded. Howell A. Lloyd summarized the relevant passages as follows:

32. Kenneth D. McRae, "Ramist Tendencies in the Thought of Jean Bodin," *Journal of the History of Ideas* 16 (1955): 306–23, at 309.

33. Kenneth D. McRae, "A Postscript on Bodin's Connections with Ramism," *Journal of the History of Ideas* 24 (1963): 569–71.

34. McRae, "Ramist Tendencies," 323.

35. The demonstration that Bodin was familiar with and influenced by Ramus's ideas on method does not, of course, prove that he was acquainted with Ramus himself, or even that he had ever seen him. Given Bodin's often-expressed opposition to venal office, however, and the fact that he was in Paris again in the 1560s pursuing a career as a lawyer, it would be strange if he had not heard of Ramus's suit against Charpentier over the royal chair of mathematics and sympathized with his ideas. It is not just that Bodin was an outspoken opponent of venal office, although of course he was. His published opinions on the subject are expressed with some warmth, and the high point of his public career came when he spoke out against venality at the Estates General of Blois in 1576. It is in what he suggests to replace venal office holding that the similarity of his thought to Ramus's appears most obviously.

governmental offices were given to all men, whether baseborn or noble, according to their "merits" and "virtues," and yet "with sufficient discretion for nobles to retain some advantage over the commoners." While the proposition was backed by some rudimentary social psychology, it was founded upon an elaborate number mysticism. Aristocratic government functioned according to "geometrical proportion." Popular government operated by "arithmetical proportion." To combine them was to achieve "harmonical proportion...."[36]

Mere arithmetical proportion would be disastrous, Bodin wrote, because under such a scheme "the voices in an assembly are counted without being weighed; and always the number of fools, rascals and ignorant men is a thousand times greater than that of good men."

Where did Bodin get this idea? He might well have gotten it from Ramus. The letter in which De Lestre reported Ramus's scheme for the French Church contains the same idea in strikingly similar phrases. Could Ramus and Bodin have arrived independently at such a scheme, and only a few years apart? They could have, or Ramus might have borrowed it from Bodin rather than vice versa. After all, Bodin was in Paris in the 1560s; he seems to have flirted with Calvinism while he was there; and he undoubtedly knew of Ramus as a champion of meritocratic recruitment to royal office. (It is curious, and conceivably significant, that when Bodin attended the Estates General at Blois, he went as the elected representative of the Vermandois, Ramus's homeland.) How the connection between Ramus and Bodin occurred, and which way the influence between them ran, is impossible to say. But that they shared more than a fondness for Ramist method is clear.

Ramus's work on the ancient Gauls and his program for the French Reformed Church suggest that he was seeking a theoretical underpinning for his efforts to halt the spread of oligarchy among the elites of French society. He borrowed from his readings in the classics and in mathematics to do so, and he lifted a term from Plato—"timocracy"—to describe his vision. In the last analysis, however, his theories and their possible connections with those of other political and social writers of his time are of secondary importance. Ramus was not especially interested in theory. What he cared about was preserving the role of merit in the French social order through open and participatory institutions, not because such a course was dictated by theory but because his own experiences and desires required it. His textbooks, his attempted reforms of the University and of French Protestantism, and his interpretation of the past were all prompted by a purely practical end: to halt the growth of the rigid, hierarchical, and oligarchic Old Régime in France.

36. Howell A. Lloyd, *The State, France, and the Sixteenth Century* (London: George Allen and Unwin, 1983), 161.

How successful was he? He was not successful at all. Few of his textbooks were translated into French, and after 1600 they were not printed in France at all, in French or in Latin. The University remained prohibitively expensive for poor students, and the royal professorships became sinecures passed on through family dynasties. The French Reformed Church remained Presbyterian, centralized, and hierarchical. Ramus was defeated on every front.

At least, he was defeated on every front in France. Elsewhere the popularity of his stands on education and ecclesiastical polity survived and even flourished. The English Puritans maintained his ideas until after the middle of the seventeenth century, and the New Englanders were still using his texts at Harvard into the Enlightenment. This may well be due to Ramus's congregationalism, but I would suggest that the nature of New England society was perhaps even more important as a reason for the continued success of Ramism there. What it implied about the importance of talent and merit, the need for widespread and accessible education, the necessity of wide participation in social institutions, and above all the ultimate value of achievement and hard work, all made it better suited to New England than to Old Régime France. There were few societies in the West in the seventeenth century where the motto "Labor Omnia Vincit" had relevance any longer. Puritan New England was one, and this is reflected in Ramus's continuing popularity there. France was most emphatically not such a society under the Old Régime. In his homeland, Ramus was unable to resist the tide of oligarchy, and all of his efforts came to nothing.

Nonetheless Ramus's life and the pedagogical system he invented are important keys to our understanding of France and of Europe as a whole in the middle of the sixteenth century. His successes and his failures mirror the most important social and cultural developments of the age. The rejection of his meritocratic vision of education reflects not only the economic downturn of the age but also the last gasp of meritocratic, optimistic, civic humanism—in fact, the end of the Renaissance. His failure to preserve the congregational character of the French Reform was only one part of the triumph of hierarchy and centralized authority in European Protestantism as a whole, at the dawn of the "Age of Orthodoxy." His appeal to merit as the only appropriate criterion for official positions in the state was lost in the rise of royal absolutism, where the king's will was, in theory at least, the only law. And, finally, his own rags-to-riches biography was, as much as any of his programs and ideals, emblematic of an age which was over by the time he died, replaced by the rigid hierarchy of Old Régime France.

APPENDIX A
Royal Professors, 1530–1610

The following table lists all of the royal professors appointed between 1530 and 1610, with biographical data including subject of their teaching, date of birth (DOB) where known, date of appointment to their chair (APPT), date of retirement (RET) where known, and country of origin. This is an abridgment of the database used to prepare the discussion of the royal professors in chapter 3.

TABLE 3: ROYAL PROFESSORS, 1530–1610

Name	Subject	DOB	APPT	RET	Origin
Akakia, Martin (I)	Medicine	1539	1574	1588	France
Akakia, Martin (II)	Medicine	?	1600	1604	France
Amboise, J.-M. d'	Philosophy	1538	1576	1611	France
Amboise, Jacques	Medicine	1558	1590	1606	France
Auge, D. d'	Greek	?	1577	1595	France
Baudichon, Simon	Medicine	?	1568	1577	France
Beauvais	Medicine	?	1547	?	?
Beyne, Rodolphe	Hebrew	?	1549	1554	England
Blanc, Vincent	Hebrew	1583	1605	1616	Italy
Boulanger, Jean	Math	?	1607	1636	France
Bressieu, Maurice	Math	1546	1581	1608	France
Caligny, A. R. de	Hebrew	?	1541	1565	France
Casaubon, Isaac	Greek	1559	1600	1610	Switzerland
Charles, Claude	Medicine	1576	1607	1623	France
Charpentier, Jacques	Math	1521	1566	1574	France
Cheradame, Jean	Greek	?	1543	?	France
Cinqarbres, Jean de	Hebrew	?	1554	1587	France
Coroné, Denis	Greek	?	1543	1551	France

TABLE 3: ROYAL PROFESSORS, 1530–1610

NAME	SUBJECT	DOB	APPT	RET	ORIGIN
Cosel, Dampestre	Math	?	1565	1566	Italy
Critton, Georges	Greek	1554	1595	1611	Scotland
Danes, Pierre	Greek	1497	1530	1534	France
de l'Isle, Arnoul	Arabic	1556	1587	1613	Germany
Dorat, Jean	Greek	1508	1556	1567	France
Dubois, Jacques	Medicine	1478	1542	1555	France
Duchesne, Leger	Latin	?	1561	1586	France
Duhamel, Pasquier	Math	?	1540	1565	France
Duret, Jean	Medicine	1563	1586	1599	France
Duret, Louis	Medicine	1527	1567	1586	France
Duval, Guillaume	Philosophy	1579	1606	1646	France
Fine, Oronce	Math	1494	1530	1555	France
Forcadel, Pierre	Math	?	1560	1573	France
Galland, Pierre	Latin	1510	1545	1559	France
Génébrard, Gilbert	Hebrew	1537	1566	1591	France
Goulu, Jerome	Greek	1581	1603	1623	France
Goulu, Nicolas	Greek	1530	1567	1601	France
Goupil, Jean	Medicine	1525	1555	1564	France
Gourmelen, Etienne	Medicine	1530	1578	1594	France
Guidacerius, A.	Hebrew	?	1530	1540	Italy
Harambour, Auguste	Math	?	1556	1558	France
Helias, Jacques	Greek	?	1572	1590	France
Hubert, Etienne	Arabic	1568	1600	1614	France
Jourdain, François	Hebrew	?	1587	1599	France
Laetus, Jacques	Medicine	?	1605	1628	Scotland
Lambin, Denis	Latin	1516	1560	1572	France
La Ramée, Pierre de	Eloquence & Philosophy	1515	1551	1572	France
Latomus, Barthélemy	Latin	1485	1534	1541	Germany
Le Roy, Louis	Greek	1510	1572	1577	France
Lecomte, Bertin	Hebrew	?	1547	1560	France
Lecomte, Jean	Medicine	?	1577	1585	France
Lefevre, J.	Medicine	1526	1582	1590	France

TABLE 3: ROYAL PROFESSORS, 1530–1610

NAME	SUBJECT	DOB	APPT	RET	ORIGIN
Lemaistre, Paul	Medicine	?	1590	1596	France
Magnien, Jean	Math	?	1555	1556	Germany
Malmedy, Simon	Philosophy	?	1572	1584	France
Marcile, Theodore	Latin	1548	1602	1617	Germany
Martin, Jacques	Math	?	1609	1625	France
Martin, Jean	Medicine	?	1588	1608	France
Mercier, Jean	Hebrew	?	1547	1570	France
Merlieres, J. de	Math	?	1577	1580	France
Monantheuil, Henri	Math	1536	1573	1606	France
Morel, Frederick	Latin	1558	1586	1629	France
Palma Cayet, P.-V.	Hebrew	1525	1596	1610	France
Paradis, Paul	Hebrew	?	1530	1549	Italy
Parent, François	Philosophy	?	1594	1622	France
Passerat, Jean	Latin	1534	1572	1601	France
Pellerin, J.	Philosophy	?	1567	1611	France
Péna, Jean	Math	1528	1557	1558	France
Pietre, Simon	Medicine	1565	1594	1607	France
Poblacion, J.-M.	Math	?	1530	1554	Spain
Poncon, P.	Medicine	?	1595	1603	France
Postel, Guillaume	Oriental Languages	1510	1538	1543	France
Raffar, Vincent	Philosophy	?	1589	1606	France
Riolan, Jean	Medicine	1580	1604	1657	France
Sainclair, David de	Math	?	1599	1629	Scotland
Seguin, Pierre	Medicine	1566	1599	1633	France
Stadius, Jean	Math	1527	1576	1579	Germany
Strazel, Jean	Greek	?	1535	1539	Germany
Toussaint, Jacques	Greek	?	1530	1547	France
Turnebe, Adrien	Philosophy	1512	1547	1565	France
Vatable, François	Hebrew	?	1530	1547	France
Vicomercato, F. de	Philosophy	1512	1542	1561	Italy
Vidius, Vidus	Medicine	?	1542	1547	Italy
Vignal, Pierre	Hebrew	1538	1592	1640	France

APPENDIX B
Editions of Ramus's Works, 1540–1640

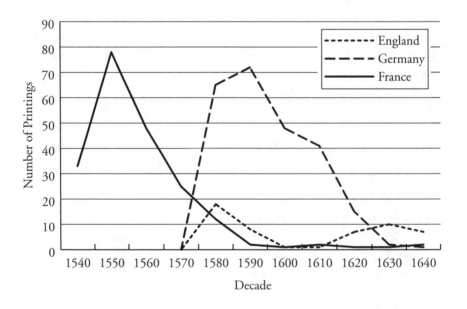

The graph is based on the census of Ramus's works in Walter Ong's *Ramus and Talon Inventory* (Cambridge: Harvard University Press, 1958).

Selected Bibliography

Manuscript Sources

Bibliothèque Nationale (Paris):

Fonds Dupuy 137, fol. 121r: Ramus to the University of Paris, Aug. 1568.

Fonds Dupuy 268, fols. 237r–238r: De Lestre to Beza, 19 March 1572.

Fonds Dupuy 581, fol. 113: Edict of Francis I against Ramus, 10 March 1543.

Fonds Dupuy 837, 951: epigrams and poems relating to Ramus.

MS français 24526: Martin Billet du Fanière, "Extraits de l'histoire du College de France de Guillaume Duval (Paris, 1644? in 4°) et notes pour l'histoire de cet établissement que Fanière se proposait d'écrire."

Archives Nationales (Paris):

A.N. H^{3}2874^2: "College of Presles 1546–1572" [Accounts].

A.N. M186, no. 66: "Extrait des registres du Conseil privé du roi, 3 octobre 1572."

A.N. MM432: "Inventaire des Titres et Papiers du College de Presles."

A.N. X^{1a}1605: Parlement de Paris. Conseils.

A.N. Minutier central des notaires, Etude XLIX liasse 63 fols. 545v–546v. Testament of Pierre de la Ramée, 3 November 1559.

Bibliothèque de la Société de l'Histoire du Protestantisme français (Paris):

MS 563^1: Synodes Provinciaux. Procès-verbaux des Synodes tenus dans l'Ile de France, la Brie, la Champagne, le Pays Chartrin, en 1564, 1605, 1623... [Collection Auzière].

MS 880: Copies of letters to and from Theodore Beza [Collection Guillaume Baum].

MS 730: Copies of letters to and from Ramus.

Print Sources

Argentré, Charles du Plessis d'. *Collectio judiciorum de novis erroribus, qui ab initio duodecimi seculi post incarnationem Verbi usque ad annum 1632 in Ecclesia proscripti sunt & notati.... Tomus Secundus; in quo exquisita monumenta ab anno 1521 usque ad annum 1632 continentur.* Paris: Cailleau, 1728.

Aristotle. *The Basic Works of Aristotle*. Edited by Richard McKeon. New York: Random House, 1941.

Ascham, Roger. *The Whole Works of Roger Ascham*. Edited with a life of Ascham by the Rev. Dr. J. A. Giles, 1864. Reprint, New York: AMS Press, 1965.

Banos, Théophile de [Theophilus Banosius]. *Petri Rami Vita*. Unpaginated introduction to Ramus, *Commentariorum de religione Christiana libri quatuor*. Frankfurt a. M.: A. Wechel, 1576.

Baum, G., and E. Cunitz. *Histoire ecclésiastique des Églises réformées au royaume de France*. 1580. Reprint, Paris: 1883–89.

Beza, Theodore. *Correspondance de Théodore de Bèze*. Collected by Hippolyte Aubert. Published by Alain Dufour, Claire Chimelli, Béatrice Nicollier and Mario Turchetti. Geneva: Droz, 1980. vol. 10 (1569), 1980; vol. 11 (1570), 1983; vol. 12 (1571), 1986; vol. 13 (1572), 1988.

Bodin, Jean. *La Vie chère au XVIe siècle: La response de Jean Bodin à M. de Malestroit: 1568*. Edited by Henri Hauser. Paris: Colin, 1932.

Bon, Mathurin. "Mathurin Bon, Lieutenant du Cappitaine Grassin, sur l'evasion du principal du collège de Presle." [A.N. Z6826, f. 50 v°, 5 February 1563.] In Alexandre Tuetey, ed., *Registres des délibérations du Bureau de la Ville de Paris, Tome 5: 1558–1567*. Paris: Imprimerie nationale, 1892, n° CCXCV.

Bonnardot, François, ed. *Registres des délibérations du Bureau de la Ville de Paris, Tome 7, 1572–1576*. Paris: Imprimerie Nationale, 1843.

Budé, Guillaume. *L'Institution du Prince*. In Bontems, Claude, Léon-Pierre Raybaud, and Jean-Pierre Brancourt, *Le Prince dans la France des XVIe et XVIIe siècles*. Paris: Presses Universitaires de France, 1965.

Bullinger, Heinrich. *Diarium*. Edited by E. Egli. Basel: n.p., 1901.

Cassirer, Ernst, Paul Oskar Kristeller, and John Herman Randall Jr. *The Renaissance Philosophy of Man*. Chicago: University of Chicago Press, 1948.

Castiglione, Baldesar. *The Book of the Courtier*. Translated by Charles S. Singleton. Garden City, New York: Anchor Books, 1959.

Charpentier, Jacques. *Ia. Carpentarii, Claromontani Bellovaci, Regii Professoris, Orationes Tres: Pro iure professionis suae, in Senatu ex tempore habitae, contra importunas Rami actiones: Ad illustrissimum Cardinalem & princepem Carolum Lotaringum*. Paris: Gabriel Buon, 1566.

———. *Ia. Carpentarii, Claromontani, Bellovaci, Philosophiae & Mathematicarum artium Regii professoris, contra importunas Rami actiones, Senatus Decreto nuper confirmati, oration. Cal. Apr. 1566*. Paris: Gabriel Buon, 1566.

Coyecque, Ernest, ed. *Recueil d'actes notariés relatifs à l'histoire de Paris et de ses environs au XVIe siècle. Tome 2, 1532–1555*. Paris: Imprimerie Nationale, 1923.

De Thou, Jacques-Auguste. *Historiarum sui temporis libri CXXXVIII*. Geneva: P. Roviere, 1626–30.

———. *Histoire universelle de Jacques-Auguste de Thou.... Vol. 4, 1567–1573*. The Hague: H. Scheusleer, 1740.

Dorat, Jean. *Iohannis Aurati Lemovicis Poetae et Interpretis Regii Epigrammatum.* Paris: Guillaume Linocer, 1586.

———. *Iohannis Aurati Lemovicis Poetae et Interpretis Regii Poematia.* Paris: Guillaume Linocer, 1586.

Drouot, Henri. "Documents sur Dorat et Hélias." *Revue du XVIe siècle* 17 (1930): 126–27.

Du Bellay, Joachim. *Oeuvres poétiques.* Paris: Henri Chamard/Librairie Hachette, 1923.

Freigius, Johannes. *Petri Rami Vita per Joannem Thoman Freigium* in *Collectaneae*, 580–625. Abridgment by John Milton in *Artis Logica Plenior Institutio* (London, 1672), reprinted and translated in Allan H. Gilbert, ed., as *A Fuller Institution of the Art of Logic by John Milton, an Englishman.* An analytic praxis and a life of Peter Ramus are appended in *Works of John Milton*, vol. 11. New York: Columbia University Press, 1935.

———. *Petri Rami Professio regia, hoc est septem artes liberales in regia cathedra per ipsum apodictico docendi genere propositae...* Basel: Henricpetri, 1576.

Galland, Pierre. *P. Gallandi literarum latinarum professoris Regii, contra novam academiam Petri Rami oratio: Ad illustrissimum Cardinalem & Principem Carolum a Lotharingia.* Paris: Vascosan, 1551.

Garin, Eugenio, Paolo Rossi, and Cesare Vasoli, eds. *Testi Umanistici su la Retorica: Testi editi e inediti su Retorica e Dialettica di Mario Nizolio, Francesco Patrizi e Pietro Ramo....* Rome/Milan: Fratelli Bocca Editori, 1953 [*Archivio di Filosofia* 3 (1953)].

Grunwald, M., ed. "C. J. Curio Petro Ramo suo S. D." *Archiv für Geschichte der Philosophie* (Berlin) 9 (1896): 335.

Hill, Henry Bertram, trans. *The Political Testament of Cardinal Richelieu.* Madison, Wisconsin: University of Wisconsin Press, 1961.

Kennedy, Leonard A., ed. *Renaissance Philosophy: New Translations.* The Hague: Mouton, 1973.

Kepler, Johannes. *Gesammelte Werke.* Herausgegeben von Max Caspar. Munich: C.H. Beck'sche Verlagsbuchhandlung, 1937.

Languet, Hubert. *Viri Clarissimi Huberti Langueti Burgundi, ad Joachimum Camerarium patrem, & Joachimum Camerarium filium, Medicum, Scriptae Epistolae....* Groningen: Nicolas, 1646.

Leishman, J. B., ed. *The Three Parnassus Plays, 1598–1601.* London: Nicholson & Watson, 1949.

Marlowe, Christopher. *The Complete Works of Christopher Marlowe.* Edited by Fredson Bowers. Cambridge: Cambridge University Press, 1973.

Nancel, Nicolas de. "Nicolaus Nancelius, *Petri Rami Vita*: Edited with an English Translation." Peter Sharratt, ed. *Humanistica Lovaniensia: Journal of Neo-Latin Studies* 24 (1975): 161–277.

Pasquier, Estienne. *Le Catéchisme des jésuites: Examen de leur doctrine*. Ville-Franche: Guillaume Grenier, 1602.

———. *Les Recherches de la France*. Paris: Laurens Sonnius, 1621.

———. *Choix de lettres sur la littérature, la langue et la traduction*. Edited and annotated by D. Thickett. Geneva: Droz, 1956.

Perkins, William. *The Work of William Perkins*. Edited by Ian Breward. Courtenay Library of Reformation Classics, 3. Abingdon: Sutton Courtenay Press, 1970.

Quick, John. *Synodicon in Gallia Reformata: Or, The Acts, Decisions, Decrees and Canons of those Famous National Councils of the Reformed Churches in France….* London: T. Parkhurst and J. Robinson, 1692.

Rabelais, François. *Oeuvres complètes*. Paris: Éditions Garnier Frères, 1962.

Raemond, Florimond de. *L'Histoire de la naissance, progrez et decadence de l'heresie de ce siecle: Divisee en huict livres….* Rouen: Berthelin, 1623.

Registres de la Compagnie des Pasteurs de Genève. Tome 3, 1565–1574. Edited by Olivier Fatio and Olivier Labarthe. Geneva: Droz, 1969.

Scaliger, J. *Scaligerana ou bons mots, rencontres agreables, et remarques judicieuses & sçavants de J. Scaliger avec des notes de Mr. le Fevre, & de Mr. de Colomies….* Cologne: Chez les Huguetans, 1695.

Seyssel, Claude de. *The Monarchy of France*. Translated by J. H. Hexter; edited, annotated, and introduced by Donald R. Kelley; additional translations by Michael Sherman. New Haven: Yale University Press, 1981.

Sterne, A. "Deux lettres de Ramus à Tremellius." *Revue critique d'histoire et de littérature*, n.s. 13, no. 15 (10 April 1882): 295–96.

Talon, Omer. *Audomari Talaei, quem petri rami Theseum dicere jure possis, Opera, Socraticae Methodicaeque Philosophiae Studiosis pernecessaria….* Basel: Waldkirch, 1584.

———. "Audomari Talaei admonitio ad Adrianum Turnebum, regium graecae linguae professorem." In his *Opera* (1584).

———. "Audomari Talaei Academia, ad Carolum Lotharingum." In his *Opera* (1584).

———. *M.T. Ciceronis de Oratore ad Quintum Fratrem Dialogi tres, Audomari Talaei praelectionibus illustrati*. In his *Opera* (1584).

Temple, William. *A Logical Analysis of Twenty Select Psalmes*. London: 1605.

Index

V

venality, 63–64, 78
vernacular, 56

W

Waddington, Charles, 3–4, 6, 27, 30,
    34, 102, 119–20
Walker, D. P., "ancient theology," 152

Z

Zwingli, Huldreich, 107, 130–31